'I CAN *PLOD* ... '

The Hooghli river from William Carey's house

'I CAN *PLOD* ... '

William Carey and the early years of
the first Baptist missionary Society

JOHN APPLEBY

Foreword by
Dr PETER NAYLOR

Grace Publications

GRACE PUBLICATIONS TRUST
7 Arlington Way
London EC1R 1XA
England
e-mail: AGBCSE@aol.com

Managing Editors:
T. I. Curnow
M. J. Adams

© Grace Publications Trust

First published 2007

ISBN 10: 0-94646-274-7
ISBN 13: 978-0-946462-74-2

Distributed by

EVANGELICAL PRESS
Faverdale North Industrial Estate
Darlington DL3 0PH
England
e-mail: sales@evangelicalpress.org
www.evangelicalpress.org

Printed and bound in Great Britain by
Biddles Ltd, King's Lynn, Norfolk

Contents

Foreword	9
Acknowledgements	11
Sources consulted	13
Prologue	21

PART ONE   'First the stalk ...'

1.	William Carey's England	25
2.	Light shines in the darkness	30
3.	William's younger years	34
4.	Into the world of work	38
5.	Family life and a business to run	42
6.	Entering the pastoral ministry	46

PART TWO   '... then the ear ...'

7.	'Our petitions may prove like seeds'	52
8.	'Sit down, young man'	60
9.	The obligation of Christians	66
10.	Happy village fellowship to troubled city church	74
11.	God's clock strikes the hour!	80
12.	The Aftermath	86
13.	In the beginning was God	90
14.	Light and shade of farewell days	96
15.	'If you will hold the rope ...'	108
16.	'For those in peril on the sea'	114
17.	Africa too? The Caribbean also?	120
18.	The abominable East India Company	128
19.	The struggle to begin!	148
20.	Blue dye	154
21.	The valley of the shadow	160
22.	'Dying, yet we live on'	166

PART THREE   '… then the full grain in the ear.'

23. A new beginning in Serampore	172
24. Culture shock!	180
25. Krishna Pal and the first-fruits	186
26. Carey the Translator	194
27. Carey the Educationalist	204
28. The Form of Agreement	212
29. The Mission family grows	222
30. Sunshine and shadows	230
31. Growing pains and a disaster	238
32. The serious quarrel and other sorrows	246
33. Carey the Botanist	256
34. Carey the Social Reformer	266
35. Epilogue	274

APPENDICES

A. The Leicester Covenant	284
B. Carey's catholicity	289
C. The communion question	293
D. William Carey's will	296
E. Extract from Sumachar Durpun	298
F. A N Groves and his unwilling wife	300
G. The Society and *Home Mission*	303
H. Grace Baptist Mission	306

*Dedicated to our daughters
Kathryn and Jacqueline who,
not of their own choice,
had to endure the trials of being
brought up as 'mish kids'*

The Applebys - India - 1964

Foreword

So why yet another biography of William Carey, British pastor, pioneer missionary, good friend of India, married man and parent? In certain libraries you would be able to find some shelves almost filled with the commodity. Yet, to my mind, there is ample justification for the present book, which would be inadequate were it not for the special qualifications possessed by its author, John Appleby, who looks at Carey through his own distinctive spectacles. His perceptions make all the difference.

Firstly, John lived in South India, serving the Lord there for many years. He knows the land, the people and – which is so important – the problems generated by the all-embracing British Raj in Carey's time, and by the vanishing British Raj in the mid-twentieth century. These problems may have had side effects which, albeit unconsciously, inconspicuously and gently, tended to impact UK-sourced missionary work in the sub-continent.

Secondly, like William Carey in his time, John Appleby embraces a sensible, biblical Calvinism. It may be that not all past biographers of Carey have been able to put on his theological shoes and feel comfortable, but John can and does. Without such empathy, it would be nearly impossible to arrive at an accurate appreciation of Carey's life and work. True evangelism must be based on the unreserved acceptance and application of the doctrines of grace, and this comes over in the present book.

Last, but definitely no means least, John has been blessed with the able support of his wife, Eileen, throughout his time as a missionary in India, and since. Knowing what it can cost for Britishers to make their life's work in climes which are far from temperate (in more ways than one), he has had ample opportunity to reflect upon the demands and tensions which faced William Carey when, with his wife Dorothy, he sailed from Dover in 1793, never to return to his homeland.

In my opinion, therefore, the present pages provide a unique and needed contribution to our understanding of the cobbler from Northamptonshire. Living for a number of years in that county, and also having visited Carey's Serampore, I have been able in a very small way to touch the pulse of a man who, two centuries on, still has much to teach us. Some of those lessons are reflected in John's book, a draft of which I could not put down, and the foreword to which I am delighted to provide.

Peter Naylor
Wellingborough
Northamptonshire

As these pages were being prepared for the press Dr Peter Naylor was taken to be with Christ, the Saviour and Lord he lived to serve. I have lost a greatly respected friend. JA.

Acknowledgements

It will become evident to the reader that the material of this book has been gathered by 'standing on the shoulders' of a number of other biographers of William Carey. Grateful acknowledgement is made to them. Their work has often been meticulous and extensive. To that extent these pages do not break startling new ground. So the question arises, Why *another* biography of Carey? The question requires answering.

1. The biographers of historical figures tend each to write from their own individual perspectives, rather like the four evangelists who wrote their individual Gospels of the New Testament. Those four accounts of the life of Christ do not contradict one another; rather they are complementary. Hence the usefulness of *A Harmony of the Gospels* to bring us a comprehensive picture of Christ's life. A more inclusive harmony of biographies of Carey is the aim of the pages that follow here. This hopefully does provide a fresh approach to the life and work of Carey, here set within the context of story of the early years of 'The Particular Baptist Society for the Propagation of the Gospel among the Heathen'.

2. Biographies that deal with understanding and sympathy for the unhappy breakdown of Dorothy Carey's mental health have been rather rare until early in the 20th century. Later accounts now take a more knowledgeable view and are more helpful. Such problems can still occur on the mission field among either men or women. Is there something we can now learn from Dorothy's case?

3. Some biographies focus particularly on Carey's evangelicalism; others make more of his agricultural, social and cultural achievements and their outstanding benefit to the India of his day. Yet Carey was not an 'either/or' man. He was a 'both/and' Christian. He had a holistic view of Christian mission that evangelicals have not always emulated.[1]

4. A conference in 1993, held at Serampore, brought together some thirty-one contributors to a symposium entitled *Carey's Obligation and India's Renaissance*, published by Serampore College, in which all aspects of Carey's work were evaluated through Indian eyes. In the same year a history of the Baptist Missionary Society 1792-1992 was published by T & T Clark, written for the BMS by Dr Brian Stanley. These publications provide a new source of valuable insights into Carey's work and into the early years of the original Particular Baptist Society, information not available to any previous biographer, but which can be included here.

5. Some biographers place little emphasis on William Carey's theological background, and on his friends of the early Particular Baptist Society or the churches that rallied to support generously the work of mission. In ignorance it has been said that 'Calvinism severs the nerve of evangelism'. The evangelistic zeal of that Calvinistic Baptist Society and their supporting churches refutes that, and so must we. The theology behind Carey's missionary vision has sometimes been

---

[1] *The mission of salvation and the task of humanisation are integrally related to each other, even if they cannot be considered identical ... great evangelical missionaries of the past, notably William Carey, carried out their mission in precisely this comprehensive way.* Thomas, M M quoted in Boyd, Robin pp 319-320

[2] *Although Carey is honoured as 'The Father of modern Missions' his connection to the Particular Baptist tradition and the theological concerns that motivated his mission are ignored or downplayed.* George, Timothy, in Haykin, Michael (Ed.) p143.

ignored despite the fact that biblical sovereign grace theology is a firmer foundation for evangelism than any other – it produced Paul the Apostle, no less![2]

6. There has not been a biography of Carey emanating from the stream of Particular Baptist church life in which he was nurtured. Surely that is the family best qualified to understand one of its sons and his colleagues?

7. The language former biographers have used, describing the past, is sometimes more romantic than prosaic, suitable to the social ethos of their day. There is a need for every generation of Christian believers to face afresh the challenge of Carey's vision and indefatigable enthusiasm, in the contemporary language of their own day and age, for the world that Carey sought to win is not yet won.

8. In the preparation of these pages I have had the benefit of encouragement, suggestions, corrections and additions from helpful friends. The work is the better for them all. The patient persistence of David Kingdon, formerly joint managing editor of Grace Publications whose library of Carey books was made available to me, has kept me going when other circumstances could easily have hindered that. Nor may I neglect to mention my deep appreciation of the patience and secretarial skills of my wife, who must frequently have thought that William Carey was actually living somewhere in our house, so much did he engage her husband's attention. Truly, no man is an island – least of all this author. My grateful thanks to all who have helped in any way, and to Dr Peter Naylor for his generous foreword.

John Appleby
Telford
2007

Sources consulted

1. Bebbington, DW
Evangelicalism in Modern Britain (1730s – 1980s)
Routledge, London, 1979

2. Beck, James R
Dorothy Carey; the Tragic and Untold story
Baker Book House, USA, 1992

3. Boyd, Robin
An Introduction to Indian Christian Theology
ISPCK, Delhi, India, revised edition, 2000

4. Brown, Raymond
The English Baptists of the 18th century
Baptist Historical Society, London, 1986

5. Carey, Eustace
Memoir of William Carey
Gould, Kendal and Lincoln, Boston, USA

6. Carey, S Pearce
William Carey
Eighth edition (revised), Carey Press, London, 1934

7. Churchill, Winston
A History of the English Speaking Peoples
Cassell & Co. Ltd., London 1956

8. Conant, T. Jefferson
The Meaning and Use of 'Baptizein'
Kregel Publications, Grand Rapids, USA, 1977

9. Daniel, J K & Hedlund, R E (Eds.)
Carey's Obligation and India's Renaissance
Council of Serampore College, West Bengal, India, 1992

10. Davis, Walter Bruce
William Carey, Father of Modern Missions
Moody Press, Chicago, USA, 1963

11. De, Susil Kumar
A History of Bengali Literature, 1800 – 1825
Delhi, India, 1919

12. Dutta, Krishna
Calcutta, a Cultural and Literary history
Signal Books, Oxford, 2003

13. Elwyn, TSH
The Northamptonshire Baptist Association
Carey Kingsgate Press, London, 1964

14. Fuller, Thomas Ekins
Memoir of the Life and Writings of Andrew Fuller
J Heaton & Sons, London, 1863

15. George, Timothy
Faithful Witness – the life and mission of William Carey
Inter-varsity Press, Leicester, 1991

16. Haykin, Michael
One Heart and One Soul
Evangelical Press, Darlington, 1994

17. Haykin, Michael (Ed)
British Particular Baptists, 1638 – 1910 Vols. 1,2,3.
P B Press, Springfield, Missouri, USA, 1988,2000,2003

18. Kingdon, David
William Carey & the Origins of the Modern Missionary Movement
Westminster Conference paper, 1992

19. Kurlansky, Mark
Salt, a World History
Jonathan Cape, London, 2002

20. Lang, GH
Anthony Norris Groves, Saint and Pioneer
Thynne & Co Ltd, London, 1939

21. Marshman, John Clark
The Story of Carey, Marshman and Ward
(Abridged edition) J Heaton & Son, London, 1864

22. Masters, Peter *Missionary Triumph over Slavery*
The Wakeman Trust, London, 2006

23. Murray, Iain H
William Carey, Climbing a Rainbow
Banner of Truth magazine Issue 349, Oct 1992

24. Naylor, Peter
Calvinism, Communion and Baptism
Paternoster Press, Carlisle, 2003

25. Needham, NR
2000 years of Christ's Power Vol.1
Grace Publications, Evangelical Press, Darlington, 1998

26. Oliver, Robert W
History of the English Calvinistic Baptists 1771-1892
Banner of Truth Trust, Edinburgh, 2006

27. Ousseren, AH
William Carey, especially his missionary principles
Leiden, 1945

28. Owen, John
Works. Vol.16
Banner of Truth Trust, London, 1968

29. Purnell
New English Encyclopedia
Purnell, London, 1970

30. Pease, Paul
Travel with William Carey
Day One, Leominster, 2005

31. Rippon, John
Pages from *The Baptist Register, 1790 – 1802*
Private correspondence with Dr K Dix

32. Schama, Simon
A History of Britain Vol. 3
BBC Worldwide Ltd., London, 2001

33. Sherring
The History of Protestant Missions in India
London, 1875

34. Smith, George
The Life of William Carey, Shoemaker and Missionary
Everyman's Library, JM Dent & Sons, London, 1935

35. Stanley, Brian
The History of the BMS, 1792 – 1992
T & T Clark, Edinburgh, 1992

36. Stuart, John
Nestorian Missionary Enterprise
T & T Clark, Edinburgh, 1928

37. Strong, Roy
The Story of Britain
Pimlico. London, 1998

38. Valentine, Theo F *Concern for the Ministry*
Particular Baptist Fund, London, 1967

Also, archive material has kindly been made available from:

Royal Botanic Gardens, Kew, by permission of the Trustees.

Bristol Baptist College, by permission of the Principal.

Strict Baptist Historical Society, with thanks to the Society for the Librarian's help.

Leicestershire County records office, with thanks for a photocopy supplied of Carey's Leicester Church Covenant.

Prologue

Any writer of a biography inevitably walks a metaphorical tightrope between iconoclasm and idolisation, between revisionism and flattery, and there is always the danger of an unbalanced emphasis. For some Carey was 'The great Evangelical' who awoke the churches to their responsibility for world mission. For others Carey was 'The great Liberal' who sparked off a tremendous renaissance of India's welfare in social, educational and botanical knowledge. Each of these views is partial and inadequate. To Carey his 'calling' was never just one or the other but always both together, as he made clear in his ground-breaking book of 1792, *An Enquiry into the Obligations of Christians to Use Means for the Conversion of the Heathens*. Nor must it be forgotten that to write the story of another *Christian* brother or sister means writing the story of one whom the Lord Jesus uniquely loved. That surely calls for *Christian* care. As also does the fact that scattered in different parts of the world today are more than one hundred descendants of William Carey.[1] All these things ought to give the biographer pause for thought.

And in respect of Carey there is a further caveat – the voice of the man himself. To his nephew Eustace, Carey wrote:

> Eustace, if after my removal anyone should think it worth his while to write my life, I will give you a criterion by which you may judge its correctness. If he gives me the credit for being a plodder, he will describe me justly.

---

[1] Carey, W M in Daniel, JK & Hedlund, RE (Eds.) p354

Anything beyond this will be too much. ***I can plod****. I can persevere in any pursuit. To this I owe everything.*[2]

In 1800, the year that Carey joined Marshman and Ward to form the 'Serampore Trio', he wrote to Andrew Fuller, the Secretary of the UK missionary Society supporting him:

> *... respecting myself, I have much proof of the vileness of my heart, much more than I thought of till lately: instead I often fear that instead of being instrumental in the conversion of the heathen, I may sometimes dishonour the cause in which I am engaged. I have hitherto had much experience of the daily supports of a gracious God, but am conscious that if those supports were intermitted but for a little time, my sinful dispositions would infallibly predominate. At present I am kept, but am not one of those who are strong and do exploits.*[3]

Toward the end of his life Carey wrote to his friend Dr Ryland, member of the governing body of the Missionary Society:

> *Should you outlive me and have any influence to prevent it, I must earnestly request that no epithets of praise may ever accompany my name, such as 'the faithful servant of God' etc. All such expressions would convey a falsehood. May I but be accepted at last, I am sure all the glory must be given to divine grace from first to last. To me belongeth shame and confusion of face.*[4]

---

[2] Massey, A K in Daniel JK & Hedlund RE (Eds.) p306 (emphasis mine). Eustace wrote of his uncle: *He could clearly discern and firmly grasp ... whatever fixed his attention and invited his pursuit; and could follow it up with inexhaustible patience and untiring diligence ... his mind could submit to the same unvarying routine everyday, for 30 years, without relaxation and without tedium.*

[3] From a paper read at the Strict Baptist Historical Society annual meeting, 1992

[4] Ibid

There speaks William himself. Let the biographer beware how he writes of his subject.

Let the reader also beware. There are wrong motives for looking back into past history. We can look back with the longing to have lived then ourselves. Were there not 'giants in the earth' in those days? Who would not wish to have lived, for example, in times when the affairs of Kingdom of God were stirring with excitement and new spiritual vigour. But that would be to challenge the sovereign Providence which has deliberately set us in *our* day and age. Longing to have lived in some other time disputes God's present will for us.

We can look back with a reactionary longing seeking to preserve, or re-create, that past age in our own time. But that would deny our Christian responsibility to be relevant to our own day. God has always shown himself meticulously relevant in every age in which he has spoken. Jesus was Jewish among Jews. If we are rightly to represent him we too, as his people, must be relevant to people around us *today*.

Alternatively we could firmly refuse ever to look back into past history. But, as someone has rightly said, *The world that is can best be understood by those conversant with the world that was.* To ignore the mistakes of the past may well lead to repeating them again.

There is a right motive for looking back into history. We must look back for our *spiritual* instruction, seeking to learn from what we see; to watch in adoration at how God prepared his people for what he required of them; to watch them struggle to be relevant messengers of the timeless Truth in *their* day and age. We should covet their humility, their patience and perseverance in the things of the kingdom of God despite all the setbacks they had to contend with. Such commitment as theirs is a virtue we need to nurture today. My purpose in these pages is therefore not merely to present a simple chronological record of William Carey's life, but also to show how God's providences so evidently shaped that life and the early years of his missionary Society; to try to understand what he believed and the principles by which he lived; and even sometimes to seek to feel, as a fellow-Christian, what he must have felt.

Part One

'First the stalk'
(Mark 4:28)

Therefore missionaries who have no results to show are not to be discouraged … the seed is being sown and the time of harvest will come.

On Mark 4:28, from *The One Volume Bible Commentary*
edited by Rev R J Dummelow, MA
Macmillan & Co 1950

1
William Carey's England

The date was 17 August, the year was 1761, when in the little Northamptonshire village of Paulerspury the cry of a newborn baby boy was heard. But the change he brought to that humble home was little compared to the ferment of radical change which was abroad in the land. A turmoil of things was bringing new ideas to birth. Industries were being revolutionised by new machinery driven by steam power.[1] Canals were being cut, road surfaces improved, the first newspapers began to be published and scientific knowledge was leaping ahead. A Royal Mail postal service began in 1784. As Sir Roy Strong indicates, in his book *The Story of Britain*, new skills developed in farming, new metal tools were appearing, new fertilisers, better rotation of crops, and, indeed, new crops. The increasing availability of cheap and plentiful food was one factor which supported a considerable rise in the population of many parts of the country from 1760 to the end of the century. Added to all these new things were the discoveries Captain James Cook made on his worldwide voyages. His writings about his adventures created great excitement as readers learned about 'the big wide world' and its many strange peoples.

The new wealth being produced by all these advances did not, however, benefit the whole population. For at least half the people, especially in rural areas, life was a struggle to survive. Illiteracy was common especially among women. Employment

---

[1] 'A long series of inventions revolutionised the manufacture, above all, of textiles ... James Hargreave's Spinning Jenny (1768)Richard Arkwright's Water Frame (1769) and Samuel Crompton's Mule (1779) ... In 1769 James Watt patented a more energy efficient use of the steam engine'. Strong, Roy p331.

depended upon such casual work as could be obtained, which was often seasonal and menial. Sweated labour, wages paid in pubs where cheap gin was plentiful, disease spawned from lack of sanitation, and crowded housing, education largely restricted to charity schools; all these contributed to the sad conditions in which too many lived who were thought of by the wealthy upper classes as 'illiterate rabble'.[2] Outside London there was no police force; lawlessness was widespread; but that lack of law enforcement was fortunate for many, since something like two hundred offences in law were punishable by death.

In October 1760 King George II died. Like his father George I, he too had been more German than English. Both father and son were:

> ... *aliens in language, outlook, upbringing and sympathy. Their court was predominantly German, their interests and ambitions had centred on Hanover and on the continent of Europe.*[3]

As a result, power in the country rested in the not too capable hands of Parliament, a Parliament described as an 'irresponsible autocracy, and a corrupt House of Commons'.[4] But George III was different. He thought of himself as born and bred an Englishman. He had been educated in England. He intended to be an active King. Some in Parliament were prepared to give him that authority and some were not. Continual royal manoeuvring to dominate Parliament; war with the French; rebellion in the American colonies; revolution in France; and an intermittent madness troubling the king – all these factors finally compelled the regency of the Prince of Wales in 1810. These were unset-

---

[2] 'This was a vast, shifting and shiftless part of the population, made up of agricultural and industrial labourers, cottagers, domestic servants, ordinary soldiers and seamen, and the poor. Their conditions of life fluctuated widely but were often extremely primitive'. Strong, Roy p336.
[3] Churchill, Winston vol 3 p135.
[4] Ibid. p131.

tling influences upon the country. John Wesley, well qualified to make such a judgement from his preaching journeys the length and breadth of the land,[5] wrote in his Journal:

> *England is in a flame! A flame of malice and rage against the King, and almost all in authority under him. I labour to put out this flame. Ought not every patriot to do the same?*

Until Carey left for India, this was the political and social unrest that he lived through, which made him more a republican than a royalist. Another writer, E D Potts, observes of the England which Carey and Dr Thomas left as they sailed for India:

> *... they left a land of corrupt and unrepresentative politics, outrageous penal laws, grave economic injustices brought about by the well-under-way Industrial Revolution, and much deep rooted religious and social bigotry.*[6]

In the area of Carey's birth and upbringing – Northamptonshire – there was little industry at that time, save shoe making. A village lad could expect only to be an agricultural worker, a shoemaker (each village and hamlet had its own in those days) or possibly a simple schoolmaster. All these factors making up the ambience of Carey's England, both at large and locally, were providential influences upon his later life and thinking. As George Smith perceptively comments:

> *Poverty, which the grace of God made him a preacher, also, from his eighteenth year, compelled him to work with his hands in leather all the week and to tramp many a weary mile to Northampton and Kettering carrying the product of his labour.*[7]

---

[5] In 1773 Wesley visited Northampton and preached there. It is tempting to wonder if Carey might have heard him preach.
[6] Quoted in Daniel, JK & Hedlund RE (Eds) p270.
[7] Smith, George p7.

2
Light shines in the darkness

Stars shine brightest on darkest nights. In all the upheavals of early eighteenth century English life God was also working out *his* purposes. There were significant changes being made in the religious sphere. The Toleration Act of 1689 granted freedom of worship to Dissenters, on certain conditions. The laws passed under the previous Clarendon Code (1660-1670) had made it illegal to worship or evangelise outside the control of the Anglican Church. But Dissenters could now enjoy new freedoms providing they took an oath of allegiance to the Crown and signed the Thirty Nine Articles of the Church of England – excepting the two articles concerning Infant Baptism. A consequence of this was that the Anglican Church began to lose its authority since it was no longer regarded as the state church to which everyone must adhere.

Over the succeeding years, now freed from the threat of persecution and attack by angry mobs, different meetings of Dissenters were developing in many places, including those of General Baptist, Strict Baptist and Particular Baptist persuasions.[1] Although all held to the practice of baptising believers by immersion there were differences of opinion among them over such theological matters as:

1. The logical order in which God's decrees were formed with regard to the salvation of his elect.
2. Whether faith in Christ was a duty to be laid upon all persons indiscriminately or limited to the elect alone.
3. Whether unbaptised persons (even if believers) should enjoy the privilege of taking church communion, or not.

---
[1] See for example Naylor, Peter p10f.

By Carey's time Particular (ie Calvinistic) Baptist churches had begun to come together in inter-church associations, making them distinct from General (ie Arminian) Baptists. In 1765 in Kettering, Northamptonshire, six ministers met together and resolved to form:

> *An Association of Particular Baptist ministers and churches in adjacent counties ... formed on the principles of Christianity.*[2]

From that beginning the Association expanded quite rapidly and soon included a number of leading Particular Baptist ministers. Among them were men whose names are now closely associated with Carey as 'rope holders' in the work of mission: men such as John Sutcliff of Olney, Andrew Fuller of Kettering, John Ryland Senior of Northampton and his son John Ryland Junior, later to be Principal of Bristol Baptist College.[3] Although these men were Association men, they found no difficulty in having personal friendships with a wider circle of well-known Christian leaders who, while not Particular Baptists in denomination, yet were of similar Calvinistic thinking.[4] As Matthew Henry remarks in his Bible commentary (upon Numbers 3:7), *Those whom God finds work for he will find help for* – a truth well illustrated, more than once, in Carey's life.

Also during these years an outreach of the Moravian Brethren had reached England from Europe, establishing a 'religious society' in Fetter Lane, London, in 1738. It was through one of their meetings in Aldersgate Street, London, that John Wesley had a spiritual experience that radically changed his life, leading to his great preaching ministry up and down the land, which was doubtless one of the factors that later prevented French revolutionary thinking from sweeping across the British Isles. In Carey's time there was a Moravian meeting in Northampton,

---

[2] Elwyn, TSH p11.
[3] Sutcliff 1752-1814; Fuller 1754-1815; Ryland Snr.1723-1792; Ryland Jnr. 1753-1825.
[4] A number of these influential contacts are described by Haykin, Michael pp 69,133,172.

whose ideas clearly had an influence on his thinking. A pattern of living together as a community was the Moravian practice which was, in many respects, the model upon which the Serampore Trio's community life style was subsequently based.[5]

In these first two chapters we now have traced, in brief outline, the political, cultural, social and religious situations forming the 'atmosphere' of Carey's England. And amid all the turmoil of the great changes taking place in the land we have seen God also at work, surrounding his future servant with those circumstances that would fit him for the task which awaited, though as yet unknown to him. Thus God gives the necessary 'boots' to all those he calls upon to make a journey. But William is not ready for that journey yet.

---

[5] In the Moravian communities decisions were made by the head of the family, which all members were required to follow, but the Serampore Trio made decisions by a process of consensus. See Chapter 25.

3
William's younger years

Paulerspury, the place of William's birth, was fortunate to possess a village school. The first schoolmaster and parish clerk was William's grandfather, Peter Carey. The school was situated at the east, or 'Church' end of the village, which then stretched about a mile to its 'Pury' or lower end. Here, in a little two-storied cottage, William's father, Edmund, set up his weaver's handloom for the production of coarse woollen cloth. An unlikely beginning, one might think, for the remarkable achiever William Carey was to become. But a providential change in the family's circumstances provided young William with opportunities that many other village children lacked.

William was just six years old when his grandfather died, and his father was appointed to succeed him in the same post – that of parish clerk and schoolmaster. The little family – wife Elizabeth, husband Edmund and son William – moved to the larger schoolhouse in the 'Church' end of the village. William now had the luxury of a room to himself, access to a few books, a place as a pupil in the school and a sight of the local newspaper, the hand-printed *Northampton Mercury*, delivered regularly.[1] These were all rare privileges for a village boy of his time. 'The child is the father of the man' it is said; the preparation of the man has begun in the stimulation of this child!

In those early years some of the characteristics which flowered to perfection in William as a man were already to be seen. Accounts of his childhood are scarce; the only sources of information that we have consist of some letters from his sister

---

[1] 'There were, for example, newspapers, for no provincial town was without its weekly paper, full of national and local news as well as advertisements of cultural events.' Strong, Roy p342.

Mary and some brief autobiographical notes that he wrote from India. William was the eldest of the five children born to Elizabeth and Edmund: Ann, Mary (nicknamed 'Polly'), Thomas and Elizabeth (who died in infancy). Mary seems to have been his favourite sister, often accompanying her brother on his walks in the country for nature study and happily caring for the specimens of plants, insects and caged birds which he kept in his room. The Northamptonshire countryside provided William with a rich source of study material and brought to birth the future naturalist. Mary wrote:

> *He often took me over the dirtiest roads to get at a plant or insect ... though I was but a child I well remember his pursuits. He never walked out, I think, when quite a boy, without observation of the hedges as he passed ...he always seemed in earnest in his recreations as well as in school ... he was always beloved by the boys about his own age.*[2]

Mary recorded an example of William's dogged perseverance, refusing to give up a thing until it was done. The boys of the village challenged each other to climb a certain tree. William joined in, at first falling a number of times but persevering until, at last, he was successful.

Edmund's brother, William's uncle Peter, left the army and also settled in the village of Paulerspury. As a soldier in the British Army he had had many adventures which he could now relate to a fascinated William. It seems that William became closer to him than to his rather parochial father, learning from Peter about botany and gardening, as well as about foreign lands and peoples. Presently William took over his father's garden and made it one of the best in the village.

In his own autobiographical notes William tells us that in his early school years he:

---

[2] Smith, George p4.

> ...*chose to read books of science, history, voyages etc. more than any others. Novels and plays always disgusted me and I avoided them as much as I did books of religion, and perhaps from the same motive. I was better pleased with romances,[3] and this circumstance made me read Pilgrim's Progress with eagerness, though to no purpose.*[4]

His father having become parish clerk with regular duties during church services, such as leading the singing and reading the Scriptures, meant that William became familiar with the text of the Bible and the Prayer Book from an early age. He was christened, served as a choirboy, was confirmed as a member of the Anglican Church and was trained to be a strict churchman. At that point he had no love for Dissenters, many of whom had been driven from the Anglican Church by its empty formality and lack of spirituality. Carey's own comment, in later life, was that ... *of real experimental religion I scarcely heard anything until I was fourteen years of age.*[5] There was one exception to this. Since her widowhood William's grandmother was living with the family. Her devout and spiritual behaviour was the only example of a deeply religious life that William would have been able to observe closely.

---

[3] In the old sense of 'a tale with characters, scenery and incidents more or less remote from ordinary life'.
[4] Smith, George p5.
[5] Carey, Eustace p7.

4
Into the world of work

At the age of twelve William left school and, as might be expected from his love of gardening and the influence of Uncle Peter, he chose to work as a farm labourer. He loved the natural world. From the time he was seven, however, a skin disease had developed which was aggravated by exposure to sunlight causing him subsequent painful nights.[1] It soon became apparent that an outdoor life was not for him. When he was fourteen years of age, therefore, his father apprenticed him to Clark Nichols, a shoemaker of good reputation in the village of Hackleton – nine miles from Paulerspury.

By this time William had found a Latin vocabulary the contents of which, with the grammar notes attached to it, he committed to memory. In Clarke Nichols' shop he found a few more books, one of which was a commentary on the New Testament. There William found a number of Greek words in the text that made him curious about that language. He remembered that in Paulerspury there was a certain Thomas Jones who, having had a good education (though now it was wasted by his disorderly life), had learned Greek. When William was allowed to make occasional visits home from his workplace in Hackleton, he went to Mr Jones for an explanation of these puzzling letters and words. So now he was learning Greek! His remarkable ability for learning languages was already beginning to show.

But it was more than books that Carey found in the Hackleton workshop as he learned his trade as a shoemaker. He was working alongside an older fellow apprentice named John Warr who was a Congregational Dissenter and an eager Christian.

---

[1] 'A scorbutic [ie scurvy-like] disorder, which his constitution eventually surmounted'. Marshman, John Clark p2.

John lent William more books, the reading of which brought him to the conviction that he was a sinner unable to save himself. Such guilty feelings were greatly increased by his knowingly passing on a counterfeit shilling coin (in those days a capital offence). The deception was soon discovered by his master, to William's shame. He was learning that his attempts to reform his own character continually failed; but through reading his Bible and other religious books and in conversations with other believers, Carey was presently brought, in his own words:

> ...to depend upon a crucified Saviour for pardon and salvation, and to seek a system of doctrines from the Word of God.[2]

Two years of apprenticeship in the Hackleton workshop had brought life-changing experiences to William: he was now an eager Christian believer and a qualified shoemaker. When Clarke Nichols died, William joined the employ of Mr Thomas Old, shoemaker and Congregationalist of the same village. The well-known Bible commentator, the evangelical Anglican minister Thomas Scott[3] was in the habit, from time to time, of visiting the home of Mr Old and preaching to the villagers. Through this ministry William's desire to 'seek a system of doctrines from the Word of God' was being well answered. Many years later, when Carey was established in India, Mr Scott was heard to remark to a friend as they passed Mr Old's house:

> That was Mr Carey's college.[4]

Robert Hall, pastor of the church in Arnsby (and father of the more famous Robert Hall Junior) published a book which had the title *Help to Zion's Travellers; an attempt to remove various stumbling blocks out of the way relating to doctrinal, experimental and practical religion*. This book began as a sermon preached by Robert Hall at the Northamptonshire Baptist

---

[2] George, Timothy p8.
[3] 1747-1821
[4] Marshman, John Clark p2.

Ministers' Fraternal in 1779. The book was a great help to William at this time. He studied it meticulously, making summary notes of the content of each page on the page margins. He later wrote of it:

> *I do not remember to have read any book with such rapture as I did that. If it was poison, as some then said, it was so sweet to me that I drank it greedily to the bottom of the cup; and I rejoice to say that those doctrines are the choice of my heart, to this day.*[5]

Not all Calvinistic Baptists would have agreed with Carey's love of that book, because it urged the presentation of gospel invitations to all readers of it. Those of High Calvinistic persuasion did not approve of Hall's book for they did not feel free to present gospel invitations to the ungodly without discrimination, but only to God's elect. Hall had argued that the way to Jesus is graciously open for everyone who chooses to come to him. An *evangelical* Calvinism thus became Carey's doctrinal thinking and practice.[6] Being a Christian, for William, was not merely an experience one seeks for oneself but an experience which fires one with a spiritual concern to present the gospel to *everyone*. He wrote home, bluntly expressing concern for the unconverted spiritual state of his family, so that even friendly sister Mary was at first offended as she battled with her personal pride, feeling that:

> *William thought his family filthy and not himself or his party.*[7]

Happily, within a short while, Mary understood and joined William in her commitment to Christ as her Saviour too.

Overseas, things were not going well for the British Army in the war with the American colonists. George III called for a

---
[5] Carey, Eustace p36, quoted by George, Timothy p57.
[6] See later (chapter 7) for further information on *The modern question* as it was called among Calvinists.
[7] George, Timothy p8.

national day of prayer, set for 10 February 1779. William was to be found with the Hackleton congregation, listening to a sermon based upon Hebrews 13:13.[8] In Carey's mind this was understood as a call to leave the lifeless Anglican Church and bear the reproach of being a despised Dissenter. He joined with the Hackleton Congregational Church in 1781 and subsequently began to preach there from time to time and also in the nearby village of Barton. The parish clerk's son had now become a Congregational Dissenter. And that was not the only change in his life.

---

[8] *Let us go forth therefore unto him* [Jesus] *without the camp, bearing his reproach.* (AV)

5
Family life and a business to run

Daniel Plackett was a leader of the Hackleton meeting. He had a family of daughters, the eldest of them being the wife of Thomas Old, who was the owner of the business that Carey joined after the sudden death of Clarke Nichols. Daniel's home is described as:

> ... Puritan, and the sisters earnest and lovable.[1]

That latter fact had not escaped William's notice. In 1781 William and Dorothy Plackett (a younger sister of Thomas Old's wife) were married in Piddington church. Dorothy was five years older than twenty-year old William and, like many village women of that time, was illiterate. The marriage register bears the mark of an X in the place of her signature, though even the officiating clergyman hardly excelled, writing her name as 'Dority'! The happiness of the early years of their married life was marred by the death of their little daughter Ann in 1782 and the unexpected death of Thomas Old in 1783.

William now assumed the care of Mr Old's widow and family, taking over Thomas Old's business, and relocated the shop in the village of Piddington where he and Dorothy were now living. A large order of boots, nearly completed when Old died, was suddenly cancelled, leaving William with a struggle to dispose of them. The little family knew what it was to be in want in those early years. Yet William never lost the appetite for learning; he was studying Dutch, French, Italian and, with the help of a nearby minister, being introduced to Hebrew. That he should

---
[1] Carey, S Pearce p39.

have married an illiterate village woman has sometimes been criticised as a great mistake. For example:

> *Never had a minister, missionary, or scholar a less sympathetic mate, due largely to that latent mental disease which in India carried her off.*[2]

Or again:

> *This imprudent union proved a severe clog on his exertions for more than twenty-five years. His illiterate wife, who possessed no feeling in unison with his own, was altogether unsuited for his companionship.*[3]

As James R Beck has pointed out in his book, Dorothy has been variously described as 'a dull, commonplace woman', 'a dull, ignorant woman', and 'an illiterate, weak-minded woman'. Yet there is no evidence to support such statements. To be illiterate is not the same as being unintelligent or weak-minded. Many villages in her day had no village school and so illiteracy was common among the women. In any case, Dorothy subsequently learned to read and write with William's help. Nor is there evidence that there was 'latent' mental disorder in her. There is no trace, before her being in India, of such mental disorder in her parentage or sisters nor, later, in her children.

> *The mental illness of Dorothy's mother, her own erratic behaviour in England and the early death of her mother … are pure fiction. Tragically these distortions needlessly colour the Christian public's perception of Dorothy.*[4]

And it certainly is not true that 'never had a minister, missionary or scholar a less sympathetic mate'. History tells of other leading Christian men whose wives succumbed to mental

---
[2] Smith, George p16.
[3] Marshman, John Clark p4.
[4] Beck, James R p19.

illness, including the wife of Carey's dear friend of later years, Andrew Fuller.

Dorothy's mental ill health is not without parallel in the records of a number of different missions since then, even where circumstances were less harsh than hers. One comment made by John Clark Marshman is worthy of note:

> *... the great tenderness which always marked his* [ie Carey's] *conduct towards her places the nobleness and meekness of his character in a strong light.*[5]

Since that was Carey's blameless attitude toward Dorothy, uninformed speculation about her character seems at best unwise; at worst, insulting. Carey's great grandson, S Pearce Carey, movingly comments:

> *I have most rejoiced to rescue the name of the mother of all his children from the cruel wrongs that have been done to her. Now that the facts will be known, feeling will rebound in her favour ... Carey would wish me to lay this wreath upon her grave.*[6]

The question of the nature of Biblical baptism began to occupy William's mind. He had been christened as a baby and confirmed when a boy, but continuing study of his Bible eventually brought him to the conviction of the rightness of baptism by total immersion as a committed believer. He sought advice from John Ryland Snr of the Northampton Particular Baptist church who provided him with a helpful pamphlet on the subject. It was on 7 October 1783 that John Ryland Jnr, then assistant to his father, baptized a 'poor journeyman shoemaker'[7] in the river Nene, as he later recalled it. William had walked five miles to get there by six o-clock in the morning for the ceremony. So the son of an Anglican parish clerk was now a trained shoemaker

---

[5] Marshman, John Clark p5.
[6] Carey, S Pearce (8th edition), preface.
[7] A journeyman was a fully qualified tradesman having completed an apprenticeship successfully.

and a Baptist believer. Yet he was not an isolationist; he was still pleased to have fellowship with several evangelical Anglican friends who shared his love for Bible truth – a trait of *evangelical ecumenism* which never left him.

The newly married couple were clearly faced with traumatic circumstances in those early years. Shoemaking had become a poor trade, possibly because the mounting costs of the unsuccessful war in the American colonies was damaging the country's economy. Their home in Piddington had attracted William as a desirable residence because of its garden but it suffered from the fact that it stood on low lying ground near marshland. Little Ann, their firstborn, dying of a fever was not an uncommon event in such a location and Carey himself fell dangerously ill, which resulted in the loss of his hair at the age of twenty two. Infant mortality was a common enough tragedy in those days but, none the less, the pain of such a loss must have deeply affected both William and Dorothy. It was three years before baby Felix appeared on the scene to constitute them a family again. Their poverty was such that William knew what it was to starve himself to save money to buy a few books, but books he must have! And his being eager to listen to good preaching often meant a walk for miles to reach the advertised meeting place. To maintain his family he opened an evening school in the village, the income from which, together with small amounts earned by his preaching and his shoemaking, kept them all alive.

6
Entering the pastoral ministry

The Baptist church in the village of Moulton came to hear of the acceptable preaching of a young man by the name of William Carey. Being without regular ministry for some years, the church there had fallen upon lean times. The few that remained in the membership called this young man to be their pastor. Their previous ministers had been of the General (Arminian) Baptist persuasion. William was undaunted by the challenge and early in 1785 the Careys moved to the village. Their low family income meant that a certificate had to be obtained from the Paulerspury authorities promising to accept financial responsibility for the family if they should become so poor as to need support from Moulton village funds, in which case Moulton would send them back to Paulerspury.[1] With William's father as the Paulerspury parish clerk, and with two other friends, the required certificate was obtained. Moulton accepted William and Dorothy as new residents.

But the Moulton church was unable to pay a living wage to their pastor.[2] William was obliged again to continue his shoemaking and open a small village school. His occasional ministry at the church in Earl's Barton involved a five or six mile walk, which cost him more in shoe leather than that church could reimburse! Despite these problems the church at Moulton began to prosper, eventually requiring the repair and enlargement of the building, which expense involved the church in debt for a while despite gifts from friends.

---

[1] By the terms of the Act of Settlement 1662.
[2] The amount the church offered is variously said to have been £10, £11, £12 a year, together with a small annual grant of five guineas and one small grant for books, both from the Particular Baptist Fund in London. (See the Additional Note at the end of this chapter).

Although serving as Moulton's pastor, Carey was not officially recognised as an ordained minister of the Particular (Calvinistic) Baptist group of churches. John Sutcliff, the pastor of Olney Baptist church[3] had urged William to consider *...the propriety of joining some respectable church, and being appointed to the ministry in a more regular way.*[4]

Carey applied to the Olney church for membership and turned to Sutcliff for advice about ordination. At a business meeting of the church on 14 July 1785 Carey shared with them the spiritual experience of his conversion. The church happily received his testimony and he was invited to preach for them the following Sunday evening. This he did, though his own estimate of that sermon was that it was *...as crude and weak as anything could be, which is called, or has been called, a sermon.*[5]

Nevertheless the church encouraged him to persevere and on 17 July they resolved:

> ... that he should be allowed to go on preaching at those places where he has been for sometime employed, and that he should engage again on suitable occasions for some time before us, in order that farther [sic] trial may be made of his ministerial gifts.[6]

It was a whole year (June 1786) before the church could come to a unanimous agreement as to William's ministerial gifts and commit him to the work of ministry wherever God in his Providence might call him. A year later (1787) the church dismissed him from the membership which they had granted him at Olney, for him to become a member at the Moulton church and to be ordained there. His ability humbly to accept church

---

[3] Olney was a village favoured by evangelical and Calvinistic ministries. The Baptist church under Sutcliff had a membership of hundreds. The Anglican church had had the ministries of John Newton and Thomas Scott and the poetry of William Cowper.
[4] George, Timothy p17.
[5] Marshman, John Clark p4. His nephew Eustace did not speak very highly of his sermons.
[6] Smith, George p19.

discipline and to persevere through those three years, when many others might have been offended and critical, augured well for the young man's future.

To see the church at Moulton flourishing under his care must have been a great encouragement to William. He had to give up his occasional preaching visits to Earl's Barton since his church was steadily growing, and the village school and shoemaking business more than filled his days together with his pastoral work in Moulton. Every fortnight he could be found walking to Kettering, with a bundle of boots for the businessman Thomas Gotch. Yet Carey still found time to devote to reading, to improving his knowledge of Greek and Hebrew, and to systematic Bible study. Not content that his family relatives[7] and his village people should come to a commitment to his Lord and Saviour, Carey knew that in the foreign lands his uncle Peter had told him about there were millions of men and women who had never heard that there ever was a Jesus Christ. And he could not forget that his Lord had commanded that all nations should hear of the forgiveness of sins through Jesus Christ. Reading a borrowed book about Captain Cook's travels, Carey was stung by a comment concerning missionary work overseas:

> *It is very unlikely that any measure of this kind should ever be seriously thought of, as it can neither serve the purpose of public ambition or private avarice; and without such inducements, I may pronounce that it will never be undertaken.*[8]

Carey was not the man to be deterred from obedience to his Lord's command by the opinions of a mere Captain Cook. His shoemaker's workshop wall was covered with papers where he had drawn a map of the world on which was written data concerning the population and religions of the various countries. On his workbench rested a leather globe with the outlines of the countries of the world scratched upon it. As he worked, he

---

[7] He had written quite a bold letter to his parents urging them as to the necessity of a living, spiritual experience. George, Timothy p8.
[8] Carey, S Pearce (8th edition) p43.

prayed. For the sake of the Lord's glory, Captain Cook *must* be shown to be wrong, wrong, wrong!

Carey was ordained to the ministry in Moulton in August 1787, once the repair and enlargement of the chapel building were completed. A number of ministers from the Northamptonshire Particular Baptist Association were present and his three friends, Sutcliff, Ryland Jnr, and Fuller, led the ordination. Michael Haykin makes the interesting point in his book that John Stanger, the son and grandson of the two previous General Baptist pastors of the church, also took part – at the invitation of Carey himself.[9]

Stanger wrote in his diary:

> *A large congregation attended. I prayed with laying on of hands. I rejoiced in the prosperity of the Cause, as it was the spot where I preached my first sermon, and where my father laboured twenty years.*[10]

Clearly William Carey's evangelistic Calvinism was an attractive rather than isolationist theology. A few years later Stanger and his church became members of the Particular Baptist Association in Kent, now being Calvinistic Baptist.[11]

But life in Moulton still had its struggles for William and Dorothy. A former Anglican schoolmaster in the village, who had closed his school and moved away, suddenly returned. There was no room for two schools in the village and as William's Baptist school lost favour it had to be closed. By now the Carey family had grown – William and Peter had arrived to join Felix – making more mouths to feed and more bodies to clothe. The shoemaking business was even more necessary though not very profitable. The church was growing in numbers and spiritual knowledge but still could not support their pastor fully. There were some matters of church discipline that required to be dealt with – never a pleasant task. One brighter moment was Dorothy's baptism at the hands of her husband in October 1787.

---

[9] Haykin, Michael p188.
[10] Carey, S Pearce p51.
[11] Haykin, Michael p188-9.

Dorothy, as a member of the Congregational church at Hackleton, was there under the influence of paedo-baptist thinking. Her baptism as a believer at Moulton represented a clear break from her former church's baptismal practice; whether or not that was difficult for her is unclear.[12] That this baptism indicated the *beginning* of Dorothy's spiritual experience seems unlikely since it is surely improbable that William, who was so 'on fire' with evangelistic enthusiasm, would have chosen a girl as his wife to whom such spirituality was unknown.

Despite growing church and family commitments, Carey still budgeted time for language learning, improving his knowledge of Latin, Greek and Hebrew, with the help of knowledgeable friends, and studying French, Dutch and Italian by himself. At least the task of shoemaking was an opportunity for him to study a book poised on his workbench. Journeys taken to purchase leather and for the sale of boots, provided opportunity for mental revision of what had been learnt and for thinking about how to meet the need of millions of heathen overseas to hear about Jesus Christ. His sister Mary once wrote:

> *He was always, from his first being thoughtful, remarkably impressed about heathen lands and the slave trade. I never remember his engaging in prayer, in his family or in public, without praying for those poor creatures. The first time I ever recollect my feeling for the heathen world, was from a discourse I heard my brother preach at Moulton ... it was a day to be remembered by me.*[13]

Many an observer of Pastor William Carey must have wondered what would be the outcome of this young man's remarkable ability with languages and his passionate concern for the spiritual welfare of far-away heathen peoples. As we look back

---

[12] When baby Ann was born the Careys did not have her christened in Piddington church. When she died in 1784 William and Dorothy were faced with the problem of burying an unbaptised child. We might conclude from this that already the Careys were considering the concept of baptism by immersion for believers alone.

[13] Smith, George p.23

now, is it not surprising that someone allergic to sunshine and being a leather worker as well should have been sent by Providence to spend a lifetime in India where the former is constant and the latter is a trade of the despised lower caste?[14] And what could Dorothy have made of her husband's most unusual missionary enthusiasm? With three young boys to care for, and William so often occupied with his work to earn the family's keep or away to hear preaching, was there much time for him to discuss these things with her?

Additional Note

An extract from the history of the Particular Baptist Fund provides the following note:

> William Carey received considerable help, and appears to have had more educational and book grants than anyone else. We list below the grants made to William Carey. **1786** – £5-5-0 for books and an extra £5-5-0; **1787** – a special grant of £5-5-0; **1788** – Moulton church to help the pastor's stipend £5-5-0; **1789/1790** – the Leicester church to help the pastor's stipend each year £5-5-0; **1791** – a grant in the name of William Carey £5-5-0; **1792** – Extra-ordinary grant of £5-5-0 to William Carey …This was an investment indeed and the Fundees surely have some cause for feeling that this ancient Fund had a real share in Carey's amazing achievements.[15]

The Particular Baptist Fund, according to the earliest surviving documents, had its origin and design in 1717, some years after the Toleration Act had received Royal Assent in 1689 (which had given Dissenters a new liberty of worship). The fund was begun to help those desiring to enter the ministry and to assist Particular Baptist churches in supporting their pastors.

---
[14] See 1 Corinthians 1:25
[15] Valentine, TF p36

Part Two

'... then the ear'

(Mark 4:28)

A beautiful allusion to the succession of similar stages,
though not definitely marked periods, in the Christian life
and generally in the Kingdom of God.

(Jamieson, Fausset & Brown, Commentary op.cit.)

7
'Our petitions may prove like seeds in the earth'[1]

On the road between the towns of Northampton and Kettering lies the village of Moulton where the 'new' idea of missionary outreach to the whole world was increasingly capturing the mind of the young Baptist pastor, William Carey. And not his mind alone: for the providence of God was carefully moving into place other people concerned with the same vision who, in due time, would unite to bring to birth the first Baptist missionary society. One of the most remarkable factors which were foundational to the success of their eventual missionary effort was the depth of the trust and commitment of three or four men to William, to the missionary project and mutually to one another. That such a closeness of fellowship and intensity of purpose could flower so rapidly and so beautifully between those men is surely a sign of a divine purpose, which is fascinating to watch take shape.

Over in Kettering, perhaps ten miles north east of Moulton, a young Baptist pastor named Andrew Fuller had been ministering since 1782. He had moved there, after considerable heart searching, from serving as pastor to a little group of believers in Soham, Cambridgeshire, who were scarcely able to support him financially. Fuller not merely agonised (for something like two

---

[1] From a sermon preached by Andrew Fuller eight years *before* the Particular Baptist Society for the Promulgation of the Gospel was founded in 1792.

years) over the rightness of a move to Kettering[2] but also had, during his time at Soham, been grappling with what was known as 'the Calvinistic controversy' or 'the Modern Question', so called from a pamphlet published by a certain Abraham Taylor. The High Calvinistic teaching that Fuller had absorbed in his early years as a Christian was that:

> *Nothing was to be addressed to the unregenerate but exhortations to external obedience ...Attendance of the means of grace, abstinence from gross evil might be enforced, but nothing was to be said to sinful men about Christ's salvation, or fleeing from the wrath to come.*[3]

When taking the pastorate at Soham (his ordination was in 1775 after a year of ministry there) Fuller had felt a serious responsibility as to what he should preach as God's truth. In his diary he describes himself as 'feeling his way out of a labyrinth', being embarrassed about whether he should, or should not, address invitations to sinners 'to come to Christ'. Conversations with Mr Hall of Arnesby, the author of *Helps for Zion's Travellers,* a book which William Carey valued so much, led Fuller to read the 1754 work by the Calvinist and philosopher Jonathan Edwards of Northampton, Massachusetts, entitled *Inquiry into the modern prevailing notions respecting the freedom of the will which it is supposed to be essential to moral agency.* Edwards' view was that the inability to do a thing does not negate the duty to do it. Fuller also read of the missionary ministries of Elliot and Brainerd who seemed to have no problem with freely preaching the full gospel message to the native Indians of America. And Abraham's pamphlet which outlined the New Testament ministries of John Baptist, Jesus Christ and the apostles (all of whom called for the ungodly to repent of their ungodliness and believe

---

[2] 'The thought of my situation now returns and overpowers me ... Oh! Lord, if thou wilt give me so much light as plainly to see in this case what is my duty, then, if I do not obey the dictates of my conscience, let my tongue cleave for ever to the roof of my mouth'. From Andrew Fuller's diary, quoted in Fuller, Thomas Ekins pp38-39.
[3] Ibid p24.

in Christ for salvation) confirmed Fuller's slowly forming view that 'the gospel *was* worthy of all acceptation'.[4]

This 'modern' view was the cause of division among Calvinists because of its practical consequences.

> If believing was an obligation, preachers could press it on whole congregations; if it was not they could only describe it in the hope that God would rouse certain pre-determined hearers to faith. Those on the modern side had a rationale for evangelism systematically expounded by Andrew Fuller. The logic of Evangelical activism was founded on the doctrine of duty faith.[5]

Fuller could now write in his diary:

> I found a suspicion that we shackle ourselves too much in our addresses; that we have bewildered and lost ourselves in taking the decrees of God as the rules of action. Surely Peter and Paul never felt such scruples in their addresses as we do. They addressed their hearers as men – fallen men.[6]

Andrew Fuller and William Carey were now standing on the same ground. Andrew, through much soul searching and careful Bible study which had led him out from under what he called 'ultra-Calvinistic' teaching; William, because he had come early into an evangelistic Calvinism which allowed him to have the whole world in his sight.

> At his first setting out, he [Carey] was much perplexed between the statements of the Arminians on some theological points, and the crude representations of some

---

[4] The title of his book, published in 1785.
[5] Bebbington, D W, p64. 'Duty faith' was the term used to describe the doctrine that belief *was* the duty of all persons hearing the gospel message preached.
[6] Fuller, Thomas Ekins, p29.

> Calvinists; but having adopted a satisfactory medium between the two extremes, his mind was fully prepared for the doctrine so successfully pleaded by Mr Fuller.[7]

The circle of Carey's immediate friends was slowly growing. Carey's introduction to the Northamptonshire Particular Baptist Association has already been mentioned. Among those leading the affairs of that Association were John Sutcliff of Olney, with whom Carey already had a close friendship; John Ryland Snr and his son, both of Northampton, who had both helped Carey in the matter of his baptism; and Robert Hall of Arnesby, whose book had been such a blessing to Carey during his early years as a Christian. Along with these, and some others, William now had Andrew Fuller as another sympathetic and valuable friend.

From its beginning the Association was regularly concerned to invite member churches to frequent fasting and prayer for God's blessing on their congregations – but not the Association churches alone. The vision was widening. A summary from a meeting in 1769, four years after the founding of the Association, reads:

> We have agreed to keep a day of solemn fasting and prayer through all our congregations on account of national affairs on Wednesday the 4th of October. We beg that you would seriously attend upon it and should rejoice to find that any of our dear brethren who are not in the compass of this Association shall be willing to meet us at the throne of grace that day.[8]

A sermon by Andrew Fuller at the Association meetings in Nottingham in 1784 seems to have given added emphasis to this widening concern. The third point of his sermon was summarised as *Let the present religious state of the world be considered to this end*.[9] And the Association circular letter of 1784,

---

[7] Morris, J W, *Life of Andrew Fuller* p99.
[8] Elwyn, TSH, p16.
[9] Ibid p17.

written that year by John Sutcliff, underlines this missionary outlook, containing as it did the significant words:

> *We trust that you will not confine your requests to your own societies or to your immediate connection; let the whole interest of the Redeemer be affectionately remembered, and the spread of the Gospel to the most distant parts of the habitable globe be the object of your most fervent requests.*[10]

In his history of the Association, Elwyn makes the significant point that this growing concern for overseas missionary outreach of the churches was thus appearing in the thinking of a number of prominent Association men *before* Carey had finished compiling his now famous *Enquiry* in 1792. We surely must conclude that the gracious providence of God was steadily bringing together a company of men whose mutual companionship was ideally suited to support and nurture Carey's own convictions. 'As iron sharpens iron so one man sharpens another'.[11]

At least one other significant influence in the situation must not be overlooked. In 1784 John Ryland Jnr received from a Scottish friend a treatise by Jonathan Edwards[12] entitled: *A humble attempt to promote explicit agreement and visible union of God's people in extraordinary prayer for the revival of religion and the advancement of Christ's kingdom on earth pursuant to Scripture promises and prophecies concerning the last time.*[13] From a range of Old Testament prophecies Edwards argued for what he called 'the latter day glory' when the knowledge and glory of God would fill the earth. To this end Edwards urged a great 'concert of prayer' to begin among all Christians.[14]

---

[10] Ibid p17.
[11] Proverbs 27:17
[12] 1703-1758 A prominent minister in America.
[13] Haykin, Michael, p154.
[14] 'Post-millennialists emphasise the present aspects of God's kingdom which will reach fruition in the future ... through Christian preaching and teaching.' Evangelical Dictionary of Theology, op.cit.

John Ryland Jnr was so impressed by Edwards' arguments that he shared the treatise with his friends Sutcliff and Fuller. Perhaps it is no coincidence that later that same year a call came for regular weekly prayer for revival by the churches of the Northamptonshire Association.[15] Five years later Sutcliff himself published another edition of Edwards' original treatise to strengthen the practice of regular prayer in the churches, commenting:

> *O for thousands upon thousands, divided into small bands in their respective cities, towns, villages and neighbourhoods all at the same time and in pursuit of one end, offering up their united prayers like so many ascending clouds of incense before the most High.*[16]

Increasingly the churches of the Association adopted this practice of weekly meetings for prayer, greatly encouraged by the reasoning of Edwards' treatise to expect a time when Christ's kingdom would cover the earth as a result of the worldwide expansion of the Christian church. It would not be wrong to call these prayer meetings 'missionary prayer meetings', for they arose from the expectation of worldwide conversion. Clearly, Carey was not alone the 'Father of modern missions'. Without detracting in any way from his relentless determination for mission to the heathen which, despite early hesitations, his friends freely acknowledged, it has to be said that it was also the oxygen of these prayer groups providentially gathered around him which eventually helped to transform Carey's passionate dreams into reality. God was to use that oxygen to grow a great flame of activity to lighten the darkness of the world's ignorance of the gospel.[17]

---

[15] Elwyn, TSH, p16.
[16] Haykin, Michael, p170.
[17] 1 Corinthians 3:6,7

8
'*Sit down, young man!*'

One might think that William's days at the Moulton church were so full of activity as to leave him little time for thinking about mission to the distant heathen. There was the school to run; more language learning to pursue; preaching around the district; journeys to other churches to raise finance for repairs to the Moulton building; his business of shoe-making; eagerness to hear others preaching (sometimes involving a walk of twenty miles to hear Robert Hall of Arnesby); all in addition to his ministerial responsibilities at Moulton. A friend did challenge him for appearing to neglect his shoe-making business.

Carey answered: *Neglecting my business! My business, Sir, is to extend the Kingdom of Christ. I only make and mend shoes to help pay expenses.*[1] Clearly, the flame of missionary zeal still burned brightly.

Describing one of his visits to Carey in Moulton, Andrew Fuller wrote:

> *I remember on going into his room where he employed himself at his business, I saw hanging up against the wall a very large map, consisting of several sheets of paper pasted together by himself, on which he had drawn with a pen, a place for every nation in the known world, and entered into it whatever he met with in reading relative to its population, religion etc. The substance of this was afterwards published in his Enquiry.*[2]

---

[1] Carey, S Pearce, p56
[2] Smith, George, p22

Inevitably these researches meant some limitation on the energy spent in all Carey's other activities. Yet if the overall quantity of what he achieved had this limitation, the quality of what he did remained high. Much later William himself wrote, in a letter home from India, that he earned the reputation of 'a skilful and honest workman' in his shoe-making business during this busy period.[3]

William was constantly urging his friends Fuller and Sutcliff to take the lead in the cause of mission to the heathen, feeling them better qualified men for this task than himself. Wherever he could, Carey regularly challenged fellow ministers with the need for foreign mission. Andrew Fuller wrote:

> They mostly regarded it as a wild, impractical scheme and gave him no encouragement. Yet he would not give it up, but talked with us one by one, till he had made some impression.[4]

At a meeting of Association ministers in 1786 in Northampton, John Ryland Snr, who chaired the meeting, requested those present to suggest a topic that might be the subject of their discussion. After a period of silence Carey spoke up:

> Whether the command given to the Apostles, to teach all nations, was not obligatory on all succeeding ministers to the end of the world, seeing the accompanying promise was of equal extent.[5]

What happened next is variously reported! It was clearly a dramatic moment. George Smith records that John Ryland Snr shouted the rebuke:

> You are a miserable enthusiast for asking such a question. Certainly nothing can be done before another Pentecost, when an infusion of miraculous gifts, including

---

[3] Fuller, Thomas Ekins, p77
[4] Carey, S Pearce, p56.
[5] Smith, George p23.

> *the gift of tongues, will give effect to the commission of Christ as at first. What sir, can you preach in Arabic, in Persian, in Hindoostani, in Bengalee, that you think it your duty to preach the Gospel to the heathen?*[6]

How many a modern would-be missionary could sympathise with Ryland's argument, as he or she struggles to discipline *their* nouns, verbs and adjectives into intelligible order in some foreign earthly language, longing for another miraculous gift of foreign languages!

In his book John Clark Marshman records Carey telling him in India that Ryland Snr sprang to his feet and denounced Carey's proposal with the words:

> *Young man, sit down! When God pleases to convert the heathen he will do it without your aid or mine.*[7]

John Ryland Snr seemed subsequently unable to recall the incident at all.[8] He is reputed to have prayed and preached as much as anyone else about 'the latter day glory', being wholly in sympathy with Edwards' treatise then circulating on the subject.[9] John Ryland Jnr however is on record as denying that his father could have said any such thing as was reported, he not even being at the meeting in Northampton in 1786.[10] Another account of the incident has come from the pen of Carey's friend, John Webster Morris, of Clipstone. In his book *Life of Andrew Fuller* (1816 and 1826) he confirms having been in that meeting and supports the account of it given much later by George Smith, as noted above. However, in the later 1826 edition of his book Morris makes the further suggestion that Ryland's remarks may have been simply 'a piece of pleasantry' or even 'intended

---

[6] This last sentence only, Fuller, Thomas Ekins, p78. Previous sentences, Smith, George p23.
[7] Marshman, John Clark, p7.
[8] Smith, George, p23.
[9] Haykin, Michael, p196.
[10] Carey, S Pearce, p54.

as ironical'.[11] Carey himself, at different times, expressed the view that he had received 'an abashing rebuke', as he put it.[12]

In the light of these different accounts of what actually took place it seems unwise to consider the incident as clear evidence of the 'yoke of Hyper-Calvinism' from which Particular Baptists had not yet escaped.[13] Other reasons can be found to account for their sincere hesitation to commit themselves to Carey's dream. Those were days when the Dissenting churches generally were struggling with a number of doctrinal issues. As we look back now it is unwise to make absolute judgements about the reason for what was then said and done. It does seem clear that while there was happy agreement that *prayer* for 'the latter day glory' was something all could support, yet actually *doing* something towards the coming of that glory was too impossible to conceive. Fuller himself, who did sympathetically support Carey, is reported to have said: *If the Lord should make windows in heaven, might such a thing be?* [14] Since many Baptist churches of the time could hardly raise the finance to support their pastors adequately, how could it be expected that they could further finance a possible large 'open-ended' expense to support missions overseas?

Perhaps a not unrelated consideration to raise at this point is the teaching of the greatly renowned Puritan preacher and writer, John Owen.[15] In his study *The True Nature of a Gospel Church* he writes:

> *No church whatever hath power to ordain men ministers for the conversion of infidels ... nor is there mention of any ordinary officers in the whole Scripture but such as were fixed in the particular churches which were to be their particular charge or care.*[16]

---

[11] Haykin, Michael, p194.
[12] Carey, S Pearce, p54.
[13] Smith, George, p24.
[14] Marshman, John Clark p7.
[15] John Owen, 1616-1683.
[16] Owen, John vol 16 pp92-93.

Owen was emphasising that the apostolic practice was always to ordain ministers 'in and unto particular churches'. Ministers, ordained to serve in those specific churches, were to diffuse the knowledge of the gospel among the heathen who lived around those churches. Was there any biblical justification for Carey's concern for evangelism among pagans where there were no churches, he not being an apostle? Carey's colleagues might well have asked the question.

It must also be borne in mind that during Carey's time there was a growing fear among government authorities that the seeds of the developing anarchy of French revolutionary thought, a mere twenty miles away across the Channel, might be planted in English soil too. In such a climate it is understandable that the formation of any new society or grouping, whether for evangelistic purposes or not, could be misunderstood by the authorities. It would therefore seem to be an unwise undertaking for humble Baptist pastors to attempt to form some new movement. Wesley's preaching tours up and down the land often resulted in great crowds gathering and local authorities were fearful, not understanding that these crowds were not anarchists. William, however, seemed undaunted by all opposing arguments. In subsequent ministers' meetings he continued to provoke discussions on the subject and, possibly at Fuller's suggestion, set to work to prepare a written statement of his arguments for mission overseas which eventually became the famous *Enquiry into the Obligation of Christians to use Means for the Conversion of the Heathen.*[17]

Two very practical encouragements came to William. The footwear that he was making in his Moulton workshop was sold to Thomas Gotch, a member of Fuller's church in Kettering. Gotch had a contract with the army for the supply of soldiers' boots. After making a delivery of boots on one occasion Carey was asked by Thomas what he earned by his trade and, learning what little it was, Thomas made the kind offer to give him ten shillings a week to relieve him of the need to make shoes.

---

[17] There is a full text of this publication to be found as an appendix to *Faithful Witness* by Timothy George, p197 and following.

Instead he urged William to use his time in further studies of languages, missionary work and in preparation for his pastoral ministry. A second encouragement came through a certain Thomas Potts of Birmingham whom Carey visited in 1788, seeking to gather financial support for the refurbishment of the Moulton chapel. In discussion Thomas learned from William that he proposed to write out his thoughts on missionary enterprise in the *Enquiry*. Thomas urged him to publish the work when completed. Learning that William had no funds with which to do so, Thomas gave him £10 toward that expense. The last years at Moulton must have been years when Carey's spirit was greatly encouraged by these two men. Their help must have been some compensation for the difficulties he was facing in seeking to raise concern among his fellow pastors that something ought to be done about the spiritual need of the heathen which so burdened his own heart.

9
The obligations of Christians

For several years following his conversion Carey had been gathering information about the different peoples of the world, their various religions and the geographical details of their lands. He drew his facts from accounts such as those by Captain Cook of his voyages, from details in newspapers such as the *Northampton Mercury*, and from the tales recounted by his uncle Peter. Geography books and church history books added to his growing store of knowledge. William was compiling a survey of the state of world religions in his day and so preparing answers to the arguments of those who resisted his pleas for evangelism in the wider world. If ministers' fraternal meetings would not hear his pleas then he would present his case more widely, in writing. Perhaps the sheer size of world need and the compelling authority of Christ's words (Matthew 28:18-20) could put to shame the fears and the apathy of all the churches in this matter. What eventually emerged was a remarkable piece of writing.

> *In an obscure village, toiling save when he slept, and finding rest on Sunday only by a change of toil, far from libraries and from the society of men with more advantages than his own, this shoemaker, still under thirty, surveys the whole world, continent by continent and island by island, race by race, faith by faith, kingdom by kingdom, tabulating his results with an accuracy and following them up with a logical power of generalisation which would extort the admiration of the learned even of the present day.*[1]

---
[1] Smith, George p24.

The obligations of Christians 67

Carey's friends Sutcliff, Fuller and Ryland Jnr were themselves noted authors. But Carey failed to persuade them to write a treatise on missionary enterprise. They in turn encouraged him to attempt the task himself, perhaps more as a stratagem to direct his pleading away from themselves[2] than out of a sincere desire to consider the matter more thoroughly.

> *Do, by all means, write your thoughts down, but be not in a hurry to print them; let us look over them and see if anything need be omitted, altered or added.*[3]

That was not the last time such a stratagem, if that is what it was, has been used to curb an enthusiast; in Carey's case it signally failed!

Carey began his *Enquiry*[4] with an introduction in which he argued that ... *it becomes us to use every lawful method to spread the knowledge of the name of the Lord* since ... *he requires us to pray that his kingdom may come and his will be done on earth as in heaven*. Carey gives the instances of Christ sending out his disciples, and later the apostles, as examples of God's intention that in every age the knowledge of his kingdom should be spread throughout the earth in opposition to the kingdom of Satan which holds a considerable part of humankind in the darkness of heathenism. It must be wrong, he pleads, that ...*some think little about it, others are unacquainted with the state of the world, and others love their wealth better than the souls of their fellow creatures.*[5]

In the first section of the *Enquiry* Carey seeks to answer, one by one, the arguments raised against mission to the heathen by

---

[2] 'Fuller, Ryland and Sutcliff advised him to revise it, more however with the hope of escaping from his importunities than with any serious desire of encouraging such a project which appeared to them perfectly utopian.' Marshman, John Clark, p8.
[3] Haykin, Michael p197.
[4] Carey's *Enquiry* was not the only one of the time. William Godwin (1756-1836), a one-time nonconformist minister turned atheist philosopher, wrote a political *Enquiry,* a revolutionary work published in 1793, a year after Carey's book came out.
[5] From the Introduction to the *Enquiry*

his Baptist colleagues. It is as though he gives there his defence of the obligation to evangelise the heathen that he would have used in the Northampton ministers' meeting where Ryland Snr disallowed discussion of the subject. Some maintained that the obligation to spread the gospel message among the heathen was laid upon the apostles only. But was it only the apostles who could baptise (Matthew 28:19-20)? If so, why were Baptist ministers now baptising believers? And if Christ's presence is promised until the end of the age, how can the obligation 'to go' be restricted to the apostolic period only? Others argued the impossibility of evangelising because of language difficulties and the uncivilised nature of many heathen. Carey is unimpressed:

> *Have not the popish missionaries surmounted all those difficulties which we have generally thought to be insuperable? Have not English traders, for the sake of gain, surmounted all those things which have generally been counted insurmountable obstacles in the way of preaching the gospel?*[6]

Still others argued that the time had not yet come for the heathen to hear the word of God. William points out that that objection comes too late; the success of the gospel had been considerable in many places already.[7] But are there not many in our own country of England who are as ignorant of the Christian message as Captain Cook's South Sea savages? William concedes the fact but insists that since there are faithful ministers in every part of this land, any who wish may easily hear the preaching of God's word.

> *But with them* [ie. the heathen] *the case is widely different, who have no Bible, no written language (which many of them have not), no ministers, nor any of those advantages which we have.*[8]

---

[6] From the *Enquiry*
[7] Illustrated in detail in section 2 of the *Enquiry*
[8] From the *Enquiry*

In section two of the *Enquiry* Carey gives a review of former missionary efforts for the conversion of the heathen from Pentecost onward, through the period of the apostles and then of the early church taking the Christian message across North Africa and into Europe. He traces Catholic missionary efforts on the coast of Africa, parts of Asia and South America. Continuing to show that history reveals an unbroken continuity of missionary obedience beyond the book of Acts, he mentions:

> The Protestant Reformation, then concludes with John Elliot and David Brainerd in North America, Ziegenbalg at Tranquebar, the Moravian Brethren and Wesley's efforts in the West Indies.[9]

The whole of section two provides such an amount of detailed historical information of the worldwide effective spread of Christianity through the centuries as to be a source of astonishment that it came from a humble shoemaker's workshop and school in a small village in Northamptonshire.

Section three of the *Enquiry* provides us with:

> The first ever statistical global survey of world Christianity ever published. Carey's compilation is amazing. His tables present a comprehensive overview of every country, each region, all the inhabited islands, of the then known world ... from whatever sources available Carey carried out a painstaking task – without compensation, recognition, or appreciation.[10]

Carey's purpose is clear. He was determined to show that of the estimated 731 million inhabitants of the world more than 430 million were pagans.[11] He pointed out that pagans were not merely ignorant of the Christian message but more importantly

---

[9] Daniel, JK & Hedlund, RE (Eds.) p.99
[10] Ibid. p100.
[11] He suggested that 44 million were Protestants, 100 million were Catholics, 30 million Greek and Armenian Christians, 7 million Jews, and possibly 130 million Muslims.

had no means of ever hearing it. He freely admits that his figures were estimates; he had calculated populations on the basis on an average per square mile, 'in some countries more and in others less'. But overall the effect is impressive and surely must expose and challenge any who, for whatever reason, fail to pay due regard to the call of the Lord 'to go'.

Sections four and five deal with practical obstacles that Carey suggested needed to be overcome. Some feared the distances involved in 'going into all the world'. The invention of the maritime compass, Carey argues, made such fears unnecessary. Safe journeys of any distance were now possible. Others spoke of the barbarous way many pagans lived. Carey replied that only those ... *whose love of ease renders them unwilling to expose themselves to inconveniences for the good of others can raise such an objection.*[12]

The spread of the gospel is precisely the way to civilise barbarous societies. But what of the danger of being killed by the heathen? The apostles were known as men who hazarded their lives for the name of the Lord Jesus Christ, he responds.[13] Should not the goodness of the cause prepare us to follow them? Carey insists that in fact Moravian missionaries and Elliot and Brainerd were seldom molested. Any who may have been attacked or killed in other lands may well have been responsible for it themselves by their arrogant, imprudent or ignorant behaviour.

There was also the question of how one might expect to procure the necessities of life in foreign places. Carey has his answer ready. A Christian minister is the servant of God. As such:

> *It is inconsistent for ministers to please themselves with thoughts of a numerous congregation, cordial friends, a civilised country, legal protection, affluence, splendour or even an income that is sufficient. The slights and hatred of men, the society of barbarians of uncouth speech, miserable accommodation in wretched wilder-*

---

[12] From the *Enquiry*.
[13] Acts 15:26

nesses, hunger and thirst, nakedness, weariness; diligence, hard work and but little worldly encouragement should rather be the objects of their expectation.[14]

Carey proposes that at least two families be involved in any venture – the men to evangelise and the women to cultivate crops for food. And one could surely use the foodstuffs which the natives ate.

Last, but by no means least, there was the problem of languages, except that trading nations had already met and conquered that problem. Like them, missionaries must mingle with the people and patiently learn their language. For good measure:

It is well known to require no very extraordinary talents to learn, in the space of a year or two at the most, the language of any people on earth, so much of it at least as to be able to convey any sentiments we wish to their understandings.[15]

A few more words about useful personal articles which he thought wise to take and how to begin relationships with the natives, and section four is done.

The duty of all Christians, and how a missionary Society might be founded, are the stuff of section five. In Carey's mind all objections to such a project have been met. Now comes the building work to launch a Society. One of the first and foremost duties is that of earnest prayer. Arising from the treatise of Jonathan Edwards on the 'latter day glory' the number of

---

[14] One cannot but wonder whether Dorothy ever caught sight of these words or heard her husband utter them. The family had suffered years of financial hardship and lack of food in *this* country. But *India?* Could such words from William lie behind Dorothy's instinctive motherly reluctance to sail away to India?

[15] Despite Carey's comment *(no very extraordinary talent)* many a Western missionary has sometimes longed for *his* extraordinary talent! As a matter of interest the Strict Baptist Mission required missionary candidates in India to occupy two years to pass qualifying exams in Tamil before assuming any field responsibilities.

churches that had responded to the concert of prayer had been on the increase. But Carey notes: *We must not be contented however with praying without exerting ourselves in the use of means for the obtaining of those things we pray for.*[16]

Carey proposes a company of serious Christians from the Particular Baptist churches, ministers and private persons, who will form themselves into a Society and make a number of rules to regulate the plan; for example, who are to be employed as missionaries, the means of defraying expenses, etc. From such a Society a committee needs to be appointed to procure all necessary information, receive contributions and carefully examine all would-be missionaries – their characters, tempers, abilities and religious views. Carey suggests that congregations should give one penny a week (more if possible) to create a fund. And those who, like William and his family, would not buy West Indian sugar as a protest against the slavery involved in its production might instead give sixpence or a shilling a week to the fund:

> *We are exhorted to lay up treasure in heaven, where neither moth nor rust doth corrupt nor thieves break through and steal* [17]*... Scriptures teach us that the enjoyments of the life to come bear a near relation to that which now is, a similar relation to that of the harvest and the seed. It is true that all reward is of mere grace, but it is nevertheless encouraging ... Surely it is worthwhile to lay ourselves out with all our might in promoting the cause and the kingdom of Christ.*

With this, the *Enquiry* is finished, though it still can challenge our lethargy.

Undoubtedly the *Enquiry* is a major document upon which much modern missionary thinking is still based. Yet, as Roger Hedlund points out:

> *Without a plan it is doubtful that the world would ever*

---
[16] From the *Enquiry*.
[17] Matthew 6:19

> have known the name of William Carey. The key is the proposal for creating a Society and committee to implement the plan. Carey's first achievement was the *Enquiry;* linked to it was his second great accomplishment, the Particular Baptist Society for the Propagation of the Gospel among the Heathen, formed in 1792.[18]

In this way Carey began not just a mission but what became a missionary *movement*. Other denominations began to follow the pattern that the Particular Baptists had begun.[19]

The *Enquiry* was published in Leicester in 1792 and sold by booksellers there, in London and in Sheffield, for one shilling and sixpence. Interestingly, the same Leicester publisher was also responsible for circulating Thomas Paine's revolutionary treatise entitled *The Rights of Man* (1791-2). As ever, the commands of Christ and the demands of unbelieving man stand opposed. But to continue Carey's story, this servant of God must pass one more test of his mettle before he ever leaves England. Can Carey survive a pastoral struggle with a church that is torn apart by indiscipline and successfully rebuild it?

---

[18] Daniel, JK & Hedlund, RE (Eds.) p103.
[19] The London Missionary Society, the Church Missionary Society, the Religious Tract Society, the British and Foreign Bible Society, the (General) Baptist Missionary Society, the Methodist Missionary Society, the Strict Baptist Mission (now Grace Baptist Mission), to name but a few.

10
Happy village fellowship to troubled city church

Aside from the family's continual financial struggle (by no means unique to them) there were happy times at Moulton. The Carey family was now a family of three boys; by her baptism Dorothy was united with William in church membership; and the chapel building was refurbished and accommodating larger congregations. Meanwhile, by 1789, the news of William's pastoral success had travelled to Leicester. An invitation from the Leicester church inviting him to take their pastorate caused William anxious concern. He wrote to his father:

> *I am exceedingly divided in my own mind. If I only regarded worldly things I should go without hesitation, but when I reflect upon the situation of things here, I know not what to do.*[1]

It was not only the happiness of the situation at Moulton that Carey was reluctant to leave; the church meeting at Harvey Lane, Leicester, described by George Smith as 'ruined by antinomianism',[2] was divided by indiscipline and disputes. The church had had a quick succession of pastors in its recent history; two deacons had been dismissed for drunkenness; the last pastor's membership was cancelled for allowing such a scandal;

---
[1] Carey, Eustace p61.
[2] Smith, George p35. 'Antinomianism is the doctrine that Christ has in such a sense fulfilled all the claims of the moral law in behalf of all believers that they are released from all obligations to fulfil its precepts as a standard of character and action.' Hodge, A A *Outlines of Theology* op.cit.

and quarrels followed within the fellowship. For nine years the church minute book had not been read to the membership,[3] a few of whom, now anxious for the future of the church, appealed to William to help them. Carey's decision to go to Leicester (May1789) was received with prayerful regret by the Moulton church. But his decision confirms something about William's character: to him a challenge was an opportunity that must be taken once he felt that it was the call of God.

In the early Leicester days things seemed to go well, but 'the honeymoon' period did not last. Old quarrels soon broke out again and people began to drift away. William concluded that such a state of affairs was the evidence that the church had lost its soul. He could see no other way forward but to disband the church as an official body and try to start again.[4] He drew up a new Church Covenant and in October 1790 invited as many as would to join him in signing it and in forming the new church. In his words members of the new fellowship were to … *bind themselves to a strict New Testament discipline, let it affect whom it might.*

For a year and ten months Carey had served the old Leicester church as a 'probationer' before being officially set apart as the pastor of the newly formed church in 1791 in a solemn service in which his friends Ryland, Sutcliff, Fuller and Samuel Pearce from Birmingham took part. Members of the new church were to cultivate an attitude of openness, honesty and respect for each other and to commit themselves to governing their behaviour by biblical principles alone.[5] Eight men and seventeen women signed the Covenant initially; curiously Dorothy's name does not appear there, though we know that she was by then a baptised believer and had learned to write.[6] With prayer and

---

[3] From a note attached to Carey's new Leicester church covenant.
[4] The church had joined the Northamptonshire Association in 1770. After Carey had been there a short while the church report to the annual Association meeting included the words *Far from enjoying harmony and peace, we are divided three against two and two against three.* George, Timothy p27.
[5] There is the full text of the Leicester Covenant in Appendix 'A'.
[6] Was the absence of her name related to the birth, or the death, of baby Lucy (born at Leicester and died in her second year)?

fasting the church began to grow again and it became necessary to construct a new gallery in the building. The whole episode gives us a further insight into William's character: having 'put his hand to the plough he would not even *look* back.'[7] That was a persistence he would certainly need in later days. Yet his success was not a cause for pride. Deeply burdened by his responsibility as a servant of God handling the profoundly precious truths of divine revelation, William thought of himself in increasingly humble terms:

> *I see more and more of my own insufficiency for the great work I am called to. When I compare myself with my work, I sink into a point, a mere despicable nothing.*[8]

The Leicester Covenant reveals Carey to have been a convinced Particular Baptist whose understanding of biblical church order was that participation in the Lord's Supper was open only to those who, obedient to the Lord's command, had been baptised by immersion on profession of their faith in Christ as Saviour and Lord. The new church members committed themselves to the teaching of the Bible that:

> *God ... from eternity chose his people in Christ to salvation ... that in the fullness of time God sent his Son to redeem his people ... that we will receive only such into our communion who make a credible profession of Repentance towards God and Faith in our Lord Jesus Christ, and who have been baptised according to the primitive Mode of administering that Ordinance, that is, by immersing them in Water, in the name of the Father, the Son, and the Holy Spirit.*[9]

---

[7] Luke 9:62
[8] George, Timothy p25.
[9] Extract from the Leicester Covenant.

There was still the need for Carey to open a school [10] and to begin making shoes again to help family finances. A little sister, Lucy, had joined the three boys Felix, William and Peter, but sadly died in her second year. Living in Leicester also brought benefits to Carey, by his introduction to a number of Leicester scholars whose friendships, together with the availability of their libraries and scientific knowledge, brought him continual academic stimulation. Among them was Dr Thomas Arnold, a recognised authority in the diagnosis and treatment of mental disorders.[11] At that time William could not have had the faintest idea how valuable that particular contact would become but a wise Providence already knew. Yet none of these things was allowed to distract William from a programme of regular study and preaching. Each day of the week was devoted to specific studies, as he wrote to his father in 1790:

> *Monday, the learned languages; Tuesday the study of science, history, composition etc.; Wednesday I preach a lecture and have been for more than twelve months on the book of Revelation; Thursday I visit my friends; Friday and Saturday, preparing for the Lord's Day ... add to this occasional journeys, ministers meeting, etc. etc.*[12]

His Sundays were not rest days either. Three times every Sunday he preached in his own chapel, or in the surrounding villages. Yet this busy weekly programme did not diminish the flame of William's zeal for evangelism *overseas* – rather the reverse, in fact. As Mr Old's house in Hackleton was William's 'theological college' (chapter four), Moulton and Leicester, with

---

[10] The school was short-lived. 'He made a second attempt to get up a scool [sic] but without success.' Marshman, John Clark p8.
[11] A copy of the first edition of Dr Arnold's book *Observations on the Nature, Kinds, Causes and Preventions of Insanity* vol 1 was kindly tracked down for me by Dr Keron Fletcher of Shrewsbury. It is kept in the Foyle Special Collection of the Kings College London Library in Chancery Lane, London WC2A 1LR.
[12] Smith, George p35.

the testing experiences which they presented, became his 'missionary training college'. Whether he realised it or not, William was being providentially prepared for his future ministry.

* * * * * * * * *

Postscript

A BBC television programme broadcast several years ago showed Hindu worship taking place in the Carey Hall, Leicester. Enquiry made of some Leicester friends resulted in the following letters being received:

10th June 2006

Yes, there was a Baptist church called Carey Hall in Catherine Street on the north side of the city. Some years ago the church at Carey Hall moved to Harrison Road (possibly to a smaller place?) and the original Carey Hall is indeed now a Hindu place of worship! ... Carey's cottage was demolished only a few decades ago; it had been a museum to his memory and the tableaux of his life were removed to Charles Street Central Baptist Church, Leicester, where I think they have a room devoted to his memory.

20th June 2006

In the 1960s, when his cottage was a museum in his memory there was talk of demolishing it, but after receiving a petition signed by 3000 Baptists in America there was a reprieve. After three or four years ... the whole site was replaced by the Holiday Inn. There is a blue plaque on the forecourt wall in memory of his cottage.

11
God's clock strikes the hour

The annual meetings of the Northamptonshire Association, when reports from the churches were received, saw the regular gathering of ministers and messengers appointed from the associated churches. But there were also other occasions in the year when associated ministers met by themselves for prayer and preaching. In such a meeting held in 1791 at Clipstone, where Carey's friend Morris was pastor, Sutcliff and Fuller preached. The former preached from 1 Kings 19:10, entitling his message *Jealousy for the Lord of Hosts illustrated*. The thrust of the sermon was that jealousy for the Lord would result in aggressive and prayerful evangelism, even to the extent of seeking to enlighten the whole earth.[1] Commenting upon the fact that believers are to be the salt of the earth Sutcliff argued that ...*it is not proper that the salt should lie all in one heap. It should be scattered abroad.*[2]

Fuller's sermon, which he entitled *The pernicious influence of delay in matters of religion*, was based upon Haggai 1:2. It was a remarkable sermon not merely in the forceful way he expounded the truth but also in appearing to be criticising the very caution he had formerly exercised in seeking to cool Carey's enthusiasm. Fuller poured scorn on those who quoted the difficulties involved as a reason for delay:

> *Instead of waiting for the removal of difficulties, we ought, in many cases, to consider them as purposely laid in our way in order to try the sincerity of our religion.*[3]

---

[1] Haykin, Michael p208.
[2] Ibid. p208.
[3] Fuller, Thomas Ekins p79.

Both of these Clipstone sermons subsequently appeared in print. They surely are like the final chimes that strike to announce the coming of the hour! Carey must have been the most excited listener in that meeting. Fuller's grandson wrote of that day in the memoir of his grandfather:

So profound was the impression produced by these words that it is said the ministers were scarcely able to speak to one another at the close.[4]

William eagerly seized the moment to urge that something be done immediately to form a Society for missionary enterprise. Sutcliff and Fuller still hesitated, more because of uncertainty that the churches in general would support such a thing than because of doubt of the rightness of it; but they urged Carey to publish *The Enquiry*. Early in 1792 it appeared in print.

The annual meeting of the Association in May 1792 was held at the Friars Lane chapel, Nottingham.[5] Reports were presented from the associated churches and prayers were made. On the morning of the second day Carey rose to preach. His text was Isaiah 54: 2-3, which he expounded in two memorable points: 'Expect great things; attempt great things'.[6] Some accounts reverse the order of the two points as though they should follow the order of the vowels in Carey's name. But Carey's point was that expectant faith, based upon God's word, should issue in great things being attempted. For William strong faith was the biblical basis for great attempts.

It is not hard to realise that the years of frustration Carey had endured, the increasing burden of awareness that the churches were neglecting to obey the Lord's clear command 'to go' and the undeniable need for the pagan world to know of Christ, all combined to pour into his words a convincing sense of godly

---

[4] Ibid. p81.
[5] That church had joined the Association in 1768. Elwyn TSH p27.
[6] Often quoted as 'Expect great things *from God*; attempt great things *for God*'. The version above, is given by Marshman, John Clark page 10 (possibly from his father, Carey's close colleague). Everyone knew Carey's whole life was already 'for God'; it hardly needed saying.

authority. John Ryland Jnr later remarked that he ... *should not have been surprised if the audience had lifted up their voice and wept.*[7]

A business session followed when time was given to matters concerning the affairs of associated churches. It looked as though the thought of a missionary Society would slip by without receiving any further attention. The awesome responsibilities involved in launching so daunting a project by such inexperienced pioneers must have seemed formidable. But, as J C Marshman tells it:

> *Mr Carey seized Fuller's hand in an agony of distress, and indignantly asked whether they were again going to separate without doing anything. The expostulation was not without effect, and he had the happiness of seeing a resolution recorded, to the effect that a plan should be prepared against the next ministers' meeting for the establishment of a Society for propagating the Gospel among the heathen.*[8]

Appended to the Association circular letter of 1792 was the following Minute, which records the momentous resolution:

> *Resolved that a plan be prepared against the next ministers' meeting at Kettering, for forming a Baptist Society for propagating the Gospel among the heathen. Brother Carey generously engaged to devote all the profits that may arise from his late publication on this interesting subject, to the use of such a Society.*[9]

One wonders how much of all this William shared with Dorothy and what she, whose horizons went no further than the few villages she knew, might have made of it all. There seems no information available to help us. It was four whole months between that great meeting in Nottingham and the proposed

---
[7] Marshman, John Clark p10.
[8] Ibid. p10.
[9] Elwyn, TSH p18.

next ministers' meeting on 2 October. For William the time must have been fraught with a mixture of impatient longing and tantalising uncertainty. God's providential 'clock' had chimed the quarters; was the hour now about to be struck?

Eventually the month of October came. Led by Andrew Fuller the host pastor, twelve other pastors, including Carey, and one divinity student gathered in a little back parlour of widow Martha Wallis' home to face the challenge set by the Nottingham resolution.[10] (Martha's husband had been treasurer for an Association fund, and a deacon at Kettering until his death earlier the same year.)[11] These fourteen men wrestled with what must have been many hesitations and uncertainties.[12] None had any experience of launching such a Society as was proposed; their own churches could scarcely support them adequately, so how could they be expected to face a new and unknown financial burden month by month? Were they now about to finally reject the High Calvinism of some of their colleagues who forbade overt evangelism? Nor was anyone among them sufficiently widely known to stir the interest of churches up and down the land. As Fuller expressed it: *There was little or no respectability amongst us, not so much as a squire to sit in the chair or an orator to address him with speeches.*[13]

The fact that 38 year-old Andrew Fuller was even present to chair that meeting was remarkable. In the May of that year his favourite daughter, a little six year-old, died after an attack of measles. Later in the same year Fuller's wife suddenly became so mentally deranged while pregnant that she regarded Andrew as an impostor and had to be kept locked up to prevent her running from the house. She would often say:

> *No, this is not my home ... you are not my husband ... these are not my children. Once I had a good home, a husband who loved me, and dear children. But where*

---
[10] 'Her back parlour measured twelve feet by ten'. Haykin, Michael p219.
[11] Elwyn, TSH p24.
[12] There are excellent thumbnail sketches of these men in Haykin, Michael pp220-223.
[13] Smith, George p39.

am I now? I am lost! I am ruined! What have I done? Oh what have I done? Lord, have mercy on me.[14]

She had given birth to a daughter at the end of that July and a few days later Andrew was at her bedside as she died. Fuller's grandson perceptively notes that after the publication of Fuller's book *The Gospel Worthy of All Acceptation* in 1785, one might think that then was the time to have founded a missionary Society, and not to have delayed until 1792. But in Fuller's case... *God had to write deeper things on the soul of his servant before he gave such an enterprise into his hands.*[15]

The spiritual fruit of these 'deeper things' was later seen, as his grandson well comments, in 'the tenderness of his letters to the missionaries, and the daily surrender by which alone such toil could be endured' as resulted in the surprising advance of the work of the Society.[16]

If others of the men then present in that little room struggled with the great problems of the task to be achieved, Carey had no doubts. He had with him a copy of the *Periodical account of the Moravian Missions.* Drawing it from his pocket he read to the group the account of Moravian missions in the West Indies, North America, Africa and the Far East.[17] If Moravians could be successful evangelists among the heathen, why not Particular Baptists? With what Fuller later described as ' fear and trembling' the little group moved to make a number of resolutions, and, as George Smith records,

The first purely English Missionary Society, which sent forth its own English founder, was thus constituted.[18]

---

[14] Fuller, Thomas Ekins p71.
[15] Ibid. p75. Fuller's sad experiences would, in later years, enable his early friendship with Carey to deepen into a profound understanding of what William was passing through in India at the death of his child and the derangement of his wife Dorothy's mind.
[16] Ibid. p75.
[17] George, Timothy p68.
[18] Smith, George p37.

They resolved, among other things, that their Society be called *The Particular (Calvinistic) Baptist Society for Propagating the Gospel among the Heathen*; [19] that members of the Society subscribe £10 sterling at once, or 10 shillings and six pence annually; that five of them (John Ryland Jnr, Reynold Hogg, William Carey, John Sutcliff and Andrew Fuller) be appointed as a committee to carry into effect the purposes of the Society; that Hogg be treasurer and Fuller the secretary. Twelve of the men present signed the resolutions and the promised subscriptions amounted to £13.2s.6d.[20] In the absence of a formal offertory bag Andrew Fuller's snuffbox was pressed into service as a receptacle for the collection of promissory notes. Carey could promise only the proceeds of the sale of his *Enquiry*. With their next meeting set for the end of October the men must have travelled back to their homes with minds full of questions, wondering at the implications of what they had done and thinking of what they must do next. And for us as we look back, a meeting of fourteen men and a fund of £13.2s.6d may seem 'small things' but they are surely not to be despised, seeing that they opened the way for much greater things. Large doors so often swing on little hinges.

---

[19] Ibid. p37.
[20] This was equivalent to the yearly salary of many workers at that time.

12
The aftermath

To all decisions there is, to a greater or lesser degree, an aftermath.[1] To the ground-breaking decisions of the Kettering meeting early that October the aftermath must have seemed daunting indeed. To function successfully, a Society such as they were launching must have a wider support base than just themselves. But how would other Baptist churches regard the venture? How would other Christian churches regard what these Baptists were doing? Some answers were not long in coming. The London Baptist ministers met to consider what their response should be. Abraham Booth was cautiously favourable but he was a lone voice among them. One London pastor, Joseph Stennett, advised his colleagues to stand aloof and not commit themselves. The aged Benjamin Beddome, pastor at Bourton-on-the-Water, later wrote to Andrew Fuller:

> *I think your scheme, considering the paucity of well-qualified ministers, hath a very unfavourable aspect with respect to destitute churches at home, where charity ought to begin. I had the pleasure once to see and hear Mr Carey; it struck me he was the most suitable person in the kingdom, at least whom I know, to supply my place, and make up my deficiencies when either disabled or removed. A different plan is formed and pursued, and I fear that the great and good man, though influenced by the most excellent motives, will meet with a disappointment ... my unbelieving heart is ready to*

---

[1] 'Aftermath' Literally: 'after-grass', that which springs up after the first cropping. Figuratively (as here): results, consequences.

The aftermath

suggest that the time is not come, the time when the Lord's house should be built.[2]

Others from Congregationalist, Presbyterian (with a few exceptions) and Anglican churches declined to commit themselves, despite the fact that the King and the Archbishop had been asked to consider giving support. It seems that in their eyes the insignificance of the twelve brave signatories of the Kettering proposals for the Society disqualified the project from gaining their support.[3]

We know how Samuel Pearce was thinking as he returned to his church in Birmingham because, in 1794, he offered to join Carey and Thomas in India but was dissuaded by the committee, who felt his wise counsel was more valuable to them at home.[4] Meanwhile, at the next meeting of the Society's committee on 31 October, he was able to present a gift of £70 to the Society fund.[5] He had been stirred by Carey's vision and had returned to his people from the Kettering meeting resolved to present the challenge of the Society to them, which he did in his sermon the very next Sunday. The honour of forming the very first auxiliary society for the support of the mission thus goes to the church in Cannon Street, Birmingham.

What were William's thoughts as he journeyed back from Kettering to Leicester and to Dorothy? The Society he dreamed of had been formed but who would their missionaries be? Should he be the first of them? But the church in Leicester was prospering markedly; their building was now enlarged and accommodating increased congregations. Was this the right time

---

[2] Smith, George p39.
[3] Years later Archdeacon Farrar of Westminster Abbey commented upon such reluctance with this stinging rebuke: 'Those who in that day sneered that England had sent a cobbler to convert the world were the direct lineal descendants of those in Palestine two thousand years ago [who said] "Is not this the carpenter's son?"' Smith, George p39.
[4] Wells, Tom in *British Particular Baptists,* Haykin, Michael AG (Ed.) vol II p188.
[5] Haykin, Michael p225 tells us that Pearce's annual salary from the church was £100. Thus £70 for the Society must have represented sacrificial giving on the part of the church.

to leave the people he had come to love? And Dorothy and the boys: what of them if he should go overseas? And where would he go? The Moravians were having some success in North America among the native Indians, in Sierra Leone and elsewhere in West Africa. Did that mean those areas were receptive to the gospel message? On the other hand there were the islands in the Pacific discovered by Captain Cook in his voyages, especially perhaps the island of Tahiti where the natives seemed friendly and welcoming. Yet it was on the island of Hawaii that similar natives had murdered Captain Cook! Then there was the reaction of William's father who, hearing of the new Society and the suggestion that his son might offer to be a missionary, suggested that William must be mad. Carey wrote in return to his father:

> *Polly tells me that you are afraid lest I should go as a missionary. I have only to say to that, that I am at the Lord's disposal, but I have very little expectation of going myself, though I have had a very considerable offer, if I should go to Sierra Leone in Africa. I however don't think that I shall go.*[6]

The committee of the Society met again on 13 November. Carey was unable to be present and perhaps that gave Fuller the opportunity to suggest that they should carefully consider where, in the heathen world, did they feel that the most promising openings for their venture might seem to be. They had before them a letter that Carey had received from a certain Dr Thomas of Bengal, India, currently in England, seeking support for his unfinished project of translating the Bible into the Bengali language.[7] Could the Society and Dr Thomas work together in mission? Mention of the translation of the Scriptures might well have seemed to William an example of God's providential leading. The committee resolved to find out what could be known of the character of Dr Thomas and to ask him to attend their

---

[6] Smith, George p69.
[7] Carey, S Pearce p96.

next meeting on 9 January. Between the memorable Association meeting of May 1792 and the planned meeting for January 1793 a mere eight months had elapsed. That was an evidence of the godly eagerness of this little band of courageous pioneers to reach into the world with the message of Christ. But what the committee did not then know was that already a longing for missionary activity existed in North India and that a suggestion had been made for Christian missionaries to be sent to Bengal.

> 'Send us', it was said, 'fit men, of free minds, disinterested, zealous and patient of labour who would ... aspire to the arduous office of a missionary ... Men who are ready to endure hardships and to suffer the loss of all things.[8]

William himself might well have written those words. Clearly, if Bengal was the place to which he was to go, the Spirit of God was already moving among some Christians in that very area! To that part of India we now turn.

---

[8] George, Timothy p71, quoted from Constance Padwick, *Henry Martyn: Confessor of the Faith* pp21-22

13
In the beginning was God

Charles Grant,[1] an officer of the East India Trading Company in Bengal and an evangelical Christian, became convinced that the Company should be concerned for the intellectual and religious improvement of the native people with whom they traded. He gathered around him a small group of men of the same persuasion and in 1786 they drew up the plan (previously mentioned) for 'A Mission to Bengal'. Dividing the whole area into eight 'Missionary Circles' they proposed that an Anglican clergyman be employed in setting up schools, superintending catechists and establishing churches.[2] The next step was to gain the approval of the Governor General, Lord Cornwallis, since the support of the government was felt to be essential to the success of the plan. Lord Cornwallis' comment was that 'he had no faith in such schemes and thought they must prove ineffectual'.[3] Despite the fact that Grant was a highly regarded government officer, much respected for his standing aloof from the prevalent corruption in official circles, the Governor General was not to be influenced by him.

Undeterred, Grant sent the proposal to the Archbishop of Canterbury, the Bishop of London and to other leaders of the evangelical movement in the Anglican Church such as William Romaine, John Newton and Charles Simeon, together with William Wilberforce MP.[4] The Archbishop received the project with 'cold caution'; the Bishop of London confessed to being so busy

---
[1] 1746-1823
[2] Marshman, John Clark p15.
[3] Ibid. p15.
[4] After his conversion to evangelicalism William Wilberforce was persuaded by John Newton to become a Member of Parliament and serve the Christian cause there. He became a strong opponent of the slave trade.

with affairs in the *West* Indies that he had no time for affairs in the East. Nothing was done to advance the project.

Presently Charles Grant returned to England and renewed his contact with the Archbishop who promised to mention the matter to the King[5] and to Mr Pitt.[6] Meanwhile Mr Wilberforce advised Grant that his proposal was too overtly religious to be received by his political friends. Reluctantly Charles revised the wording of the proposal and was then asked to revise it again, since the first revision still appeared to make the education and civilisation of the natives to include their religious conversion. The Archbishop then presented this second revision to the King. The royal response, eventually, was that the King was hesitant to countenance it ... *chiefly in consequence of the alarming progress of the French revolution and the proness* [sic] *of the times to movements subversive of the established order of things.*[7]

Perhaps it was a mistake to have revised the proposal at all, for that then made it appear purely political. But one possibility still remained which Charles proceeded to pursue. The charter of the East India Company was due for renewal by Parliament. Grant and Wilberforce sought to have a clause included requiring that the Company permit the entry of missionaries to their Indian territories. Such was the Company's hostility to that clause that in the event the India Bill of 1793 was silent on the subject, the proposed clause having been dropped. Anglican clergymen were appointed to minister to Company staff[8] but it was another twenty years before the Company officially permitted missionary activity among native Indians. So apparently the groundbreaking scheme for mission to Bengal, which the zeal and energy of Charles and his friends led them to propose, had come to nothing. Years later Charles wrote: *Many years ago I had formed the design of a mission to Bengal, and used my*

---
[5] George III (1760-1820)
[6] William Pitt, Prime Minister (1804-1806)
[7] Marshman, John Clark p17.
[8] A notable example of whom was Henry Martyn (1781-1812).

humble efforts to promote the design. Providence reserved that honour for the Baptists.[9]

Yet it was this missionary zeal of Charles Grant that God used to bring the Baptists to Bengal. For it was previously in India that Grant had met, and become friendly with, the same Dr John Thomas of whom the Society committee men were now hearing. Thomas had served as a ship's doctor on a voyage out to India but on arrival there left the ship and settled in Bengal. Beginning to learn the Bengali language, Thomas set about translating the New Testament into that language, with financial help from Charles. But Thomas' imprudence and unreliability in financial matters led Grant after a while to withdraw that help. Thomas had been in correspondence with Abraham Booth,[10] a prominent Baptist Pastor in London and a writer of theological works in defence of Particular Baptist beliefs and practice. Travelling to England, Thomas met Booth to plead for support for the work begun in Bengal and to preach at Booth's church. Booth wrote to Carey telling of this Dr Thomas and at a meeting of the committee in Kettering on 9 January 1793, a few of the Society men were eagerly waiting to meet Thomas. John Sutcliff was expected to be present but could not attend and Ryland Jnr was away in Bristol at the time. As he recorded later, Andrew Fuller was feeling a great responsibility because of the absence of these friends from the anticipated meeting. Carey preached a sermon on 'Behold, I come quickly and my reward is with me'.[11] The men prayed together ... and waited! Their faith and courage was being tested to the limit. Evening came and the committee was on the verge of dispersing when Thomas at last came limping in. He had been injured on the journey from London. An eyewitness of the scene later recorded:

It was late in the evening, and while in full deliberation, that his arrival was announced. Impatient to behold his

---

[9] Ibid. p.20
[10] (1734-1806)
[11] Revelation 22:12

colleague [ie. Carey][12] *he entered the room in haste, and Mr Carey rising from his seat, they fell on each others necks and wept.*[13]

The men heard from Thomas details of his financial difficulties and of Charles Grant's refusal to help him further. He seemed so completely open and honest about the matter that the committee, understanding the coming of Thomas to them to be the indication of where the Society was to begin missionary work, felt able to resolve that Thomas and Carey should proceed to Bengal in the spring, as missionaries of the Society.

It is clear, said Andrew Fuller to Carey, that there is a rich mine of gold in India. I will venture to go down, said Carey, but remember that you must hold the ropes. We solemnly engaged him to do so, said Fuller, nor while we live shall we desert him.[14]

While the Anglican Church, the King, Parliament and the East India Company directors all sought to prevent what was thought to be 'the most wild, extravagant, expensive and unjustifiable project of converting Indian natives to Christianity'[15] a largely unknown group of humble Baptist pastors in Kettering launched exactly such a project in trembling faith. The Society's bank account now stood at £115. 0.6d. They had accepted two missionaries, pledged themselves to their support and the support of their families, hardly knowing what would be involved. As Andrew Fuller wrote to John Ryland Jnr: *Things of great consequence are in train. My heart fears, while it is enlarged. It is a great undertaking; yet, surely it is right.*[16]

A little group of believers in Bengal, north east India, moved by God's Spirit to urge the evangelisation of the indigenous

---
[12] Carey had offered himself as a missionary in January 1793 Fuller, Thomas Ekins p82.
[13] Ibid. p83.
[14] Smith, George p83.
[15] Marshman, John Clark p19.
[16] Haykin, Michael p228.

people among whom they lived; a little group of people in the Midlands, England, fired by God's Spirit with the conviction that all the world must be told of Jesus Christ; and now Dr John Thomas proves to be the human link used by God's providence between the two groups. As we look back we can see a developing pattern in the purposes of God more clearly than could those men involved at the time. Any criticism of the Society's willingness to employ Thomas knowing, as they did, of the instability of his character, must not overlook the unique role that he played in God's purpose. Thomas was a ready-made man of experience in Bengal who had begun to learn the language, was already beginning to translate the New Testament, and was a medical man as well. Surely the committee men of the Society were right to regard him as God's gift, to accompany Carey and to define where the Society might best begin its missionary work.

14
Light and shade of the farewell days

There was an urgent need now for more funds and for petitioning the East India Company for a licence to send missionaries to the area under that Company's control in Bengal. Fuller, Carey and Thomas set out to visit other churches seeking their fellowship in prayer and in financial help. Something like £150 a year would be required, it was thought, to maintain the work, in addition to initial travel expenses for the missionaries. Nor were those the only formidable problems to be solved. The committee were now aware of Dorothy's unwillingness to leave her homeland and take the family she knew not where. And there was the problem of the church in Leicester that had so prospered under Carey's ministry and pastoral care. Fuller was not a man to delay doing what he knew must be done.[1] Within a week of the dramatic meeting of 9 January Fuller was writing to John Ryland Jnr:

> *I have this day been to Olney, to converse with brother Sutcliff to request him to go with me to Leicester ... to conciliate the church there, and to sound out Mrs Carey's mind, whether she will go and take the family, that we may know for what number of passengers to provide. If*

---

[1] We must not overlook the willing cooperation of the churches of these men, who will have often been without their pastors for some time, when Fuller, Sutcliff and Ryland were away from home on Society business, travelling by stage coach, by coastal ship, on horseback or on foot.

[the family should] *not go we must guarantee the family as well as support him in the mission.*[2]

That little extract gives us an insight into the careful pastoral concern with which Fuller handled his task as Society secretary. A church is not to be dictated to; a wife is not to be bullied; the goodwill of the church is to be sought; the dignity of Dorothy's choice is to be respected. And Fuller is anxious to have his friend Sutcliff join with him in this ministry. These men were breaking new ground, never before traversed by them or indeed by any of their fellow Particular Baptists, and they wisely sought to do so with mutual watchfulness and Christian care.

This episode also sheds some light on Dorothy's state of health at that time. Keeping in mind Andrew Fuller's sad, and so recent, experience of losing the treasured companionship of his wife, first by her mental derangement and then by her death, we can be reasonably sure that there could not have been as yet any evidence of the mental disorder which blighted Dorothy's last years of life. Fuller would have recognised the symptoms of any such disorder. He would not have written as he did to Ryland if he had any suspicion that Dorothy was anything less than a perfectly capable mother and valuable pastor's wife. Dorothy was already successfully 'holding the fort' at home during William's frequent absences on his shoemaker's business, school teaching, pastoral ministry and fellowship with other pastors.

In the event Dorothy opted to stay in this country and not to accompany William overseas. With three young boys clutching at her skirts, and another baby 'on the way' such a decision is not hard to understand. Since we have no record of the precise reason or reasons for Dorothy's decision[3] it needs to be said that she was certainly not the only wife to decline to accompany her husband overseas. Dr John Thomas had twice visited India alone, each time leaving his wife and family in England. It was not uncommon for officials of the East India Company to go out alone.

---

[2] Beck, James R p70.
[3] Beck, James R offers several *possible* suggestions that could have influenced Dorothy pp71-76.

A voyage to India at that period was considered, even in educated circles, a far more formidable undertaking than at the present time. It was regarded in the light of a perpetual banishment from home.[4]

As Richard Holmes in his book 'Sahib: the British soldier in India, 1750-1914' informs us (p39):

Europeans who survived the sea voyage risked death from cholera, typhoid, dysentery and sunstroke, snakes and tigers, and undermined their health by eating and drinking to excess ... the mortality rate amongst Europeans, mostly due to cholera, was 69 in every 1,000 – more than five times that of the Manchester slums. Of the Company's officers, from 1760 to 1834, only 10% survived to draw their pensions.

Dorothy may well not have known of any of these cases but they show us that her decision to let her husband go to India alone was not an unusual one for women faced with similar choices at that time.

There were many in the church at Leicester not at all happy with the news that they were about to lose their beloved pastor. The growth of the church during Carey's ministry meant that many of the new members were his spiritual 'children'. The building had been enlarged to accommodate the bigger congregations but the debt was not yet cleared. How could it be right that their pastor should leave them now? But one of the church members, by his brave and challenging words, helped his Christian brothers and sisters to grapple with the problem. He reminded the church meeting how often they had prayed for Christ's kingdom to come. God was now calling them, he argued, to make the sacrifice that would prove the sincerity of their prayers. They must not just be content to let their pastor

---

[4] Quoted by Beck, James R p72, from the unabridged two-volume edition of *The life and times of the Serampore Missionaries* by Marshman, John Clark, 1859.

go; they must *send* him. A note in the church book (24 March 1793) reads:

> Mr Carey, our minister, left Leicester to go on a mission to the East Indies, to take and propagate the gospel among those idolatrous and superstitious heathens. This is inserted to show his love to his poor miserable fellow creatures. In this we concurred with him, though it is at the expense of losing one whom we love as our own souls.[5]

Carey's comment, in a letter to his father, is illuminating: *Never did I see such sorrow manifested as reigned through our place of worship last Lord's day.*[6]

20 March was appointed for the farewell meeting at Leicester which was attended by many people from all parts of the Midlands and even further afield. Dr Thomas gave a rousing talk to the crowded chapel on life in India as illustrating the truth of Psalm 16:4.[7] He spoke of ... *the crying needs of humanity there, the idolatries of the natives, the learned Hindus he had nearly led to faith in Christ, the translation of the Scriptures already begun* ...[8]

The Society's treasurer, Reynold Hogg, preached from *The will of the Lord be done.*[9]

Andrew Fuller concluded the meeting with an address to the two missionaries based upon John 20:21.[10] So richly was the missionary spirit poured out upon the assembled congregation that the collection from the meeting amounted to £600![11] After that meeting William moved his family from Leicester back to Hackleton, to the area and the people with whom Dorothy and the boys would be most familiar. Dorothy's young sister Kath-

---

[5] Smith, George p42.
[6] Ibid. p45.
[7] *Their sorrows shall be multiplied that hasten after another God.*
[8] George, Timothy p77.
[9] Acts 21:14
[10] *As my Father hath sent me, so send I you.*
[11] Fuller, Thomas Ekins p84.

erine Plackett, known as Kitty, came to live with them there for mutual companionship.

A third problem remained to be solved – that of gaining a licence from 'The Company of Merchants of London trading into the East Indies' (generally known as The East India Company) for two missionaries to travel to Bengal and take up residence there for the purpose of evangelism among the natives. Formed on 31 December 1600 by Elizabeth I, the Company, though a purely commercial enterprise, could function like an independent nation. It could mint its own money, govern its employees as it saw fit, raise its own army and navy, and declare war or negotiate peace at will with other nations, *providing they were not Christian nations.*[12] Trading posts were established at Surat, 1608; Madras, 1639; Bombay, 1687; and Calcutta, 1690. These were all answerable to the Board of Directors in London.[13] The problem was that there was no clause in the Company charter permitting them to allow missionaries to use Company ships or to reside in Company trading areas. A strong effort by Wilberforce and others to add such a clause was refused by Parliament, as we have seen, because it was opposed by the Board of Directors of the Company. Nevertheless, Fuller was concerned that the missionaries should avoid appearing to be smuggled into Bengal. Carey met his former mentor Thomas Scott and asked him to plead with Charles Grant for help. But when Grant learned that Dr Thomas was to accompany William he felt unable to oblige Scott on account of former experiences in India with Thomas.[14]

Two Society committee men were sent to London to explore whether anything might be achieved by applying for a Company licence. It quickly became clear that there was no hope of a licence being granted and that it would be indiscreet even to apply for one. It was concluded that Carey and Thomas would have to run the risk involved in sailing without a licence. Just then, as though confirming the rightness of that decision, news

---

[12] Kurlansky, Mark pp333-4. Emphasis mine – HJA.
[13] Not until 1858 did the British *government* assume control of Company affairs in India
[14] George, Timothy p82.

came that a ship, *The Earl of Oxford,* was due to leave for India in a few weeks. Captain White knew Dr Thomas; as ship's doctor he had twice before served under him. He was prepared to take the missionaries without advising India House of their presence. A flurry of activity followed: farewells at Hackleton, leaving Dorothy within five weeks of being delivered of her baby; a farewell meeting at Olney, once Carey's home church. Carey's plan was that he would return for Dorothy and the rest of the family sometime in the future once he had settled in Bengal with suitable accommodation. William and the eldest son Felix, age ten, then set out together with Dr and Mrs Thomas, their daughter and two of Thomas' cousins. They boarded *The Earl of Oxford* on the Thames, a few committee friends waving them off from the water's edge.[15] A few months earlier France had declared war on Britain with the consequence that the French navy could attack British vessels anywhere on the high seas. So *The Earl of Oxford* sailed to the Isle of Wight and waited for six weeks to form a convoy under the protection of navy vessels. William and Felix found a lodging for that time in Ryde.

This delay of six weeks meant that news could reach William there, in a letter from Dorothy, of the safe delivery of a son whom she named Jabez.[16] For William this was good news which helped him to bear the heavy disappointment of the delay before the voyage could begin.

> *This is pleasant news indeed to me; such goodness and mercy follow me all my days. My stay here was very painful and unpleasant, but now I see the goodness of God in it ... You wish to know in what state my mind is. I answer, it is much as when I left you. If I had all the world I would freely give it all, to have you and my dear children with me, but the sense of duty is so strong as to*

---

[15] Ibid. p82. Curiously the account in Marshman (p23) is different. He seems to suggest that Thomas, Carey and Felix made their way to the Isle of Wight to wait for *The Earl of Oxford* and boarded her there.

[16] See 1 Chronicles 4:10. Does that choice of name hint at what Dorothy was thinking, now being apart from her husband?

overpower all other considerations; I could not turn back without guilt on my soul.[17]

Evidently Dorothy asked in her letter how Mrs Thomas was thinking about this journey to India and William responds that to stay in England would have been her preference but that 'she thinks it right to go with her husband'. Was Dorothy beginning to waver in her determination to stay, now that the baby was born? Was William still gently pleading with her to come with him? It surely cannot be wrong for us to sense an emotional 'tug of war' here. Many Christian couples, seeking to work for God and his kingdom, will understand exactly the heartache that William and Dorothy must have known in having to choose just then between the command of the Lord 'to go' on the one hand and the obligation of rightful human commitments on the other.

That delay of six weeks brought what looked like bad news, too. Captain White suddenly received an anonymous 'whistle-blowing' letter, possibly from one of Dr Thomas' unsatisfied creditors, threatening to expose him to India House for carrying missionary passengers on his ship to India without the required licence. With his captaincy obviously at stake Captain White was compelled to send William, Felix and Dr Thomas off the ship, together with their luggage, and to refund their passage monies. Mrs Thomas, daughter and cousins remained aboard and eventually sailed leaving William and Dr Thomas to follow later. Carey wrote to Fuller:

Our plans are frustrated for the present; but however the dealings of Providence, I have no doubt that they are directed by an infinitely wise God.[18]

Fuller, in turn, wrote to Ryland Jnr (now Dr John Ryland – the doctorate was awarded by Brown University in the USA, as was Carey's doctorate in 1807):

---
[17] George, Timothy p83.
[18] Marshman, John Clark p23.

We are all undone. I am grieved; but perhaps it is best. Thomas' debts and embarrassments dampened my pleasure before. Perhaps it is best he should not go out. I am afraid leave will never be obtained now for Carey, or any other.[19]

But Carey was right: in more ways than one the wise providence of God was at work. At least the missionaries would not now be smuggled into India by an act of deliberate deception; and the further delay, while a foreign ship was sought, allowed for a complete change of circumstances for both William and Dorothy.

Leaving their luggage in Portsmouth, Felix and the two men hurried to London where, touring the coffee houses, they found an agent for a Danish vessel bound for Calcutta, which was shortly expected to arrive at Dover. The same night they journeyed to Northampton to meet Dr Ryland and then, by foot, to Hackleton to surprise Dorothy and the children at breakfast! For William there was the unexpected joy of seeing his baby son. But despite pleas and tears Dorothy still seemed unmoved. The two men set off walking back to Northampton to ask Dr Ryland for more funds since the fares on the Danish vessel were more than on *The Earl of Oxford*. Ryland gave them what Society monies he held and an authority to borrow, on the security of the Society, from any London church that could help. Dr Thomas was resolved to try once more to persuade Dorothy to change her mind. The two men returned to Hackleton. While (according to sister Polly) William wept and wondered, Thomas in blunt language suggested to Dorothy that if she did not go she would repent all her life for the fact that her family was divided forever.[20] Perhaps the fear of going was now replaced by the fear of not going! Time would tell if this was a wise basis on which to change her mind, but change she did, only insisting that her sister Kitty go with them for company and to help with

---

[19] Ibid. p24.
[20] George, Timothy p83.

the children. This, of course, meant that even further finance was required to cover the cost of a larger party.

Astonishingly, within twenty-four hours the family was packed and ready to go, leaving John Sutcliff of Olney to arrange for the disposal of their heavier house furniture. So to London, to negotiate with Abraham Booth and Dr John Rippon for loans from their churches[21] to meet the extra cost of new passengers and then to negotiate the passage monies with the shipping agent. The monies raised were still short of the amount required so, to save some expense, Dr Thomas offered that he and Kitty should serve on board as assistants and so work their passage, which was agreed. The party left for Dover, while Thomas went to Portsmouth to pick up the luggage left there when they disembarked from *The Earl of Oxford*. It was a near miracle that the whole party and their luggage finally gathered in Dover by the expected embarkation date. They were not to know that the *Krön Princessa Maria* would be two weeks late arriving at Dover. They eventually boarded her on 13 June 1793, sailing under the captaincy of an English-born, Danish naturalised, Captain Christmas.[22] Once at sea the generous captain allowed Thomas and Kitty to take their meals with him and the family, rather than eat in the steward's mess, despite the fact that they were working their passage. He allowed William and Thomas to conduct daily worship on the ship and in various ways proved to be very friendly to them throughout the five months at sea.

This is a point in our unfolding story at which we need to stand back from the pretty picture of the *Krön Princessa Maria* and her passengers as she spreads her sails and comes alive under her passengers' feet, responding to the restlessness of the sea by her slow lifting, pitching and rolling. They were leaving behind a restless society in Britain and the effects of stormy winds blowing across Europe after the bloody French Revolution of 1789. Society in both countries, Britain and France, was forming into warring factions in a struggle for liberty and equality among their peoples; in the former, often by heated argument

---

[21] Marshman, John Clark p25.
[22] Ibid. p25.

Light and shade of farewell days 105

and public disorder; in the latter, by riot, fire and bloodshed. In January 1792, another shoemaker, Thomas Hardy by name, established *The London Corresponding Society*.[23] With a subscription of one penny a week members up and down the land met for the study of Thomas Paine's revolutionary book *The Rights of Man*. Through such societies and working men's clubs his secular teachings and French revolutionary propaganda spread throughout the land to cottagers, weavers and miners.

> *To the government, fretting about national as well as social disintegration, it suddenly seemed sinister. Part of the savagery of the government's counter attack — arresting its leaders, trying them for sedition and sentencing them to fourteen years Australian transportation — was undoubtedly due to the fact that ... an attempt to replace Parliament with a British 'Convention'* [24] *might begin ... agents also noticed that the Corresponding Societies were packed with rowdy, violent, verbose types; a new generation of uppity weavers, godly nailmakers, republican tailors and, most ominously for those who felt the hairs rise on the nape of their necks, Sheffield cutlers.*[25]

In 1793 Napoleon Bonaparte rose to prominence in France as an outstanding military leader, gaining fame for his suppression of a revolt by the Paris Convention. Later, being given the leadership of the army, Bonaparte began to fulfil his dreams of bringing the whole of Europe under his authority by the might of his army and the skill of his leadership. Wellington was reported to have said that Napoleon's presence on a battle field was worth 40,000 men! Slowly the whole of Europe — and beyond — came to experience the tragedy of war at his hands.

And there, sailing away from all these disturbing scenes of turmoil, was an insignificant, weak little band, but carrying

---

[23] Schama, Simon vol 3 p60.
[24] 'Convention' — a term used in revolutionary France of the body set up to govern a specific area of the country.
[25] Schama, Simon vol 3 pp60-61.

with them to India 'the power of the healing creed of Jesus of Nazareth'. With struggles, tears and prayers they were to lay the foundation of a spiritual kingdom in India which is still today slowly gathering power (and not only there but also worldwide) and steadily proceeding toward 'the one far-off, divine event, to which the whole Creation moves in the hands of the great Disposer of all events'.[26] Not Thomas Paine, nor Thomas Hardy, with their secular reasonings, not Napoleon Bonaparte with his brutal force of arms, but God and his Christ alone shall have the glory of this world's history. *God chose the foolish things of the world to shame the wise; God chose the weak things of the world to shame the strong.*[27] But as the little party continues their long, wearisome voyage we look back, briefly, to watch their friends who were left behind, as they begin to take up 'the rope' of support they had promised to hold. Would they be faithful?

---

[26] Fuller, Thomas Ekins p87. Similar words are carved around the dome of the Capitol in Washington DC. Compare Titus 2:12-13
[27] 1 Corinthians 1:27

15
'If you will hold the rope'

Those words were not lightly spoken; nor were they lightly received. Soon after the missionaries had set sail Fuller, speaking to a meeting of friends, said:

> *Our undertaking to India really appeared to me, on its commencement, to be somewhat like a few men deliberating about the importance of penetrating into a deep mine which had never before been explored.*[1] *We had no one to guide us; and while we were thus deliberating Carey, as it were, said, 'Well, I will go down if you will hold the rope!' But before he went down, he, as it seemed to me, took an oath from each of us at the mouth of the pit, to this effect, that while we lived we should never let go the rope. You understand me. There was a great responsibility attached to us who began the business.*[2]

Clearly, the committee men of the Society regarded the relationship between themselves and Carey almost as a holy sacrament, to endure as long as life should last. Likewise Carey regarded himself as indissolubly bound to them. A remarkable trust existed between them all. There was a precious spiritual uniting of minds. Even when individual committee officers had

---

[1] Carey and Thomas were not, in fact, the first missionaries to India. 'The history of Protestant missions in India begins with the Lutheran missionaries Ziegenbalg and Plutschau, who landed in Tranquebar, South India, in July 1706. By 1711 Ziegenbalg had translated the New Testament into Tamil'. Boyd, Robin p15. The Moravians had worked in Calcutta until just before Carey arrived there.
[2] Fuller, Thomas Ekins p88.

to make decisions in the absence of opportunity to consult others they seemed able to do so without damaging their fellowship together. The means of communicating with one another were slow and tedious; their individual pastoral responsibilities allowed them to meet as a committee only infrequently.

Contact with the missionaries, once they were established in Bengal, was a time-consuming business. The sea journey, to carry goods and mail, meant many months of delay before delivery. There were many months more before a reply could be received. War with the French meant that English ships were sometimes sunk at sea and mail was lost. The situation demanded an indestructible confidence and trust between all concerned. A letter home in January 1795[3] illustrates Carey's dependence upon such trust:

> *Much engaged in writing, having begun to write letters to Europe; but having received none, I feel that hope deferred makes the heart sick. However, I am fully satisfied of the firmness of their friendship that I feel a sweet pleasure in writing to them, though rather of a forlorn kind; and having nothing but myself to write about, feel the awkwardness of being an egotist.*[4]

Friends in England had no knowledge of what their two missionaries had been doing for over a year. Carey's first letter to the Society, written on board ship as they approached India, was not received by them until a year later.[5] For his part, we can understand Carey's excitement when he received answering mail from England and was able to write, in May 1795:

> *Blessed be God, I have at last received letters and other articles from our friends in England ... from our dear brethren Fuller, Morris and Ripon.*[6]

---

[3] They had landed in Calcutta in November 1793.
[4] Smith, George p70.
[5] They had embarked June 1793; Carey's letter reached them July 1794. George, Timothy p106.
[6] Smith, George p71.

The value of an unfaltering trust, earned and given between Christian brethren, was the golden cord which held firm the tiny fledgling endeavour across the thousands of miles of ocean that separated them from one another. No less remarkable was the fact that growing numbers of churches were ready to support the work prayerfully and financially when there was no news from the field to share.[7] Only a bare trust that the Society and its missionaries were rightly interpreting the command of Christ 'to go' provided the stimulus for growing support among an increasing number of churches of different denominations. The spirit of Carey himself was spreading among Christians up and down the land: 'Expect ... Attempt'.

The successful growth of the Society during this long wait for news is much to the credit of Andrew Fuller, the Society's secretary, sometimes with the support of Ryland and Sutcliff. As one has described Fuller's prodigious efforts:

> *His deputation ministry took him into almost all the counties of England, Ireland and Scotland. His cause required frequent advocacy with cabinet ministers, members of Parliament and East India Company directors. Nor were there wanting bitter and subtle enemies, both at home and abroad, who left no means untried to accomplish the ruin of the Mission. Moreover his journeys were the more irksome because his writings had already gone before, stirring up discussions and strife in all parts.[8] Some would seek advice on personal or ecclesiastical matters, for it was not often that one so wise in counsel journeyed through the country.[9]*

---

[7] 13 November was declared among the churches as a day of fasting and prayer for the missionaries although there was no news of their whereabouts. Beck, J R p90.

[8] Notably *The Gospel Worthy of all Acceptation*, in which he showed biblical justification for actively presenting the gospel to sinners, as opposed to the view of High or Hyper Calvinism prevailing in some churches.

[9] Fuller, Thomas Ekins pp 88-9.

Fuller, a man known to be shy and retiring, who often suffered bouts of ill-health, to say nothing of the time involved in his frequent writing of articles and letters,[10] added to his formidable ministerial responsibilities at Kettering, now added to all this, by a solemn vow once given to God and before his fellow men, the secretaryship of the Society.

One of Fuller's first journeys, as Society secretary, was to Scotland, where he sometimes preached to large congregations of four or five thousand people, returning to Kettering with over £900 for the work of the Mission and with promises of further help.[11] On four further occasions (1802, 1805, 1808, 1819) he repeated the journey to Scotland with similar success. But he also faced opposition on these journeys. When accused of schism by an Anglican clergyman known for his low opinion of Dissenters, Fuller crisply replied:

> *I never felt it; for it did not appear to be aimed to hurt us, but merely to screen yourselves, in the view of your bishop, from the suspicion of favouring us ... Before you can fix the guilt of schism on us, you must prove (i) that the Church of England is a true church; (ii) that it is the only true church in the kingdom.*[12]

The following extract indicates something of the pressure under which Andrew Fuller laboured during all these exertions:

> *My wife*[13] *looks at me, with a tear ready to drop, 'My dear you have hardly time to speak to me'. My friends at home are kind, but they also say, 'You have no time to*

---

[10] Many of his letters have survived and they reveal an intense pastoral concern for his many contacts, for the missionaries and their converts in India, and also many loving letters to his wife written while away on his deputation journeys.

[11] When preaching at James Haldane's church (Edinburgh) Andrew Fuller records that : *My heart was dismayed at the sight ... nearly 5000 people attended, and some thousands went away unable to get in.* Haykin, Michael (ed.) vol 2 p225.

[12] Fuller, Thomas Ekins p91.

[13] This was Fuller's second wife, Ann, whom he married in 1795.

see or know us, and you will soon be worn out'. Amidst all this, there is, 'Come again to Scotland; come again to Plymouth; come to Bristol'. My heart is ready to do everything you desire, but my hands fail me.[14]

And unseen, but none the less persistent, was the pressure of the fact that it was seven long years before any news was received at home of a single convert resulting from the missionaries' work.

But this intense personal devotion of the Society's committee men to Carey and the mission was not without its dangers. When some of the London Particular Baptist churches, for example, suggested forming an 'assistant' committee among themselves, Fuller thought it unwise, arguing that it would 'dilute' the sense of responsibility which the Northamptonshire men felt, having bound themselves by solemn oath to Carey. He also suspected that many of the London churches were of a Hyper Calvinist persuasion.[15] Later when new men composed the Society committee, who had not known Carey as intimately as the original founders of the society had known him, Fuller more than once had to oppose their suggestions, arguing that they did not reflect the same confidence in Carey as he had. After Fuller's death the sad breach that developed between Carey and his colleagues and the new committee members clearly demonstrated the loss of that former close personal fellowship between the senders and the sent. The fact that Carey himself never once returned to England during his long years of service in Bengal undoubtedly contributed to a loss of unquestioning trust in him by those who never knew him, even though it also demonstrated his fierce determination not to lose a single day, or hour, from the work on which he had set his heart. Who is to say if, or indeed how, this loss of trust could have been avoided without hindering Carey's remarkable progress in the work in Serampore?

---

[14] Ibid. p97.
[15] Ibid. p106.

It is clear that Fuller's selfless pouring out of his energies in support of the Society was an indispensable contribution to the success of the work. Nor may we forget the patient support of the churches for which men like Fuller, Ryland and Sutcliff had ministerial responsibility. It was often the case that Fuller was away on deputation for a month or more at a time; so also, sometimes, were Ryland and Sutcliff. On one occasion Ryland had to write explaining the absence of Fuller and Sutcliff from their chapels:

> *They are so out of reach that their people begin to complain. Others therefore must bestir themselves.*[16]

All that Carey and his colleagues were able to do was built upon the secure foundation of all that was being done in England. There is a point where there is little difference between the spiritual demands of the commitment 'to send' (as Fuller and his friends understood it) and that of the commitment actually 'to go'. Both make demands which are equally serious when properly understood. But now we must return to Carey and Thomas aboard the good ship *Krön Princessa Maria* at the mercy of the wind and the waves.

---

[16] Haykin, Michael p267.

16
'For those in peril on the sea'

What must have been the emotions that stirred Carey's mind as the *Krön Princessa Maria* unfurled her sails and pulled away from Dover to head down the British Channel? The seemingly forbidding hurdles of the past few months had all been overcome and his vision of 'into all the world' was becoming a reality. He now had an unexpected colleague in Dr Thomas, whose experience of life in Bengal could be so valuable; the supporting churches had proved equal to the task of raising the funds to make the voyage possible; his wife, together with helpful sister Kitty and all the children, were with him on the journey; the British navy frigate was accompanying them as protection from the French navy; being on a Danish vessel meant that they were for a while beyond the reach of the hostile East India Company; and the captain of the ship was very friendly towards them. Truly, God had been *so* good!

For the older Carey children the whole experience must have been exciting and very different from anything they had known before. New sights and unusual sounds to become familiar with, the activities of the sailors to watch, the few other passengers to learn about – a German, a Norwegian, a Dane and a Frenchman[1] – all must have intrigued the children. Carey was able to write:

> *Our infant* [baby Jabez, a few months old] *has thrived more than if it had been on land and the children are*

---

[1] The Frenchman was a Deist who had several argumentative sessions with Carey during the voyage. Deism was the view that natural reason is the only source of religious knowledge. Having created the world God leaves it to run by its own inherent rules.

well satisfied. The children were complete sailors and the women were much better than ever I expected.[2]

For Dorothy and her sister things were not so easy. Both suffered from the misery of seasickness from time to time, though they must have been grateful for the kindly captain's concern in having soup sent to their cabin, which was in fact the largest cabin on the ship. But for simple village women as they were, unaccustomed to the movements of a ship, the dancing horizon, the creaking of the ship's timbers, the noise of the wind in the rigging and the shouts of the crew, must all have seemed unnerving. The captain permitted William and Thomas to conduct a service of worship each Sunday in their spacious cabin. It was open to any on the ship, though few ever attended. The family had their own private prayer time daily.

As the days passed it seems that Carey's initial excitement changed to a time of soul-searching. The godless behaviour of the crew was a trial to him and haunting him at the back of his mind was the looming problem of the East India Company's declared hostility to missionaries working in their trading areas. After the busy life of a pastor and the hectic months leading up to this point in his life, his enforced inactivity as a passenger at sea must have been hard for him to bear. A couple of entries in his *Journal* are significant:

> *I feel myself to be much declined, upon the whole, in the more spiritual exercises of religion ... sometimes I am quite dejected when I see the impenetrability of the hearts of those with us. They hear us preach on the Lord's Day, but we are forced to witness their disregard all the week. I have reason to lament over the barrenness of soul, and am sometimes much discouraged; for if I am so dead and stupid, how can I expect to be of any use among the heathen?*[3]

---

[2] Beck, James R p89.
[3] Smith, George p46.

After a week or two on the voyage William had begun to learn Bengali from Dr Thomas and, with his own knowledge of Hebrew, had been assisting Thomas with a translation of Genesis. That must have helped him to feel that he was really beginning the work on which he had set his heart. Carey is able to write:

> *I think that I have had more liberty in prayer, and more converse with God, than for sometime before; but have not withstanding been a very unfruitful creature, and so remain.*[4]

The journey to South Africa was without serious incident. Yet for Dorothy it was a steady sailing away from all she had known. Thomas wrote of her:

> *Poor Mrs Carey has had many fears and troubles; so that she was like Lot's wife, until we passed the Cape; but ever since, it seems so far to look back to Piddington, that she turns her hopes and wishes to our safe arrival in Bengal. She has had good health all the passage, and her little babe has grown a stout fellow.*[5]

With a fair wind prospering their journey the captain decided not to stop at the Cape but to push on while he could. Carey was disappointed for he had hoped to meet some Christians there. Soon after leaving the Cape they encountered a violent storm that tossed the ship about like a tiny cork in a whirlpool. The pitching and the rolling from side to side must have provoked fear in the hearts of the passengers, unfamiliar as they were with the raging of the sea. Even Carey wondered if they could survive, facing great waves that he thought must be fifty yards high.[6] The ship's masts and rigging were damaged. Instructing his wife and the children to stay in bed, he went on deck to see if there was any way he could help:

---

[4] Ibid. p46.
[5] Beck, James R p89.
[6] George, Timothy p89.

I saw her going, [ie.sinking] *and with others, concluded she could not recover it. I felt resigned to the will of God; and to prevent being tossed overboard by the motion, caught hold of what was nearest to me ...at last we cleared the wreck*[age] *and set our main sail, which kept the ship a little steady.*[7]

The storm passed on its way and after some days masts and rigging were repaired and the journey continued without further incident across the Arabian sea to the tip of India and up into the Bay of Bengal. But if Dorothy's original refusal to go with William arose from a fear of the unknown, she could now add to her anxieties the fear of the known consequences of having agreed to go with him.

The nearer they approached their destination the wider became William's understanding of *world* mission. In his first letter to the Society,[8] reprinted and circulated among the supporters of the Society, Carey wrote:

I hope the Society will go on and increase ... Africa is but a little way from England; Madagascar but a little way further; South America and all the numerous and large islands in the Indian and Chinese seas, I hope will not be passed over. A large field opens on every side, and millions of perishing heathen, tormented in this life by idolatry, superstition, and ignorance and exposed to eternal miseries in the world to come, are pleading, yea, all their miseries plead as soon as they are known, with every heart that loves God, and with all the churches of the living God.[9]

Carey was already, before setting foot in Bengal, thinking of what his family could do to enlarge their missionary outreach; he thought one of his sons might study Sanskrit and another

---
[7] Ibid p89.
[8] Written on board in October 1793; the letter reached Fuller on 29 July 1794
[9] George, Timothy p90.

Persian while he concentrated on Bengali. It is such thinking which marks out Carey as a pioneer of world evangelisation. Bengal, even India as a whole, was not to be the end of his thinking.

Various parts of India had previously been visited by Christian missionaries long before Carey's coming. There was the (suggested) visit and death of St Thomas the apostle to the South (between AD 51-72). Clement of Alexandria (AD60-120) speaks of a missionary from Alexandria visiting India. There was the arrival of Mar Thomas and 400 refugee Syrian Christians who set up a Nestorian[10] Community in south west India under the protection of the local king, with further reinforcements in AD 774. They used a Syriac liturgy that did not lend itself to evangelism outside their own community. The Portuguese arrived in Western India in AD 1500 bringing the Franciscans and finding the Nestorians already present. St Francis Xavier visited the same coast in AD 1542 bringing the Jesuits with him.[11] On the south east coast of India there was the work of the Lutheran missionaries in Tranquebar from AD 1706 who confined themselves to the Tamil community, concentrating on the translation of the Scriptures and other Christian writings into Tamil. Yet nothing of all these various efforts reached further than the limits of India and showed no vision for *world* mission. Only the Moravian Brethren could be said to have begun what Carey was proposing in their outreach to a number of different countries. In Carey's mind Bengal was not an end to be reached but was to be the beginning of a worldwide movement yet to be attempted.

> *Convinced Calvinistic Baptist that he was, Carey's intended strategy saw his own denomination as a mere initial 'trial project' in his comprehensive plan for a world-*

---

[10] Named after Nestorius (AD 381-451) who taught heretically that Christ was *two* persons – the divine Son of God indwelling the human son of Mary, not *one* divine Person with two natures.

[11] There are detailed accounts of early Christianity in India in *The Nestorian Missionary Enterprise* by Revd. Stewart, John pp. 101-135 and in *An introduction to Indian Christian theology* by Boyd, Robin pp 7-14.

wide dissemination for Jesus Christ's message ... his desire was to unleash the resources of the world Church for the complete welfare of the whole of humanity.[12]

Such thinking lay behind Carey's proposal to Fuller (1806) for a conference in South Africa 'of all denominations of Christians from the four quarters of the world about every ten years – the first to be in 1810 or 1812 at the furthest'. Fuller's response was however less than sympathetic: he called the proposal 'Carey's pleasing dream'.[13] It was a hundred years (1910) before an International Missionary Conference such as Carey 'dreamed' of actually took place in Edinburgh.

But to return to the *Krön Princessa Maria*; a contrary wind (the North West monsoon?) frustratingly delayed the ship's arrival in Calcutta by a couple of weeks but eventually, on 11 November 1793, they arrived in port. To avoid the problem of the captain being required to include them on his passenger list for the East India Company, Dorothy, Carey, the children and Dr Thomas disembarked onto a small riverboat and landed separately from the other passengers, so slipping into Calcutta without the knowledge of the Company. The rightness of such a secret entry into the Company area had been a cause of earnest debate in the Society committee meetings. They had resolved that since their missionaries had no subversive intentions against the Company, but only wished for the good of the people of Bengal, they must be right to obey the command of Christ to go everywhere with the Christian message, being prepared for whatever consequences might follow. Such was the practice, they felt, of the apostles and early Christian believers. But now, with Carey and Thomas 'on the ground' in India, was Bengal to be the only area in the world for the Society's concern?

---

[12] Hedlund, R E in Daniel J K and Hedlund, R E (eds.) p96.
[13] George, Timothy p163.

17
Africa too? The Caribbean also?

In his *Enquiry* Carey referred to the 'noble efforts made to abolish the inhuman slave trade' and, while regretting that they had not yet been wholly successful, pointed to the establishment in 1788 of a free settlement for liberated slaves at Sierra Leone on the west coast of Africa. The colony was founded by an English trading company with the aims of introducing Christianity there and of giving employment to destitute blacks living in London.[1] Carey writes of that event as:

> *An effort which, if followed with a divine blessing, not only promises to open a way for honourable commerce with that extensive country, and for the civilization of its inhabitants, but may prove the happy means of introducing amongst them the gospel of our Lord Jesus Christ.*[2]

During committee meetings after the departure of Carey and Thomas and their families for Bengal, discussion arose as to the possibilities of openings for the Society elsewhere in the world. Parts of Canada and Sierra Leone were considered but no decision was made. By 1795 however certain events had become known to the Society men which led to a fresh discussion of the matter by the committee meeting at Arnesby in April of that year. John Ryland and Samuel Pearce had been visited by a former slave, David George from Virginia, America, who had become a Baptist preacher and pastor of a Calvinistic Baptist church he had founded in Nova Scotia. In 1792 he had sailed

---
[1] Haykin, Michael A G p243. A number of freed slaves from Nova Scotia also came there.
[2] The *Enquiry*, section five.

with his family to Sierra Leone and founded a Calvinistic Baptist church in Freetown, the capital of the country. Ryland and Pearce therefore proposed that Sierra Leone should be the next country for the Society to consider since any missionaries sent there could have George David and his church to help them.

One of Ryland's students at the Bristol Baptist Academy, Jacob Grigg, offered to go. A former student at the Academy, James Rodway, then pastor at Burton-upon-Trent, also volunteered to go. Both men were 'set apart for the work of the Lord' at a meeting in September 1795 and sailed in November, reaching Sierra Leone on 1 December.[3]

In the mystery of divine Providence, however, the high hopes with which this venture began were soon to be dashed. Rodway fell seriously ill and was compelled to return to England, which he did in 1796. Grigg's problem was political: he was much influenced by the thinking of the French Revolution and was not only strongly opposed to slavery but went further in his views to the extent of regarding the rule of the English government as tyrannical. Unwilling to keep these opinions to himself for the sake of the gospel, he clashed repeatedly with the Governor of the colony, an Evangelical Anglican, who complained to Fuller. This caused Fuller to write in a letter to his friend Sutcliff:

> *There is great danger of the African Mission being utterly destroyed through Grigg's imprudence. I must call a small committee at Guilsborough next Thursday. Your company is absolutely necessary.*[4]

At the Guilsborough meeting a decision was reached which led to Fuller writing to Carey:

> *The African Mission has utterly failed, partly through the affliction of Rodway, who could not stand the climate, and ... partly owing to Grigg's imprudence, who has in-*

---
[3] Haykin, Michael A G p244. Much of the information here is from Haykin pp243-245.
[4] Ibid. p245.

terfered in the disputes of the colony and stirred up the people to oppose the Governor.[5]

Early in 1797 the Governor presented Grigg with an ultimatum, either to return to England or sail to America; Grigg took the latter course. We can only guess how news of this failure will have disappointed Carey who must by that time have been coping with the emotional stress caused by the death of his son Peter and the beginnings of Dorothy's mental derangement. Was the work in Bengal similarly to come to an untimely end?

From the Society's point of view this event confirmed, in the thinking of the committee men, the importance of missionaries refraining from becoming involved in the politics of any country and instead strictly concerning themselves with the spread of Christian truth. It was this policy that justified to them the entry into Bengal despite the Trading Company's objections. But it was also this policy that caused a great deal of heartache in the work later begun in Jamaica, to which we now turn.

In 1791 a letter to John Rippon of the Carter Lane church in London brought the existence of Baptist churches in Jamaica to the attention of Particular Baptists in England. Rippon publicised the letter in his *Baptist Annual Register,* a newssheet recording Particular Baptist affairs that he published for several years. The letter came from George Liele, one of thousands of slaves and their masters who because of the War of Independence emigrated from America in 1783 and came to Jamaica. His letter indicated that he had founded a Baptist church of over three hundred members in Kingston. Liele was appealing for help to enable the building of his chapel to be completed. He reported that the total Baptist community on the island was about one thousand five hundred persons.[6] Liele had baptised a man of mixed race (Negro and White) who planted his own church on an estate owned by a Quaker planter. Later the Jamaica House of Assembly passed a law prohibiting the teaching of Christianity on the plantations and opposition to such activity developed among many of the planters. This prompted Moses

---
[5] Ibid. p245.
[6] This, and other relevant information, taken from Stanley, Brian pp69-82.

Africa too? The Carribean also? 123

Baker, an immigrant whom Liele had baptised and who had founded a church near New York, to report regularly to John Ryland. In December 1813 the Society appointed one of Ryland's students at the Bristol Baptist Academy, John Rowe, to the task of helping Moses Baker. Rowe landed in Jamaica in February 1814 – marking the beginning of the Society's official interest in Jamaica.

What Rowe found when he landed was less than encouraging. Because of the House of Assembly law Baker had not been able to teach his people for eight years, no baptisms had happened for three years and no celebration of the Lord's Supper for ten years. Yet the estimated total of Baptists on the island had risen to around eight thousand. Under the Society committee's instructions 'to avoid interference in political matters and to endeavour by a respectful demeanour to recommend himself to the white inhabitants of the island'[7] Rowe settled on the opposite side of the island from Kingston and, with the approval of the planters, established a day and Sunday school in Falmouth for teaching the slave children to read and learn the basic truths of Christianity. By the time of Rowe's death in 1816, he had gained the respect of the district magistrate. The more tolerant attitude towards missionary activity which Rowe had succeeded in earning was, however, not to last. His successor, Lee Compere, sent out to join Rowe in 1815, was less compliant with the Committee's required policy. Receiving a desperate appeal from the church in Kingston for teaching on 'the way of God more perfectly', Compere complied in 1816 but a year later was disowned by the Society, apparently for refusing to keep silent on the subject of slavery. For the next ten years hostility against missionary activity by the planters grew in strength and Baptists in particular were regarded as allies to the abolitionist cause. Yet the number of Baptists on the island grew steadily. William Knibb,[8] who had been sent by the Society to the island in 1825 after volunteering as a replacement for his brother Thomas (who had died in Jamaica only fifteen months

---

[7] Ibid. p71.
[8] A full account of the life of William Knibb is available in Haykin, Michael (Ed.) vol 3 pp211-231.

after arriving), wrote to his mother that thousands were flocking to hear the Word. A correspondent writing to John Dyer (who after Andrew Fuller's death had succeeded as secretary to the Society) wrote: *With you the blessings of the Gospel descend like dew; but with us they are heavy showers of rain.*[9]

Talks in England about the abolition of slavery in the British colonies were regarded in Jamaica as if they were an official policy and Sam Sharpe, a Jamaican Baptist deacon, organised a strike of the slaves in anticipation of the presumed event. Knibb vigorously opposed the strike and warned the strikers that their action was inopportune. But the strike became violent; crops were fired, some factories were destroyed and a few white owners were killed. Retaliation was swift: hundreds of slaves were slaughtered. The Baptist missionaries were blamed and Knibb was arrested; many Baptist chapels were destroyed including Knibb's chapel in Falmouth. The news reaching England resulted in blame being attached to the Jamaican missionaries, with the result that the Baptist missionaries appealed to the Society:

> *... that one of our brethren be appointed as a deputation to proceed forthwith to England, to act under the direction of the committee; and that brother Knibb, on account of his intimate acquaintance with the mission in the disturbed part of the island, and his knowledge of the circumstances immediately connected with the rebellion, be appointed for that purpose.*[10]

William Knibb and family arrived back in England on 26 April 1832.

The Society committee was united in trying to dissuade Knibb from the course he was proposing to take. They urged that slavery was political and the Christian message alone was his business. Finding himself unable to persuade the Committee otherwise Knibb could contain himself no longer and addressed them with these impassioned words:

---

[9] Stanley, Brian p74.
[10] Haykin, Michael AG vol.3 p217.

> *Myself, my wife and my children, are entirely dependent upon the Baptist Mission; we have landed without a shilling, and may at once be reduced to penury. But if it be necessary, I will take them by the hand, and walk barefoot throughout the Kingdom, but I will make known to the Christians of England what their brethren in Jamaica are suffering.*[11]

Two days later the annual meeting of the Society was held and Knibb was one of the speakers. He did not hesitate:

> *... the embassy on which I am sent by my brother missionaries is so intimately connected with the best interests of 800,000 of our suffering fellow creatures held in the chains of slavery ... I plead for liberty to worship God on behalf of 30,000 Christian slaves, of the same faith as your selves; and if the friends of missions will not hear me, I hope the God of missions will.*[12]

The congregation was persuaded; the committee was persuaded; and for the next two years Knibb was sent throughout England and Scotland with his burning message. The British Government promised to help the Society by financing the rebuilding of some of the destroyed chapels and in 1834 a partial freedom was declared to all slaves under British rule. In 1838 complete freedom was declared. In October 1834 Knibb returned to Jamaica to a triumphant welcome. People exclaimed:

> *It* [is] *him, it him for true. But see how him stand! Him make two of what him was when him left ...God bless you, massa, for all the good you do for we. God, him too good.*[13]

Knibb died in 1845 and was buried in the Falmouth churchyard. The history of the work in the Caribbean is beyond the re-

---
[11] Ibid. p218.
[12] Ibid. p221.
[13] Ibid. p222.

mit of this book.[14] The whole West Indies venture presented the Society with problems very different from those arising in the work in India since the missionaries in the Caribbean came not so much as evangelists but more as pastors and teachers to an *existing* Christian Negro community. And the Caribbean work compelled the Society to recognise that the gospel message has its proper social, as well as its spiritual, implications. How else can you love your neighbour as yourself? But we have been away from Bengal for too long and must return there without delay. Except to make the point that Sam Sharpe, the Baptist deacon who organised the strike in anticipation of a freedom that did not then come and was one of those executed as a result, was made 'A National Hero' and honoured at the Independence of Jamaica in August 1962.[15]

---

[14] See Stanley, Brian p.68-96; 240-264.
[15] Shown in a BBC television documentary programme

18
'The abominable East Indian monopoly'[1]

Elizabeth 1st granted a Royal Charter in 1600 to 'The Company of Merchants of London trading into the East Indies'. The first East India Company base in India was established at Surat in 1608 on the West coast. This was subsequently superseded by trading posts in Bombay in 1689, on the West coast and by Madras in1639 and Calcutta in 1690, both on the East coast.[2] Calcutta developed as the chief of these trading centres and became the place where the West first truly encountered the East. The wealth of the Company increased yearly, trading in spices, rice, sugar, saltpetre, opium, tobacco, chintz, ginger and jute sacking. Some fifty vessels a year were calling at the East India docks in London with produce from India. Gradually the Company assumed political responsibilities in addition to commercial interests and after Robert Clive's victories became the virtual colonial government of large parts of India under him. Company employees were allowed to trade privately for themselves and many amassed large fortunes uncontrolled by English law. Eventually a Governing Council of the Company, presided over by a Governor General in Calcutta, was appointed in 1773 responsible to the Court of Directors in London. In 1774 Warren Hastings was appointed the first of a long line of Governor Generals to represent the British Government in India.[3] It was against this background and into this situation that Carey and

---
[1] Quoted from William Carey's journal
[2] Madras, Bombay and Calcutta are now known by their vernacular names Chennai, Mumbai and Kolkata respectively.
[3] Information drawn from Krishna Dutta pp1-15.

Thomas, uninvited and unwelcome, dared to bring the light of the Christian message.

When Clive eventually returned to England – a sick man – a chorus of accusations was brought against him:

> ... charging him with bribery, embezzlement and general abuse of his position. There was some substance to the charges brought against Clive; he did accept huge presents from Indian princes, but bribery was endemic in all forms of government in the 18th century.[4]

In his famous defence, when brought to trial by the House of Commons and being unabashed by the charges against him, he – then one of the richest men in Britain – retorted:

> A great prince was dependent upon my pleasure, an opulent city lay at my mercy; its richest bankers bid against each other for my smiles; I walked through vaults which were thrown open to me alone, piled on either hand with gold and jewels! Mr Chairman, at this moment I stand astonished at my own moderation.[5]

The well known axiom 'power corrupts and absolute power corrupts absolutely' was true at all levels of the administration of the Company, despite the fact that Governor Generals were appointed by the British Government in an attempt to deal with corruption in the Company. A system of governing in the style of British courts, police and regulations was introduced to replace what had been the Indian system of Muslim justice. The result was that a few hundred British civilians attempted to govern the millions of Bengalis by means of a legal system foreign to them, thus providing fertile soil for further abuses and injustices.

> Warren Hastings[6] lived in open adultery. The majority of the officials had native women ... the pollution, springing

---

[4] Purnell, op. cit.
[5] Sharma, Simon vol 2 p505.
[6] Governor General 1773-1785

from England originally, was rolled out to corrupt social and political life, till Pitt cried out.[7]

The original 'Pious Clause' (making the improvement and education of the natives by Christian missionaries one of the obligations of the Company) had been struck out of the charter, for who could tell what harm might be done to Company affairs by the interference of missionaries and their Christian principles, especially their evangelistic aims? Hence the persistent opposition of the Company Directors to missionary outreach in their areas. Company chaplains were allowed to minister to Company staff but on the strict understanding that they were forbidden to teach Indian natives.

The Calcutta scene had much to displease Carey and Thomas. The Company was:

> *... as the vituperative critics of the East India Company's rule claimed, so steeped in venal selfishness, a racket disguised as a business, as to be entirely beyond redemption.*[8]

In addition to the moral decadence rife among European employees of the Company, hardly recommending the Christianity for which England was supposedly known, there was the problem of the luxury in which many of them were living, creating a huge gulf between themselves and the native people of Bengal (to whom Carey was eager to present Christian truth) and also between themselves and the missionary. Writing to Andrew Fuller in 1794 Carey expressed his concern at the situation:

> *In a country like this, settled by Europeans, the grandeur, the customs and prejudices of the Europeans are exceedingly dangerous ... all their discourse is about the vices of the Natives: so that a missionary must*

---
[7] Smith, George p56.
[8] Sharma, Simon vol.2 p481.

see thousands of people treating him with the greatest kindness [ie. fellow Europeans] *but whom he must be entirely different from in his life, his appearance and everything.*[9]

In his *Enquiry* Carey had formulated two principles that he felt should define the missionary's lifestyle. First, a missionary must be one of the companions and an equal of the people to whom he is sent; second, a missionary and his converts must, as soon as possible, become indigenous and self-supporting. Now, at the age of thirty-three, Carey faced the hard task of working out those principles in the most unhelpful environment. He writes:

It will be very important to missionaries to be men of calmness and evenness of temper, and rather inclined to suffer hardships than to court the favour of men, and such who will be indefatigably employed in the work set before them, an inconstancy of mind being quite injurious to it.[10]

As we continue with events in Calcutta we shall see what was involved for Carey as he strove to pass his own test.

---
[9] Beck, James R p91.
[10] Smith, George p60.

The house Carey lived in through the later years of his life

photo: Naylor

Carey Baptist Church, Calcutta

photo: Naylor

Carey Baptist Church, interior

photo: Naylor

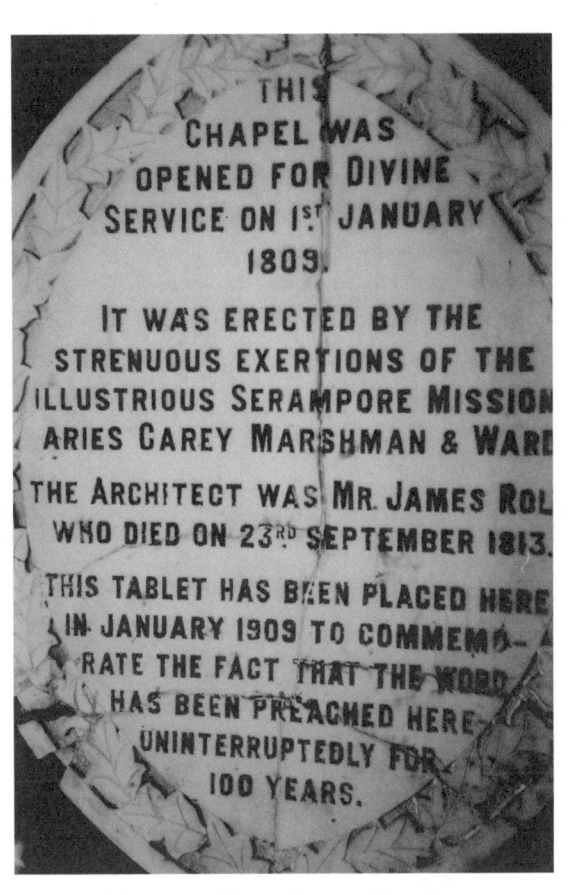

THIS CHAPEL WAS OPENED FOR DIVINE SERVICE ON 1ST JANUARY 1809.

IT WAS ERECTED BY THE STRENUOUS EXERTIONS OF THE ILLUSTRIOUS SERAMPORE MISSIONARIES CAREY MARSHMAN & WARD

THE ARCHITECT WAS MR. JAMES ROL WHO DIED ON 23RD SEPTEMBER 1813.

THIS TABLET HAS BEEN PLACED HERE IN JANUARY 1909 TO COMMEMORATE THE FACT THAT THE WORD HAS BEEN PREACHED HERE UNINTERRUPTEDLY FOR 100 YEARS.

Plaque in Carey Baptist Church

photo: Naylor

Judson Memorial plaque, Carey Baptist Church

photo: Naylor

Danish church, Serampore, where Carey preached occasionally

photo: Naylor

> SACRED TO THE MEMORY
> OF
> HIS EXCELLENCY
> **LT. COLONEL OLE (OLAVE) BIE**
> GOVERNOR OF FREDERICSNAGORE
> BORN AT TRONDHJEM, NORWAY IN FEBRUARY, 1733
> DIED AT SERAMPUR, 18TH MAY 1805
> COLONEL BIE WAS A DISCIPLE OF
> SWARTZ OF TRANQUEBAR
> HE RECEIVED AND SHELTERED THE
> BAPTIST MISSIONARIES IN 1799
> AND BUILT THE CHURCH HERE.

Colonel Bie Memorial plaque, Danish church, Serampore

photo: Naylor

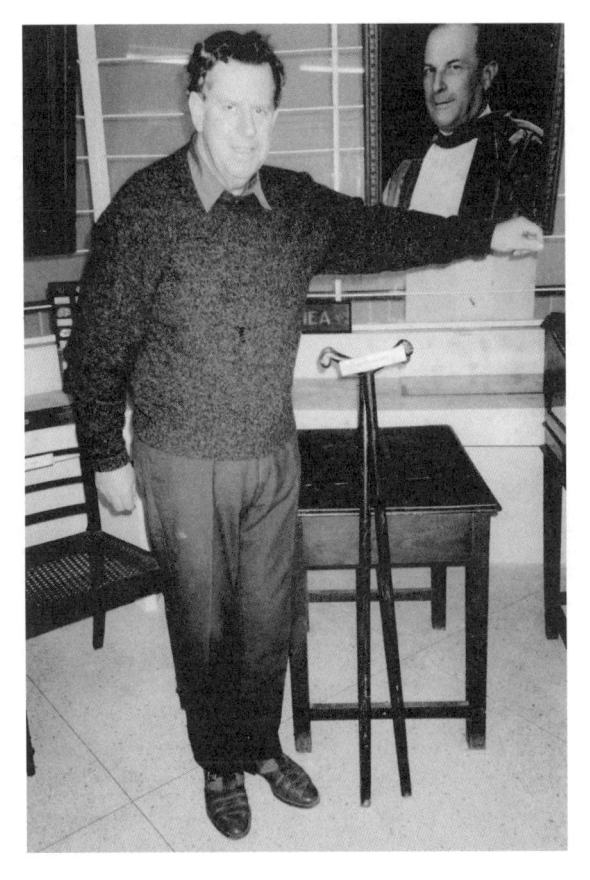

Carey Library, the College. Peter Naylor's left arm indicates Carey's height. Naylor was six feet tall.

photo: Naylor

Carey's tomb, Serampore

photo: Naylor

Serampore College, 2006

photo: Wikipedia

Indian Post Office First Day Commemorative Cover

NOTTINGHAM

LEICESTER

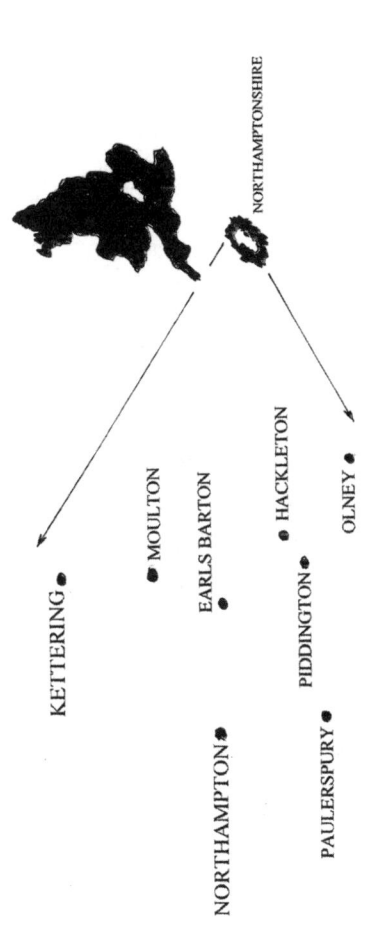

KETTERING

MOULTON

EARLS BARTON

HACKLETON

NORTHAMPTON

PIDDINGTON

OLNEY

PAULERSPURY

NORTHAMPTONSHIRE

Carey's English 'World'

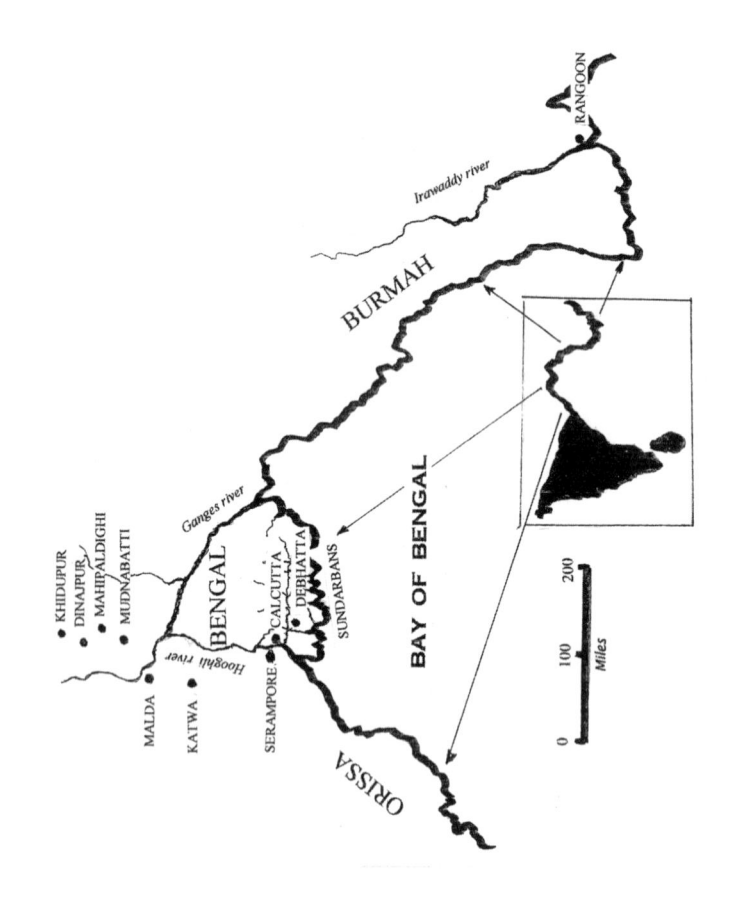

Carey's Indian 'World'

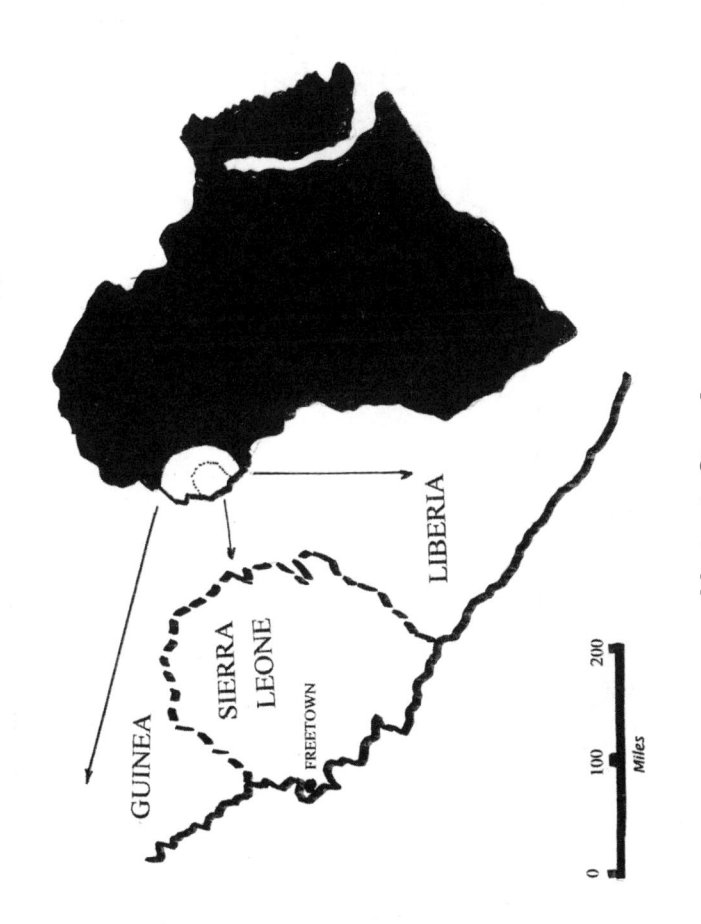

Mission to Sierra Leone

Mission to Jamaica

19
The struggle to begin

Mrs Thomas, with her daughter and two cousins, had remained on *The Earl of Oxford* when it left the Isle of Wight (chapter fourteen); Carey and Dr Thomas were to follow later when a ship was available. Now that the Carey family and Thomas had arrived in Calcutta their first duty was to locate Dr Thomas' family. Mr and Mrs Udney, who were already acquainted with Thomas from the days when they and Charles Grant were helping to finance his translation work prior to his linking with the Particular Baptist Society, had given hospitality to Mrs Thomas and her party. Now that the Thomas family was united again they and the Carey family began living by themselves as a community. Problems soon arose however largely due to Thomas' mismanagement of the funds which they had brought from England to support them until they found means of employment. A quantity of goods such as scissors, penknives and some silverware items, thought to be saleable in Calcutta market, had been brought with the intention of selling them for cash. But it became clear that Thomas' estimate of what quantity of goods would suffice was inadequate and the market proved to be disinterested. The large house and the staff engaged by Dr Thomas were fast consuming their reduced funds. Dorothy, her sister and Felix all contracted dysentery and were very ill.[1] In her case, as some of William's letters suggest, Dorothy had recurring wearisome bouts of the disease for twelve years, which must have been very enervating. It must have been a hard struggle for

---

[1] Both amoebic and bacillary dysentery were commonly contracted in India, the former a more serious form that attacks the liver and produces lasting damage. In Carey's time the cause of 'the bloody flux' as it was called was unknown. Nowadays the cause is known to be the lack of proper sanitation, and both forms can be dealt with successfully if treated early with modern drugs.

Dorothy to care for four boys, even with Kitty's help, since one of the boys was also ill. Carey was embarrassed by Thomas' high standard of living and resolved to find accommodation elsewhere, moving his family to a cheaper house in a Portuguese settlement near Calcutta. But even this, he felt, was still not living like the Bengali natives.

Carey got to hear of a Brahmin settlement called Nuddea, north of Calcutta. To have planted the Christian gospel in such a centre, William felt, would have an impact throughout Hindu India. He travelled by boat to visit the place, and tried to buy a plot of land where he could build himself a hut and live like the natives. But it was not to be; no land was made available to him. Returning to Calcutta he thought of buying a plot of wasteland where he could grow sugar cane and support himself by farming but this idea came to nothing. Recommended to apply for the post of superintendent of the East India Company's botanical gardens in Calcutta, he offered himself, only to find that the post was already filled. It was a tiring experience trudging about in Calcutta seeking some means of employment. Carey records in his diary one occasion when 'he was very weary, having walked in the sun about fifteen or sixteen miles'.[2] But then help came from an unexpected source. Nelu Dutt, a Bengali banker, had formerly loaned money to Dr Thomas and now offered Carey the free use of a small house in a suburb of Calcutta. His wife, formerly a Mrs Carey, was one of the last survivors of the terrible Black Hole of Calcutta incident, who was said to have survived by drinking her own tears.[3] Carey had quickly discovered that Thomas was not to be depended on where money was concerned; he had used up more than his share of the money they had procured from the sale of goods, leaving Carey little, while adding to his own income by his professional work as a doctor. All these difficulties and the constant moving from place to place must have been most unsettling for Dorothy and Kitty, neither of whom knew the Bengali language. William wrote home:

---
[2] George, Timothy p99.
[3] Smith, George p61. When, years later, their circumstances were reversed Carey was pleased to be able to help them.

> My wife and sister too, who do not see the importance of mission as I do, are continually exclaiming against me, and as for Mr T. [ie. Dr Thomas] they think it hard indeed that he should live in a city in an affluent manner, and they be forced to go into a wilderness and live without many of what they call necessaries of life (bread in particular).[4]

The translation of Genesis into Bengali, which the two men had worked on while on the ship, was much delayed because Thomas was often too busy to come to Carey to continue the work. Carey wrote of spending another month when he had 'scarcely done anything'. The relationship between Carey and Thomas was deteriorating, yet every Sunday the two men were to be found in the markets of Calcutta, Thomas preaching and a less fluent Carey trying to converse. Under Thomas' previous ministry in Bengal an enquirer named Ram Basu had seemed likely to become a Christian; he now came forward to offer himself as Carey's teacher and interpreter. Through him William heard that free land was being offered to anyone who would settle in an area known as the Sunderbunds, to clear it and thus make profitable agriculture possible. This area was part of the huge delta where the Ganges flows into the Bay of Bengal, very fertile and overgrown with jungle, and renowned for its tigers. To Carey this was exactly the kind of farming situation in which he had always visualised setting up the mission. With £16 which Thomas borrowed from a native money lender, Carey bought a boat and loading his family and possessions on board he sailed for several days in the delta rivers, to reach Debhatta where he had been allocated some land.[5] An agent of the Company, Mr Charles Short; was in charge there of the manufacture of salt.[6] Lodging in his house, William and his boys began building a house of bamboo and thatch on the plot of land allotted to them nearby at a place called Hasnabad (meaning the 'smiling spot').

---

[4] Beck, James R p95.
[5] Smith, George p62.
[6] *On the East coast, near Calcutta, rivers spread out into wet lands where the sun evaporates seawater leaving crusts of salt.* Kurlansky, Mark p334.

Carey began to lay out his garden by planting some fruit trees and root crops. Food was plentiful in the area, though not the kind of food that would have been familiar to Dorothy and Kitty. Wild animals were plentiful too. In his journal Carey wrote:

> ... the Sunder Bunds ...is a very large impenetrable forest only intersected by large rivers by which our boats went; these forests are some hundreds of miles in extent, and entirely uninhabited by man. They swarm with tygers [sic], leopards, rhinoceroses, deer, buffaloes, etc. I thought I heard the roar of a tyger in the night but am not certain.[7]

To Fuller, Carey wrote that:

> Wild hogs, deer, and fowl are to be procured by the gun, and must supply us with a considerable portion of our food. I find an inconvenience in having so much of my time taken up in procuring provisions and cultivating my little farm. But when my house is built I shall have more leisure than at present, and have daily opportunities of conversing with the natives, and pursuing the work of the mission.[8]

Hearing that a white man with a gun lived there a number of natives, who had formerly left the area because of the tigers, returned to settle on the land around Carey's plot, assuming that his gun would protect them from the wild animals and perhaps provide them with food. He for his part regarded them as his 'stated congregation' once he had enough skill for preaching in Bengali. But preaching in Bengali meant he must first master the language, which was not without its peculiarities:

> It is a language of a very singular construction, having no plural except for pronouns, and not a single preposition

---

[7] Beck, James R p96.
[8] Marshman, John Clark p28.

in it; but the cases of nouns and pronouns are almost endless, all the words answering to our prepositions being put after the word, and forming a new case.[9]

Several entries in his diary from this time show that William suffered from bouts of depression. His burning desire was to translate the Bible into Bengali; but as a farmer and a hunter he had no time to do so. He complains of 'the lack of social religion' by which he meant worship with other believers; his generous host Charles Short was a Deist and eager to challenge William's understanding of religion. William's colleague Dr Thomas was in Calcutta and out of touch. William sometimes deplored the fact that it had been a whole year since he left his beloved flock at Leicester and yet conversions amongst the natives had not happened. Dorothy and Kitty he describes as 'my accusers and hinderers, enemies to the work'.[10] Yet eventually he was able to write in his journal:

Well, I have God and his Word is sure; and though the superstitions of the heathen were a million times worse than they are, if I were deserted by all, and persecuted by all, yet my hope, fixed on the sure Word of God, will rise superior to all obstruction, and triumph over all trials.[11]

But this 'smiling spot' was not to be the place where the mission to Bengal would be based and for good reason. Writing much later Marshman expressed the opinion that Carey's plan of a missionary community living there among the natives, and like the natives, would not have been successful. It was a malarial area, so that …

… if his straw huts and mud floors had not sent half the community to the grave during the first rainy season, the inconceivable distress to which European families must

---
[9] Smith, George p63.
[10] Beck, James R p99.
[11] Davis, Walter Bruce p37.

have been subjected in such a colony, in such a climate, would have broken it up within a twelvemonth.[12]

In the event, however, another turn of Providence was to involve the family in a further move to a situation offering far better circumstances. But all the many changes in their circumstances since reaching Bengal have meant that Dorothy has had to cope with a move for the family almost every month!

---
[12] Ibid. p42.

20
Blue dye!

The Carey family had been scarcely a year in Hasnabad when a letter reached William offering him a post as superintendent of a factory involved with the production of indigo, a beautiful durable blue dye used in printing on calico.[1] The dye was made from an Indian plant of the same name. This offer came about through Dr Thomas who, hearing of a tragedy in which a brother and sister-in-law of George Udney, an East India Company officer and former friend of Thomas, were drowned. Thomas wrote a consoling letter to Mr Udney.[2] This letter restored the earlier friendship between the two men and in responding George Udney offered Thomas the management of one of the indigo factories he owned personally. When Thomas mentioned the difficulties under which his colleague William Carey was labouring in the Sunderbunds Mr Udney offered Carey the management of a second factory he was building in Mudnabatti at a monthly salary of two hundred rupees.[3] Thomas resigned his medical work in Calcutta,[4] took up his new post at Mahipaldighi in the Malda area three hundred miles north of Calcutta and wrote to Carey conveying George Udney's offer, at the same time apologising for his own regrettable lapse of behaviour recently in regard to the work of mission.

Carey wrote in his journal:

> *This appearing to be a remarkable opening in divine providence for our comfortable support, I accepted it ...*

---

[1] A popular cotton cloth made in Calicut
[2] Marshman, John Clark p28.
[3] Then equivalent to about £240 a year.
[4] *The prospects of which were by no means bright.* Marshman, John Clark p29.

> I am resolved to write to the Society that my circumstances are such that I do not need future help from them and to devote a sum monthly for the printing of the Bengali Bible.[5]

Carey eagerly wrote to convey the news to the Society. To him it was good news since he could now fulfil his suggested plan that his missionary work should be financed by his own efforts. He wrote to his sister:

> It was always my opinion that missionaries may and must support themselves after having been sent out and received a little support at first, and in consequence I pursue a very little worldly employment which requires three months closish [sic] attendance in the year.[6]

He expressed the hope that the Society could now be in a financial position to send missionaries to other destinations. At the same time he wished to remain related to the Society *as if* he did still need their support. But when, eventually, the Society committee received Carey's letter some of the members, especially those newly appointed who had not known Carey personally, expressed considerable concern 'lest he should allow the spirit of the missionary to be swallowed up in the pursuits of the merchant'. Fuller was unavoidably absent from that committee or, knowing William as he did, such a letter would never have been sent to Carey. When, after long delay, that committee's letter reached Carey his response was sharp:

> I can only say that, after my family's obtaining a bare subsistence, my whole income, and some months more, goes for the purpose of the Gospel, in supporting persons to assist the translation of the Bible, and in teaching school. I am, indeed, poor, and shall always be

---
[5] Smith, George p64.
[6] Ibid. p71.

so until the Bible is published in Bengalee and Hindoostanee, and the people want no further instruction.[7]

It was over a year before either of these letters reached their destinations. Meanwhile Carey had loaded his family and possessions once more onto a boat and set out on the three day river journey north from the Sunderbunds to Malda, one more move for Dorothy to cope with. Kitty, however, had decided to remain in Sunderbunds with Charles Short who had been their host and they soon were to become man and wife.

The middle of June 1794 saw Carey and his family reaching the new factory built at Mudnabatti, about thirty miles from Malda. Dr Thomas was already installed at his factory and plantation some sixteen miles further on, near enough for the two men to meet from time to time. In Mudnabatti the Carey family could enjoy the settled comfort of a newly built house that for the next five years was to be their home. Both men could now apply for, and received, permits to reside officially in Company territory as indigo planters. Carey was now responsible for a staff of some ninety employees in the factory. He wrote, excitedly:

These will furnish a congregation immediately, and, added to the extensive engagements which I must necessarily have with the natives, will open a very wide door for activity. God grant that may not only be large but effectual.[8]

The Udneys in Malda proved to be very friendly and helpful and Carey enjoyed preaching in their home on some Sundays. The Christian message, so unwelcome to the East India Company, was there being preached in the official residence of the Company representative! But for Dorothy, still struggling with ill health from time to time, it seems that these settled circumstances had come too late. Already signs of mental instabil-

---

[7] Marshman, John Clark p29.
[8] Smith, George p66.

ity were becoming noticeable. The loss of her sister's company and practical help would surely have affected Dorothy, even if she were able to be glad that Kitty was getting married. She must have suddenly felt lonely among all the crowds of natives around her, she unable to speak or understand, much of their language. Since Dorothy had apparently never experienced William's deep convictions about mission, had he been demanding too much of her? On the other hand, Carey could never have foreseen, perhaps never expected, the kind of hardships that had befallen him and his family. Would things have been very different if the original plan had been followed for William to come to India alone and only return for Dorothy and the family once he was settled? But that would have meant at least a year or more away from Bengal for William at the very time he was getting to grips with learning the language and translating the Scriptures. That would have been a serious interruption and loss of time for the work.

Carey's love of nature and of plant life in particular gave him a great interest in the cultivation of indigo. Given a carefully prepared soil, regular rainfall and careful weeding, the plant grows from March to July, reaching a height of about five feet when it is ready for harvesting. The plant is then fermented in specially built vats and beaten until it emits a blue dye which is then drained into other vats, boiled and allowed to solidify. It was then cut into small cakes which were packed and sent off to Calcutta for sale. The whole process would leave the rest of the year free from the need for close supervision, allowing William some months to use his time with work related to mission. But, as with all agricultural work, unfavourable weather could mean that success was not always guaranteed. Some years the plantation would be more profitable than others. In the case of the Mudnabatti factory, standing on the banks of the river Tangan, the land was low lying and often marshy, with the result that the dampness of the air and the heat of the hot summer months frequently caused severe bouts of sickness among the natives of the place. Carey noted in his journal:

Several of our managing and principal people are sick. It is indeed an awful time here with us now, scarcely a day but some are seized with fevers. It is, I believe, owing to the abundance of water, so that all the country hereabouts is about a foot deep in water.[9]

In the September of the first year in Mudnabatti William, and then Felix, fell ill with fever; in William's case occasioning very severe and violent bodily spasms which seemed to bring him near to death. Providentially, Mr Udney paid them a visit just then (unaware of their illness) and was able to give them a supply of bark, the use of which helped them both recover.[10] It is not difficult to see how this illness in the family, (especially in the case of William her husband on whom she had to rely so much) could have contributed to Dorothy's worsening mental condition. How helpless, perhaps even panic-stricken, she would have felt lest her William should die, leaving her to struggle alone with frightening problems. But another heavy sorrow was soon to befall the family …

---

[9] Smith, George p69.
[10] Ibid. p69. This could refer to bark of the Cinchona tree from which quinine is obtained. If so this fever was likely to have been malaria, which commonly occurs in areas of wet and damp.

21
The valley of the shadow

Hardly had William recovered from his severe bout of fever when five year old Peter, next youngest after Felix, fell ill with a fever and a violent dysentery which within a fortnight led to his untimely death in October 1794. Described by his father as 'a fine and engaging boy' Peter had picked up Bengali with a fluency that exceeded his father's skill and led to the fond hope that he would be a fine asset to the mission.[1] But that was not to be. The sorrow of this loss was further deepened by the fact that Dorothy and William now faced the rigid taboos of the Indian caste system. Because of Hindu and Muslim religious objection to physical contact with a corpse, particularly the corpse of one neither Hindu nor Muslim, no one was willing to help with the practical details of a burial. William wrote in his journal:

> *I could induce no person to make a coffin, tho' two carpenters are constantly employed by us at the works. Four Mussulmen* [i.e. Muslim men] *to keep each other in countenance dug a grave ... no man would carry him to his grave. I concluded that I and my wife should do it ourselves, when at last our own Matu (a servant kept for the purpose of cleaning out the necessary*[2] *and of the lowest caste) and a boy who had lost caste, were prevailed upon to carry the corpse and secure the grave from jackals.*[3]

---

[1] George, Timothy p108.
[2] ie. emptying the toilet containers
[3] Beck, James R p104.

And that was not the end of the painful affair; the four who had dug the grave were penalised by the headman of their village, a censure that was only revoked when Carey, uncharacteristically, threatened to refer the matter to a district judge. Shortly after this traumatic event it seems, perhaps unsurprisingly, that Dorothy's mental illness became chronic. Despite what might have been thought to be settled and comfortable surroundings, together with a welcome financial security, the sudden loss of this young child and the insensitivity of the caste people around them provided a severe blow that Dorothy was unable to bear. For William the experience taught him that caste was a system of evil in the way that it held men and women in an inhuman bondage.

In a generous attempt to help them at this time Mr Udney proposed that William and Dr Thomas should make a survey trip in his official boat along the river Tangan as far as they could go, while Dorothy and the boys and Mrs Thomas stayed with Mrs Udney. Carey had longed to see Tibet, though in the event the river became too shallow for them to reach that far. But the break and changes of scenery seemed to help and by the Christmas of that year all the members of the Carey family were enjoying better health. Carey noted in his journal with regard to his Sunday preaching:

> *I now rejoice in seeing a regular congregation of from two to six hundred people of all descriptions – Mussulmans, Brahmans and other classes of Hindus, which I look upon as a favourable token from God.*[4]

During this time William and Dr Thomas were involved in the formation of a small Baptist church in Dinajpoor, a town to the North of Mudnabatti. The membership of this first Baptist church in Bengal consisted of the two men themselves, Thomas' cousin[5] who had been recently baptised, together with some Eurasian believers living in the area.

---

[4] Smith, George p70.
[5] Samuel Powell, who had travelled in *The Earl of Oxford* with Mrs Thomas.

Contact with Dr Thomas and his cousin had led to the conversion to Protestantism of Ignatius Fernandez, a former Portuguese Roman Catholic priest who now built a chapel beside his house in Dinajpoor and conducted the services there whenever Carey or Thomas were unable to be present. Notably the first ever celebration of the Lord's Supper by Baptists in Bengal was celebrated in that chapel. But there were still no native converts such as Carey longed for, though he was by now able to preach in Bengali for half an hour or so at a time.

Yet along with these joys came more sorrow. Although Dorothy, at last, seemed to be recovering physically from months of debilitating dysentery, her mental disorientation became much worse. For that reason she was not considered for membership of the Dinajpoor Baptist church. Writing to Andrew Fuller sometime later Dr Thomas described her harrowing state:

> *Do you know that she has taken it into her head that C. [ie.Carey] is a great whoremonger; and her jealousy burns like a fire unquenchable; and this horrible idea has, night and day, filled her heart for about 9 or 10 months past; so that if he goes out of the door by day or night, she follows him; and declares in the most solemn manner that she had catched [sic] him with his servants, with his friends, and with Mrs Thomas ... she has uttered the most blasphemous and bitter imprecations against him; she has even made some attempt upon his life ... yet she speaks highly of me as a good man, but deceived in Carey.*[6]

Some of Carey's subsequent letters and journal entries confirm Thomas' sad description of the case. It is very moving to know that Carey wrote at this time to his friend, Dr Arnold in Leicester, a psychiatrist, a copy of whose first book on 'Emotional Disturbance' he gave to Carey in Leicester. Both William and Thomas were poring over its pages now. But the slowness of communication between India and England would have

---

[6] Beck, James R p109.

meant more than a year's delay before any hope of a reply. That William should write at all, despite this known delay, indicates something of his pathetic loneliness as he watched the heartbreaking collapse of the woman he loved. To Fuller Carey wrote that Dorothy was afflicted with ... *the species of insanity described by Dr Arnold under the name of 'Ideal Insanity'.*[7]

Fuller was the most likely of his friends to understand William's plight because of his own experience with the similar illness of his first wife. But even Fuller did not have to face the embarrassment of the charge that he was promiscuous in behaviour as Dorothy asserted of Carey. The only thing to be done when she was at her most irrational was to confine her to her own room. William wrote to his sister:

> *I have been obliged to confine her some time back to prevent murder which was attempted. But she now shows no disposition to commit such violence and is at liberty.*[8]

How all this must have weighed down William's spirits can scarcely be imagined as he sought to extol the value of Christian truth and the morality that he preached, as opposed to the immorality of some Hindu gods. Added to which he was living in a land where the idea of demonic possession of an individual was commonly accepted. Would Dorothy's collapse indicate that Christianity could offer no security against such a possibility? And what would be the effect of this upon his boys? It is no surprise then to find Carey writing in his journal:

> *Oh that this day could be consigned to oblivion, what mixture of impatience, carelessness, forgetfulness of God, pride and peevishness have I felt this day. God forgive me.*[9]

---

[7] Ibid. p111 By 'Ideal Insanity' Dr Arnold meant a state of mind that imagines things that have no real existence, as opposed to 'Notional Insanity' meaning wrong ideas about things that do exist.
[8] Ibid. p116
[9] Ibid. p116

Mudnabatti was the place where baby Jonathan now made his appearance, possibly in 1796, though Carey gave various dates for this. Medical opinion in those days was that a pregnancy would either disturb, or sometimes restore, the sanity of women who were mentally ill. The latter possibility was perhaps the hope that allowed William to bring about this situation. We know that Dr Arnold was of the view that 'psychopathology was connected with sexuality, pregnancy and childbirth.'[10] Dr Thomas wrote to Fuller: *She is just ready to lie in, and then I hope she will be better.*[11]

But in the event Dorothy's health worsened rather than improved after the delivery. To this very personal sorrow was added a blow to Carey's translation work. Rama Rama Vasu, Carey's translator and preaching companion, of whose conversion Thomas had formerly had high hopes, was proved to have been guilty of adultery and the theft of monies. Carey had no option but to dismiss him from his employ.[12] Coming on top of everything else this must have seemed like a final blow. Carey had now virtually lost both a capable wife and mother and a valued translator and language teacher whom he had visualised as vital to the success of the work of the mission. How would he react to such a succession of sorrows and setbacks? Could the work even be continued?

---

[10] Ibid. p114
[11] Ibid. p115
[12] Carey, S Pearce p172

22
'Dying, and yet we live on; beaten and not yet killed'[1]

Writing to Fuller at this testing time Carey displayed something of his dogged courage:

> *We can only desert the work with our lives. We are determined to hold on, though our discouragements be a thousand times greater. We have the same ground of hope as you in England – the promise, power and faithfulness of God.*[2]

And he was not content just 'to hold on'. He wanted to grow. So he asked Fuller for more helpers, explaining that he would receive them 'with rapture'. As it happened, a helper was actually on the way to him at that very time; but the long delays affecting correspondence meant that, before the letter announcing his coming could reach Bengal, Mr John Fountain had arrived in October 1796. Carey records in his journal:

> *As I was sitting at my desk on the ground floor at Mudnabatti ... in bolted a man with a neighbour of mine, who he had picked up twelve miles off, and, before I could make enquiries, I found was a brother missionary.*[3]

---
[1] 2 Corinthians 6:9 NIV
[2] Carey, S Pearce p173.
[3] Ibid. p173.

To have a companion delighted Carey but John Fountain's radical political views, reflecting the political excitement in England arising from the French revolution, caused the Society some concern. Fuller had threatened to recall him if he did not restrain the expression of his political views in India:

> *All that we felt any hesitation about you was your too great edge for politics. The mission has awfully suffered in Africa through that folly. The loss of £300 or £400 is the least thing to be considered; though considering that as public property it was grievous that it should be so thrown away.*[4]

Carey was glad of Fountain's presence as a companion, especially as he was able soon to gain a skill in Bengali and so help with the translation work. However, the East India Company would not license Fountain as an indigo production assistant to William, whose thoughts consequently turned to the possibility of moving to Bhutan and settling the mission outside Company control. Would this be the only way in which further missionaries could come and settle? The situation was becoming urgent when news reached William of *four* new missionary families on their way to join him. Meanwhile Carey and Fountain at their own expense were running two schools and busily translating the Bible into Bengali in every spare moment of their time, as well as preaching from time to time to indigo factory employees and native people in the surrounding villages.

Translation work was now proceeding so well that Carey began to investigate how it might be printed. Appalled at the high cost of having it printed in Calcutta, he began to write to Fuller about the possibility of importing a printing press from England. Suddenly news reached him of a press for sale in Calcutta. William's excited talking about the prospect of himself printing the Bengali pages persuaded Mr Udney to purchase the £46 press

---

[4] Fuller, Thomas Ekins p111. The loss of monies referred to was in relation to expenses incurred in sending out the missionary and returning him home. Smith, George p80 comments: 'Fountain proved to be almost as dangerous to the infant mission … as Thomas had been from his debts.'

and present it to the mission as a gift. A firm producing Bengali types had recently started up in Calcutta which meant that Carey could purchase type locally, as well as paper and ink in preparation for printing to begin.

The indigo factory was not too successful during Carey's first five years of management. Three of those years had seen such natural disasters as huge floods, then drought, and finally disease in the fields destroying the crops on which the factory depended for its supplies. Mr Udney resolved to close the factory. William faced the prospect of possible unemployment. At the same time Thomas had left his post, being discontented with his work as an indigo producer, much to Mr Udney's annoyance. Finally things became even more difficult when Mr Udney received a different posting from the Company and was succeeded in Malda by an official who was known to be unfriendly toward the mission. Unknown to Carey the secret hand of Providence was in all this apparent confusion shaping events for a stable and lasting future for the mission. Carey resolved to purchase his own indigo factory as a temporary means of employment and with generous help from Mr Udney purchased a factory at Khidurpur, twelve miles north of Mudnabatti which was free from the danger of flooding and a much better area for crops. Then came the news in early 1799 that the ship carrying the expected missionary families would soon be reaching Calcutta.

Aboard the American ship *Criterion* approaching their journey's end were Mr and Mrs Grant with two children, Mr and Mrs Brunsdon, Mr and Mrs Marshman, together with the bachelor William Ward, a printer, and Miss Tidd coming to India to marry John Fountain. But news of their arrival in Calcutta came to the attention of Company officials who insisted that the missionaries return to England forthwith.[5] Carey tried to argue that since he, as an indigo producer, had a licence to be in the Company area they could all join him as assistants: the Company was not

---

[5] According to Carey, S Pearce, p185, a newspaper report had classified them as 'Papists' instead of Baptists and officials feared that they were from Catholic France who would therefore foment revolution. But it made no difference when the error was corrected.

impressed. Fuller had written suggesting an appeal be made to Governor Lord Wellesley (appointed in 1798) in order to allow the missionary community to be set up around the factory Carey had purchased. Carey smiled, it is said, and replied:

> *You must drop all your English ideas and adopt Indian ones. There can be no settlements here in the English sense of the words ... if I were to return myself as a missionary I certainly should not be allowed to remain in the country. You must not, however, suppose that we are obliged to conceal ourselves or our work. We preach before magistrates and judges ... I would not hesitate to avow myself a missionary, though I would not officially return myself as such.*[6]

In the event the situation was dramatically changed when Colonel Ole Bie, the Governor of the Danish settlement at Serampore (formed in 1755) across the Hooghli river from Calcutta, invited them to settle under his jurisdiction. Should they wish to travel in Company areas he offered them Danish passports to enable them to do so. Hearing of the arrival of his bride John Fountain hurried from Khidurpur to Serampore to meet and marry her and begin discussions as to what was next to be done by the four families to meet up with Carey. Ward and Fountain presently returned to Khidurpur to put to Carey the proposal that they should all make Serampore the centre for their community. Sadly, Carey was told, Mr Grant had died of cholera and dysentery a few weeks after landing and was buried in Serampore, leaving a widow and two children.[7] Was Carey now to leave the property he had bought in Khidurpur and suffer the financial loss that would entail? That question was answered as soon as Carey learned of the threat that Company officials would deport any of the missionaries caught travelling in their areas. And it became clear that the Company would also not permit any printing press to be set up in their trading

---

[6] Marshman, John Clark p34.
[7] Carey, S Pearce p186.

areas. William agreed to join the others in Serampore. In the first week of January 1800 Fountain and the Carey family travelled to Serampore by boat, with Dorothy 'in a hopeless state of insanity'.[8] William's six lonely years of struggle in missionary apprenticeship were over; the missionary *community* was about to begin. Yet there were those who were suggesting that there surely should have been native converts after six years of labour. Carey replied successfully to the challenge:

> *What could three ministers do, even in England, supposing it now dark and rude as Caesar discovered it; supposing them, also, to have a language to learn before they could converse with any; and them to have the Scriptures to translate and write out with their own hands; and this done to have no other means to make the Scriptures known but by preaching – with printing almost totally unknown and only here and there one able to write? May it speed your prompt help. Staying at home has become sinful for many and will be more so.*[9]

It was not that Carey was indifferent to the lack of converts; that lack weighed heavily on his heart. Just before leaving Khidurpur he wrote to John Newton:

> *I know God can use weak instruments, but I often question whether it would be for his honour to work by such as me. It might be too much sanction [for my] guilty sloth, if I were to meet with eminent blessing.*[10]

Here was a man fit for the leadership that awaited him in Serampore.

---

[8] Marshman, John Clark p50.
[9] Carey, S Pearce p180.
[10] Ibid. p181.

Part Three

'... then the full grain in the ear'
(Mark 4:28)

> "God never removes His people from this world till they are ripe and ready. He never takes them away till their work is done. They never die at the wrong time."
>
> (J C Ryle commentary, op, cit.)

Up to this point we have concentrated mainly upon William and his family.

Now the Serampore story begins: William and his family become part of a new 'family', so that what is achieved is as much the product of the whole group as of any single member of it. Who can say what Marshman and Ward gained from Carey, or he from them? They all moved together in a quite startling oneness, like that seen among the original Northamptonshire founders of the Society, a true biblical *homothumadon*.[1]

---

[1] The Greek word means 'of one accord'. It occurs ten times in the Acts of the Apostles to describe the unity of the first Christians. It is formed from homos ('same') and thumos ('mind').

23
A new beginning in Serampore

The Careys and John Fountain arrived at Serampore by boat, with all their possessions and their precious printing press aboard, on 10 January 1800. There was a remarkable providence in this, for a year or so later Serampore would not have been a refuge for them. Hostilities had sprung up between the two home countries of England and Denmark. The British fleet under Horatio Nelson bombarded Denmark's capital city after routing the Danish fleet in 1801 and again in 1807 when they captured the Danish fleet. The fear was that Napoleon might use the Danish navy to assist in the invasion of the United Kingdom. Providentially, before all that happened, the mission had already been established in Serampore and had earned the respect of the East India Company authorities. They had come to realise that the mission was not a threat to them and so permitted the missionaries to continue their work, even allowing them to make visits outside the Danish settlement.[1] In 1808 Serampore was nominally occupied by British troops but the then British Governor, Lord Minto, was favourably disposed towards the missionaries. Not until the Company's charter was amended in 1813, however, was the presence of missionaries in Company areas made legally secure.

Carey met the Danish Governor, Colonel Bie, the day after arriving in Serampore. He proved to be a friend to the mis-

---

[1] On three occasions the Company placed temporary restrictions on the mission. In 1806, because of the Vellore mutiny; in 1807, because of an ill-worded tract published by the mission; in 1821, because of a complaint against the mission from some Indian princes

sion.[2] One of the immediate tasks for the missionaries was to locate themselves in suitable premises. Gone were Carey's earlier thoughts of housing the community in a series of mud huts, for Serampore was a town of brick houses. They were able to purchase a large and suitable property from the Governor's nephew near the centre of the town, in which their little community of ten adults and nine children could be accommodated, family by family in separate rooms, with a central hall for communal meals and for worship.[3] By the end of the year the grounds of the house included Carey's experimental garden of two acres, in which he had arranged the planting of over four hundred species of plants.[4] Other buildings were available for housing the proposed printing operation and a possible school. Ward described the situation:

> *It stands by the riverside upon a pretty large piece of ground, with a garden at the bottom and in the middle a fine tank or pool of water ...we hope this will form a comfortable missionary settlement. Being near Calcutta, it is of the utmost importance to our school, our press, and our connection with England.*[5]

Physical housing was one thing but creating a harmonious community, Moravian style, was quite another. Anticipating the task, Ward wrote in his journal:

> *I tremble almost before we begin to live together. So much depends upon a disinterestedness, forbearance, meekness and self-denial. One man of wrong temper*

---

[2] The friendly Governor Bie had been taught the value of Protestant missionary work by Schwarz, a Lutheran missionary who came to work in Tranquebar

[3] The property was purchased for 6,000 rupees (about £800), partly with monies the new missionaries had brought, partly by bills on the Society and partly with a loan. (Marshman, John Clark p51).

[4] 'This Serampore garden eventually had the rarest and best collection of plants in the East'. (Davis, Walter Bruce p49).

[5] Smith, George p91. Calcutta was 16 miles north of Serampore, a journey by rowboat, up the Hooghli river, of about two hours.

could make our house a hell. Much wisdom will be necessary ... selfish passions must be crushed and the love of Christ swallow up all else.[6]

For William there was the necessary adjustment from being his own master for six years to working now with a team whose members he regarded as being equal with himself despite his seniority in age and experience.[7] In this he departed from the Moravian style, in which one person was appointed 'Housemaster' and his decisions were final. In Serampore authority was exercised by each man taking responsibility for one month. Meals were taken together; any private earnings were given to the community purse from which the work was financed; each family was allocated a small amount of 'pocket money'; one evening each week the community gathered to discuss and settle any differences of opinion and to renew their agreement to live communally; one evening was devoted to sharing spiritual experiences. Some years later a missionary passing though Serampore wrote of Carey the delightful sentence:

He is a very superior man, and appears to know nothing about it.[8]

Another visitor, ten years after the founding of the community, recorded:

Carey has attained to the happy art of ruling and overruling in connection with the others, without his asserting his authority, or others feeling their subjection.[9]

Evidently, in its early years, the Serampore system was a success. But there were sorrows too. Mr Grant had died almost as soon as reaching Serampore; John Fountain, on a visit to

---

[6] Carey, S Pearce p192.
[7] Fuller is said to have written to rebuke him for this, fearing it was an expression of the 'Equality' thinking of the French revolutionary movement
[8] George, Timothy p124.
[9] Winter, Ralph D. in Daniel and Hedlund (Eds.) p137.

Dinajpoor for ministry with Ignatius Fernandez, fell seriously ill and died. He was buried there, leaving his widow (formerly Miss Tidd) expecting a child. Mr Brunsdon contracted a serious liver complaint within a few months which also proved to be fatal. Of his remaining two colleagues Carey was able to write happily:

> *Brother Ward is the very man we wanted; he enters into the work with his whole soul. I have much pleasure in him, and expect much from him. Brother Marshman is a prodigy of diligence and prudence, as is also his wife in the latter; learning the language is mere play to him; he has already acquired as much as I did in double the time.*[10]

The reference to Marshman's wife, Hannah, indicates how much Carey valued her presence in the community. With Dorothy Carey so incapacitated it was Hannah who took over the role of 'mother of the mission' by caring for Dorothy and the Carey boys, for Mrs Brunsdon, for Mrs Grant and her two children, and for pregnant Mrs Fountain. Hannah served the whole community with skill and patience, despite having, over the years, twelve children herself – and losing six of them in infancy. She has the possible distinction of being the first female missionary in India. Christopher Smith writes of her:

> *To her, then, is profound recognition due as a leader in many respects ... there was no female precedent in mission from whom she could draw inspiration, but that did not deter her. Instead she forged ahead and became 'Mother' of the Serampore mission in local parlance, just as much as William Carey was known as the symbolic 'Father' on a broader front.*[11]

Her contribution to the community finances was the establishment, with her teacher husband, of two boarding schools

---
[10] Smith, George p92.
[11] Smith, A Christopher, in *British Particular Baptists* vol 2 (Ed.) Haykin, Michael p252.

and later a free school for poorer native children teaching all subjects in the vernacular language.

William Ward was eager to begin the printing of the Bengali Bible and was surprised and delighted to discover that so much of it was already translated. Most of what was available was Carey's work prepared during his earlier six years before Serampore. Dr Thomas and John Fountain had also completed some parts; only two of the Old Testament historical books remained to be translated. William Ward set the type with his own hands and the first page of the Bengali New Testament was pulled from the press on 17 March 1800. Just one year later the complete New Testament in Bengali was published. Thereafter, referring to Ward, Felix and Brunsdon (before his untimely death), Carey wrote:

> *They pursue me as hounds a deer. The labour is ten-fold what it would be in England – printing, writing, and spelling in Bengali being all such a new thing. We have in a manner to fix the orthography, and my pundit changes his mind so frequently. Still, I venture to say that our mss. are much correcter* [sic] *than any of their own.*[12]

It is not generally recognised how 'revolutionary' Carey's printing of books really was. Ashin Dasgupta, former Director of the Indian National Library in Calcutta, contrasting the earlier writing of books by hand with the new printing of books, commented in the Serampore Conference of 1993:

> *... take the thing with which Carey was closely associated, the introduction of printing in Bengali. It brought enormous change in our civilisation. We are now in a period of similar change. We shall be moving away from printing ... a whole new generation is being brought up on the computer. The period from Carey to ours is a*

---

[12] Carey, S Pearce p198.

> *continuum. Carey was at the beginning and we are at the end.*[13]

The group of missionaries formed themselves into a church with Carey appointed as pastor and Marshman and Ward as deacons. They celebrated the event with a Thanksgiving Day on 24 April 1800, thanking God for the remarkable spiritual and practical unity they had found among themselves. Each of them had brought various gifts and abilities, providentially honed and shaped by previous different life experiences in England, which meant that they were effectively more than just three persons. What Carey accomplished in Serampore has to be seen in that context. His concept of a missionary *community* as a means of Protestant mission has been called a 'major novelty'. The pattern was common in Roman Catholic thinking. If, instead of establishing a 'novel' community of *many* gifts, Carey, Ward and Marshman had each commenced his own individual work we should not now be celebrating the remarkable achievements of Serampore.

> *There is no way the incredible output of a handful of missionaries can be explained apart from the two chief features of the Serampore Brotherhood: the commitment to mutual accountability and interdependence, and the freedom (for a few years at least) to make its own decisions ... without the interference of an external body of directors.*[14]

---

[13] Ashin Dasgupta in Daniel and Hedlund (Eds.) p4.
[14] Ibid. p145.

24
Culture shock

Just before Carey and his new friends arrived in Serampore, the Moravian Brethren had left Calcutta disappointed at the lack of Christian converts. The work of preaching there was 'like ploughing a rock' they said. The East India Company's Anglican chaplain advised Carey and his friends that God's time for the conversion of Bengal was not yet come. Ordinary people questioned them: 'If God commissioned you, why are two of you already dead?' These were hard questions to answer for those who had come with the exciting hope that preaching the gospel there would usher in 'the latter day glory' that Jonathan Edwards had urged them to pray and work for.[1] Listening to stirring sermons in crowded English chapels about the promise of that day of glory was one thing; to toil and see no success in India was quite another. William Ward expressed something of their feelings:

> *We are often much disheartened, though we try to keep up each other's spirits. At present it is a dead calm; not one whisper, 'What must I do to be saved?'*[2]

The practical value of being able to support each other in facing hard problems is obvious, and perhaps to none more so than to Carey himself. What William and Dorothy suffered when the death of their son Peter occurred had given them an experience of the grim servitude under which the teachings of Hinduism under the Brahmins had placed the millions of India's outcaste peoples. By now Carey had also seen the callous and

---
[1] Referred to earlier in chapter seven.
[2] Carey, S Pearce p202.

violent treatment of burying lepers alive. He had seen devotees of an idol 'god' crushed to death under the clumsy wheels of the great juggernaut on which the idol was carried; he watched men swinging in the air at temple festivals suspended by iron hooks fastened in the flesh of their backs. He had watched helplessly, in an agony of his spirit, the deliberate burning of the widow of her dead husband on his funeral pyre. He knew that sometimes the sick and dying were taken and left on the banks of a 'holy' river as a sacrificial offering. He had seen that women were held in the lowest esteem[3] and denied education by child marriage.[4] An Indian historian writes:

> *The decay of knowledge and learning coupled with social degeneration helped the extensive spread of blind superstition and inhuman social customs. Polygamy, early marriage, sati rites,[5] killing female children,[6] throwing the first child into holy rivers were some of the most dreadful and inhuman practices performed in different parts of the country in varying degrees.[7]*

Carey was learning that North India's Brahmins, formidable foes indeed, were teaching that the so-called 'salvation' that *might* be obtained for any non-Brahmin individual could only be by death and rebirth as a more fortunate person. (The Hinduism of South India, against which the Lutheran missionaries had to battle, was much more a conflict for them with Animism which regarded natural objects as the supposed 'home' of spirits needing to be placated by worshippers' offerings.) To someone

---

[3] 'It has been stated often enough that in Hinduism there is no salvation for a woman until she be reborn as a man'. Mangalwadi, Ruth in Daniel and Hedlund (Eds.) p337.

[4] 'To the Hindu female all education is denied'. William Ward, quoted by Smith, George p53.

[5] The burning of widows on their husbands funeral pyres.

[6] 'In the last two decades it is estimated that ten million female foetuses have been aborted in India.' (From a report in *Evangelical Times* (UK) August 2006 p7.

[7] Nemai Sadham Bose, quoted by Ashish Kumar Massey in Daniel and Hedlund (Eds.) p299.

like William, with the experience of the incredible grace of God freely bringing the undeserved gifts of forgiveness and eternal life for Christ's sake to all who seek it, such self-harm and inhuman behaviour was appalling.

Worse still, the malevolent ignorance of Brahmin teaching made use of the cruel power of the caste system. Not to believe Brahmin teaching was daring enough, but to accept Christian teaching and publicly break with Hinduism and its customs, for example by Christian baptism, was to incur banishment from the caste of their Hindu family and their village life. Sadly, for the few Indians who seemed to be on the verge of becoming Christians, this final step was too much to take. Carey had been greatly disappointed that for those of whom he had such hopes, their family and village ties proved stronger than the call of Christ. Was the gospel message he preached not to be all-powerful? In the absence of any native converts after nearly seven years, how was the home Society to maintain interest in the work of the mission? Even before settling in Serampore Carey had expressed his disappointment to his friend Samuel Pearce, pastor in Birmingham:

> *I am almost grown callous, and am tempted to preach as if their hearts were invulnerable. But this dishonours the grace and power of God, who has promised to be with his ministers to the end; and it destroys all energy, and makes preaching stupidly formal.*[8]

And later, to the Society he wrote:

> *I hope you will not be discouraged by our little positive success, but rather regard it as a call for double exertion, and to send us more men. Hindustan must be amongst the 'all nations which shall call Him blessed'.*[9]

---

[8] Carey, S Pearce p180.
[9] Ibid. p181 Carey quotes Psalm 72:17.

One can imagine the Serampore brethren often supporting one another by prayerfully comforting and reassuring each other with the promises of Scripture.

In fact, of course, having translated most of the Bible into Bengali meant that a tremendous amount of work had been successfully done under the most difficult conditions. It was work that had to be done first, in order to put the Word of God into people's hands, before evangelistic success could be expected. Moving from place to place in the first years, learning the language and its script, the loss of their boy Peter, coping with Dorothy's mental collapse, often missing the fellowship of Dr Thomas, and facing the intimidating discoveries of what the rituals of Hinduism were really like, were all trials daunting enough to cause any lesser man to give up. Writing to a friend Carey expressed himself bluntly:

> *Never was such a combination of false principles as here. In other heathen lands conscience may often be appealed to with effect. Here God's law is erased thence, and idolatrous ceremony is engraved in its stead ... and all are bound to their present state by caste, in breaking whose chains a man must endure to be renounced and abhorred by his wife, children and friends.*[10]

But despite the human cost in renouncing caste, still to retain its distinctions within a church fellowship would surely be incongruous.[11] William had earlier discussed this issue with Andrew Fuller. Should the restrictions of caste be tolerated in church membership, or should they be abolished? On the assumption that some high caste people would be converted, Carey wrote:

> *They can join in every religious act of worship, except the eating of bread at the Lord's Supper, without losing caste, but cannot eat bread unless prepared by a Brahmin.*[12]

---

[10] Ibid. p203.
[11] Galatians 3:28
[12] Fuller, Thomas Ekins p107.

The Society men were at a loss to know what advice to give and felt the need for more information. Fuller initially replied:

> ... if there be an impossibility of their eating bread with you, or the different castes among themselves, according to what at present strikes me you have no right to allow their neglecting of Christ's institute, seeing this would be dispensing with it.[13]

Eventually the Serampore community themselves insisted that caste differences were to be abolished in church membership, unlike the Tranquebar mission of the Lutherans which took a more relaxed view of caste.[14]

Looking back now it is clear that until Carey little or nothing had been done by the East India Company to change those things in Hindu society that so appalled him as a Christian.

> We must admit that Carey was called to become the reformer of a state of society in which the worst evils of Asiatic and English rule combined.[15]

Referring to Carey's arrival in India, one Theology and Ethics lecturer wrote, at the Bicentenary Symposium in the Serampore college (1993):

> The Kairos[16] is here for one and all interested in social action, mission and evangelisation, to thank God for this 'Friend of India' to the world, to the church, to India ... Carey's contribution to the social reforms in India marks the synchronisation between preaching and practising the gospel ... the stand Carey takes ... in fact reflects the type of God he believes in.[17]

---

[13] Ibid. p108.
[14] Carey, S Pearce p211.
[15] Smith, George p52.
[16] The Greek word means 'a fixed point in time' or 'a definite and opportune period of time'
[17] Rajkumar, Evangeline in Daniel and Hedlund (Eds.) p323.

Although Carey's social activities have been criticised as being an ulterior motive for his obtaining converts to Christianity the charge cannot justly be maintained. All his actions in seeking social reform can be shown as arising naturally and necessarily from his theology; they were an integral part of his understanding of biblical truth. (See chapter 34). Carey knew well enough that mere social reform would never bring commitment to Christ, but conversion and commitment to Christ would inevitably bring social reform. But it is time for us to return to the progress of the work now established in Serampore.

25
Krishna Pal and the first fruits

William Ward, writing in his journal, confessed that he was:

> ... ready to doubt whether Europeans will ever be extensively useful in converting souls by preaching, in this country. God can do all things. Paul could become a Jew to win Jews, and a Gentile to win Gentiles, but, however needful, we cannot become Hindoos to win them, nor Mussulmans to win Mussulmans.[1]

But if it *must* be converted Hindus who were to preach successfully to Hindus, or converted Muslims to preach to Muslims, how could that ever be achieved? After more than six years of evangelism there were no converted natives. Remarkably, as events unfolded, it would become clear that the Spirit of God had already begun to provide the answer to that question some years before the missionaries had even arrived in Serampore.[2]

A member of the carpenter caste who had some years earlier come to settle in the suburbs of Serampore fell sick and was strangely troubled with a sense of sin. He began to realise that Brahminical teachings offered no spiritual relief to his troubled mind. Searching for relief he joined different sects that were opposed to the caste system and even professed belief in One God.[3] He became a guru (spiritual teacher) in one sect although still without relief from his consciousness of being a sinner in God's sight. One day, sixteen years later, he heard that these

---

[1] Stanley, Brian p48.
[2] *Before they call I will answer* Isaiah 65:24 (NIV).
[3] Sikhism is an example of a monotheistic (One God) sect which rejects Hindu teachings. Islam, Jainism, and Buddhism are other faiths also free from idolatrous rituals typical of Hinduism.

European missionaries who had recently arrived were talking about Jesus as the Saviour of sinners. He was reminded of what he had heard from the Moravian missionaries who had previously been in Calcutta. Soon afterwards, as he was about to take a ritual bath, he slipped on the steps leading to the water, fell and dislocated a shoulder. In considerable pain he sent a message to the Serampore missionaries asking for help. Providentially Dr Thomas was present just then, visiting briefly from his work as manager of a sugar factory. He was able to reduce the dislocation at once and gave gospel tracts to Krishna Pal and his accompanying friend Gokool. Subsequently Krishna Pal wrote about the effect of one of Dr Thomas' tracts:

> *In this paper I read that he who confesseth and forsaketh his sins, and trusteth in the righteousness of Christ, obtains salvation. The next morning Mr Carey came to see me, and after enquiring how I was, told me to come to his house, that he would give me some medicine ... and through the mercy of God my arm was cured.*[4]

Not only was the arm cured: Krishna Pal and Gokool also made repeated visits to the mission house where Carey and Felix had Bible studies with them. After a few weeks of this Dr Thomas asked the two men if they understood what they were being told. They both answered that they understood and had come to believe that Christ gave up his life for the salvation of sinners such as they were. What followed caused a holy joy among the missionary community. Dr Thomas was so affected mentally at the subsequent sight of the baptism of Krishna Pal that he became wildly excited and had to receive medical treatment for some days in the Calcutta mental asylum. At the same time there was horror and anger among local people that two Hindus had become 'Europeans'. They had heard that Krishna Pal and Gokool sat at table and ate food with the missionaries *and* with each other despite being from different castes. Both men were once attacked on their way home from the mission

---

[4] George, Smith p97.

for having crossed caste barriers. After some further days of instruction Krishna Pal and Felix were baptised by Carey on the last Sunday in December 1800 in the Hooghli river – just opposite the mission house – in the presence of a company of Hindus, Muslims, Europeans and the Governor of Serampore. Later that day William conducted the Lord's Supper in Bengali. That was the first communion service to include a *Bengali* baptised believer, himself the first to escape the tyranny of the caste system – though not to escape the bitterness and persecution of subsequent ostracism. (Christians were insultingly called 'feringee' meaning 'foreigner'). Carey wrote home happily:

> *Thus, you see, God is making a way for us, and giving success to the word of His grace! At last the Lord has appeared for us. May we have the true spirit of nurses, to train them up in the words of faith and sound doctrine. I think it becomes us to make the most of everyone whom the Lord gives us.*[5]

And Ward was able to write:

> *Thus the door of faith is open to the Hindoos and who shall shut it? The chain of caste is broken, and who shall mend it?*[6]

Soon, others joined with Krishna Pal and the community by baptism: the first Bengali woman, the sister of Krishna's wife; then his wife; and then, through their friendship, Gokool and his wife (who initially caused Gokool to hold back); then a widowed lady whom they had befriended committed herself to Christ – the first Bengali widow to do so. Outside this circle of friends and acquaintances came the breakthrough into the higher writer caste with the baptism of Petumber Singh, whose curiosity had been aroused through reading an early tract from Serampore, subsequently followed by a number of others from

---
[5] Smith, George page 101
[6] Marshman, John Clark page 56

his caste and their wives. By 1802 others from the Hindu 'outcaste' community, a Muslim and finally a high caste Brahmin all confessed their faith in Christ by the act of baptism.[7] As the community grew in this way certain problems emerged. For instance there was the problem of overcoming the superstitions and errors imbibed by the individuals over the years under the influence of previous beliefs. At what point is it suitable to offer the act of believer's baptism? Ward wrote in his journal:

> *We think it right to make many allowances for ignorance and for a state of mind [which is] the fruit of a corrupt superstition. We cannot think, therefore, of demanding from the candidates more than a profession of dependence on Christ, and submission to him in all things.*[8]

Clearly the work of nurturing such believers was to be important.

Other problems arose. Because becoming a Christian meant isolation from their Hindu or Muslim neighbours, how were these believers to support themselves? No one would employ them. When daughters were to be married, who but Hindus could they marry? Carey even had to draw up a form for a Christian marriage, since only Hindu customs had existed up till then. When husbands were converted, but not their wives, what was to be done if the wife refused to stay in the home? When Christians died where could they be buried? As a sign of conversion, should converts change their previous Hindu names? Initially the community tried to provide housing and some regular finance, recognised the need for divorce when mixed religion marriages failed, and purchased a plot of land to be used as a Christian cemetery. Hindu names, they argued, were to be retained so as to avoid an unnecessary gulf between them and their Hindu peers. To change their names from Indian to English, or to adopt biblical names, would give the impression that Christianity was essentially a Western faith. The Serampore

---

[7] Information drawn from Smith, George pp101-2.
[8] Smith, George p99.

Three were determined that converts should be self-supporting and not made to become unwisely dependent upon the mission. The infant Bengali Baptist church would face many more problems and each problem had to be solved in a way that would make that solution a good precedent for future Christians to follow. For problems hitherto never experienced, the Serampore community, as also the home Society, certainly needed continual biblical wisdom!

The Society committee meeting in Leicester expressed their prayerful pleasure at these beginnings of success in Bengal in a letter signed by all committee members written in August 1801 to the converts:

> *DEARLY BELOVED IN THE LORD the joy of our hearts was great when the news of your conversion reached us. In you we see the first fruits of Hindustan, the travail of our Redeemer's soul, and a rich return for our imperfect labours ... we affectionately congratulate you on your having embraced the Gospel, and united with the church of Christ.*[9]

By the end of 1801 the missionaries were able to inform the Society that they 'now had thirteen communicants and eight inquirers'. They had compiled a little volume of hymns, some adapted from English, some in native style and they had printed and circulated twenty-two thousand tracts.[10] As we have seen, they already had the use of the first edition of the Bengali New Testament. By 1803 the first convert from the Brahmin caste (already mentioned) was baptised and joined the little church. His name was Krishnu-prisad. As he removed his sacred thread from his shoulder (the emblem of his caste) before his baptism and trampled it under his feet, William Ward took possession of it noting in his journal, 'This is a more precious relic than any the Church of Rome could boast of'.[11] At the first Lord's Sup-

---

[9] Fuller, Thomas Ekins p118.
[10] Marshman, John Clark p69.
[11] Marshman, John Clark p70. Ward later purchased a new one for Krishnu-prisad since it was felt to be more of a social badge than a religious one.

per after his baptism Krishnu-prisad deliberately received the communion cup from the hand of a former outcaste believer who had just drunk from it. Not long after this he married the daughter of Krishna Pal, the carpenter and very first convert, thus completing his total rejection of the Hindu caste system. Later Krishnu-prisad and Krishna Pal became effective evangelists together, having been set apart for ministry by the laying-on of hands of the missionaries.[12] Presently Carey wrote home:

> *The number of inquirers constantly coming forward, awakened by the instrumentality of these men, fills me with joy. I do not know that I am of much use myself, but I see a work which fills me with thankfulness. Not having time to visit the people, I appropriate every Thursday evening to receiving the visits of enquirers. Seldom fewer than twenty come.*[13]

This infant church was boldly declaring that, in Christ, there is neither Englishman nor Indian, slave nor free, male nor female, Brahmin nor Muslim nor outcaste, 'for they are all one in Christ Jesus'.[14] By 1810 the mission could record that there were three hundred converts spread across a number of mission stations outside of Serampore, one hundred and five of whom had been added that year alone.[15] But there was a cost. When Carey was alone in Mudnabatti producing indigo he faced little or no persecution from Hindus and Muslims. His evangelism was apparently unsuccessful and caused no concern. But now that converts were being gathered in Serampore and from the districts around, and caste barriers were being so openly broken, persecution began. Some of the converts and sometimes the missionaries suffered verbal insults, false accusations, even physical attacks. Carey, the man who 'expected great things', made a classic statement:

---

[12] Ibid. p74.
[13] Smith, George p118.
[14] Galatians 3:28
[15] Smith, George p114.

> *I think there is such fermentation raised in Bengal by the little leaven, that there is a hope of the whole lump by degrees being leavened.*[16]

Carey was *still* expecting great things! The next two chapters comprise overall surveys of two 'great things' that Carey and his colleagues completed during their years together at Serampore – their translation projects and their educational schemes.

---
[16] Ibid. p113.

26
Carey the translator

A year after the Serampore community had come into being, in February 1801, William Ward pulled the last sheet of the Bengali New Testament from the press. The translation that Carey had begun years before in Mudnabatti with Dr Thomas' help was now completed despite the many upheavals and troubles that they had endured – not least of which in William's case was the illness of Dorothy his wife. All the precious New Testament pages were bound and the first complete book was laid on the communion table in the hall where their meetings were held. The mission 'family' and the newly baptised converts gathered to thank God that his Word was now available in the mother tongue of the Bengali people. Subsequently copies of the book were presented to, and met with the approval of, the kings of England [1] and of Denmark; copies were also sent to the home committee chairman, John Ryland Jnr, for use in the encouragement of supporters of the Society, who became much excited to see this result after years of their prayers and financial support. Fearing that too much excitement was occasioned by this event, Ward wrote modestly to Fuller:

> *I think there have been too many encomiums[2] on your last missionaries in the 6th number of your Periodical Accounts.[3] I cannot get out of my mind a public show while I read these accounts – 'very fine missionaries to be*

---
[1] England's king was George III who is reported to have said, 'I am greatly pleased that any of my subjects should be employed in this manner'. Carey, S Pearce p213.
[2] Encomium = high praise or flattery.
[3] Extracts from missionaries' letters and reports of the work were published periodically in this form

seen here; walk in, brothers and sisters'. I cannot think that any encomiums of this kind can excite public confidence, or produce the least good.[4]

Inevitably that first edition was not without its faults as Carey was realistic enough to acknowledge. In 1803 he began a revised edition which was published in 1806. This was made possible because, after the first edition was published, Carey providentially came into contact with some eminent Bengali scholars who were able to advise him of more felicitous and idiomatic expressions that he could use in order to make the meaning more easily understood by readers. Even in his seventieth year, 1831, he wrote to Fuller:

I have still two or three years of work to do particularly in putting my best corrections to my Bengali and Sanskrit versions of the Bible.[5]

The fifth revision of the Bengali Old Testament and the eighth revision of the New Testament were completed in 1832; two years later, as he lay dying, he was reading the proofs of that eighth edition of the New Testament.

Mention of a Sanskrit version of the Bible arises from the fact that William's study of Bengali had shown him that Bengali often used Sanskrit expressions. So although Bengali – the common language of some twenty-five million people – remained his priority in translation, he felt the need to master Sanskrit as well. He wrote:

Sanskrit is India's hallmark of culture, the franchise of her real aristocracy, the tongue wherein her scriptures and classics are enshrined, the speech which unlocked her many vernaculars.[6]

---

[4] Marshman, John Clark p58.
[5] Arangaden, Christopher in Daniel and Hedlund (Eds.) p178.
[6] Ibid. p179.

Carey had realised that if any inroads for Christianity were to be made among members of the Brahmin caste then a Sanskrit version of the Bible was essential, for that was the language in which their scholarly debates were held. Writing to John Ryland in 1810 Carey commented:

> *The language itself, with its copiousness and exquisite structure seems fitted to receive the divine oracles beyond almost any other, while its being a language in which the meaning ...of every individual word has been fixed for ages enables it to retain and preserve the precious treasure with as much firmness perhaps as the Greek itself.*[7]

Carey also translated several great Hindu epics[8] from Sanskrit into Bengali in order that the common people should see that they were mere myths and legends when compared with the Sanskrit Bible. Fuller was not so sure: 'wasting time on obscene literature' was his comment. Carey argued that anyone seeking to evangelise the Indian people needed to know upon what sources Hindu teachings were founded.

The complete Sanskrit Bible was published in 1818 and met with a favourable response from those Brahmins who read it. By 1820 the Serampore press had published the whole Bible in Bengali, Sanskrit, Oriya, Hindi, Marathi and later in Assamese, as well as Bible portions in more than thirty other Indian languages; a number of other translations awaited printing.[9]

> *In no country in the world and in no period of the history of Christianity was there ever displayed such an amount of energy in the translation of the sacred Scriptures from their originals into other tongues as was exhibited by a handful of earnest men in Calcutta and Serampore ... It cannot be supposed that these first attempts are to be compared with the versions which have been subse-*

---

[7] George, Timothy p142.
[8] An epic is a long poem celebrating the deeds of a legendary hero.
[9] Arangaden, Christopher in Daniel and Hedlund (Eds.) pp180-183.

quently made in these languages. But this must not diminish the intense admiration we ought to feel towards men of such boldness of design and such astounding energy of execution.[10]

It is no surprise that the first editions of these translations while basically adequate were not the best, considering the linguistic problems that had to be faced in preparing them. The frequent revisions he made indicate that Carey was aware of that. There were immense problems to be solved. Spoken Bengali was often a corrupt form of pure Bengali; quite early on Carey had written to Fuller:

I must mention some of the difficulties under which we labour, particularly myself. The language spoken by the natives of this part, though Bengali, is yet so different from the language itself that though I can preach ... so as all who speak the language well, or can write or read, perfectly understand me, yet the poor labouring people ... have scarcely a word in use about religion. They have no word for 'love', for 'repent', and a thousand other things; and every idea is expressed either by quaint phrases or tedious circumlocutions. A native who speaks the language well finds it a year's work to obtain their idiom.[11]

Writing to his friend Pearce in England Carey explained that words such as 'devil' and 'Son of God' would not convey to idol worshippers the biblical significance of those terms.[12] There was a problem to know what to do about the Greek word 'baptizien', which in English versions was not translated but simply transliterated as 'baptize'. Carey wanted to use words expressing the *meaning* of 'baptizien', as one would express the mean-

---

[10] Sherring, MA quoted by Davis, Walter Bruce p59.
[11] Smith, George p73.
[12] George, Timothy p138.

ing of any other Greek word.[13] To pour water over themselves (effusion) was the Indian custom of *bathing*; when, on special occasions, they dipped themselves under the water that would have been regarded as a ritualistic cleansing in some *sacred water* for their purification from sin. To have used a Bengali word describing either of those modes would have failed to convey the biblical concept; to simply transliterate the word, as in many English versions, would hide the true meaning of the word. Carey therefore insisted upon the meaning as 'total immersion, submerging', or even 'burying,' in order to symbolise the biblical idea of dying to an old way of life and rising to a new lifestyle. His decision meant that the Calcutta branch of the British and Foreign Bible Society (formed in 1811) felt unable to continue to finance the Serampore translation work and in 1833 withdrew their grant-in-aid. That was a severe loss to the mission since in the same year all their Indian funds were lost when two Calcutta banks collapsed. Realising the seriousness of the situation the Society's supporting churches in England arranged a special appeal for funds which resulted in finance being raised sufficient to replace the lost grant and the losses sustained from the collapse of the banks.[14]

It is obvious from the way Carey handled this experience that he was:

> *... extraordinarily cautious in retaining the scriptural sense. So the Bengali translation was not easily intelligible.*[15] *Carey was aware of this and his translation gradually improved in later editions. But in spite of its drawbacks the book was very popular in the country.*[16]

---

[13] The Greek word always refers to total submergence. See Conant, TJ p187-192.
[14] Carey, S Pearce p392.
[15] The word order in the translation tended to follow the word order of the Greek sentence, which was a sentence construction very different from Bengali usage.
[16] Chatterjee, SK in Daniel and Hedlund (Eds.) p167.

Any Bible translator faces similar problems in seeking to express biblical meanings in a language where pagan religious terms would only convey pagan meanings. For Carey there were also problems in trying to decide the best style to use for the shapes of the letters of the Bengali alphabet and the correct spellings for the words, since the language had not appeared in print before. All previous manuscripts had been handwritten. When native converts began to join the mission group a further difficulty arose over hymnology: there were no Christian hymns in Bengali. Sometimes William would translate an English hymn into Bengali, but then the poetic style would still be English and 'foreign' to Indian ears. Only after some time spent in understanding Christian truths would Bengali converts be able to compose lyrics in the Indian style.[17]

Writing to Fuller in 1808 Carey described his method of translation:

> *I never ... suffer a single word, or single mode of construction to pass, without examining it and seeing through it. I read every proof sheet twice or thrice myself, and correct every letter by my own hand. Bro. Marshman and I compose, with the Greek or Hebrew, and Bro. Ward reads every sheet. Three of the translations, viz. the Bengalee, Hindusthanee and Sanskrit I translate with my own hand ... I constantly avail myself of the help of the most learned natives, and should think it criminal not to do so, but I do not commit my judgement to anyone.*[18]

Over the years Carey employed some thirty Indian pundits[19] each of whom knew Sanskrit and some other Indian language. Sadly there seems to be no record of any of them ever

---

[17] One such composed by Krishna Pal, translated in an English style, is in a number of our hymnbooks; 'O thou, my soul, forget no more the Friend who all thy misery bore'.
[18] George, Timothy p141.
[19] Chaterjee, SK in Daniel and Hedlund (Eds.) p163. Pundits were Hindu scholars learned in Sanskrit, Hindu philosophy and religion.

becoming Christian. Interestingly it was Carey's practice, whenever a new translation was begun, first to publish the Gospel of Matthew, the Acts and the letter to the Romans. He argued that these three books gave readers the life of Christ, the lives of the first churches and then an outline of Christian truth – all together being a basic overview of the message he sought to publish. The Serampore men succeeded in jointly publishing the Bible, or some part of it, in forty languages before Carey died; of those forty publications six were complete Bibles translated by William himself.

To have produced printed books in Bengali at that time was to have gone against the popular practice of handwritten manuscripts. The success of Carey's work sparked off a renaissance in Bengali literature. Previously the language of religion was the Sanskrit, restricted to use among Brahmins. The language for legal purposes was Persian, still remaining from the previous Mohammedan rule of North India. Under British influence English was becoming the language of government. The common people's Bengali was under pressure from all these influences and was regarded as inferior:

> Carey found Bengali literature in such a dishonoured state ... so he had to toil hard, struggling to raise the status of Bengali. Everyone was astonished when he firmly observed that he was convinced that the Bengali language is superior in point of intrinsic merit to every language spoken in India and in real point of utility yields to none.[20]

In his *History of Bengali Literature* (published in 1919) Dr S K Dee comments that Carey:

> ... led the learned Bengalis whom he attracted to study the language (at a time when it was held in contempt) ... with the result that his contribution to Bengali learning can only be completely measured by adding to it the

---
[20] Chatterjee, SK in Daniel and Hedlund (Eds.) p167.

writings of an admiring public who soon took up his work with earnestness.[21]

The exertions of Carey and his colleagues can truly be said to have laid a new foundation for an era of flourishing vernacular literature and printed books. After Carey's death Marshman wrote:

Before Carey's days the Bengali language was unknown in the world of literature, and had never been reduced to grammatical rule. Pundits would not write it, and there was scarcely a book in it worth reading. It is now rich and refined and expressive. To Dr Carey and his pundits and his translations this is chiefly owing.[22]

By 1803 a chapel was opened in Calcutta where preaching in English and Bengali took place each week, together with tract distribution and open-air preaching. But Carey's vision, which Marshman and Ward came to share, was to reach wider than Serampore, wider than Calcutta, wider than Bengal. Carey wrote to Fuller (1803):

If we are given another fifteen years, we hope to translate and print the Bible in all the chief languages of Hindustan. We have fixed our eyes on the goal. The zeal of the LORD of Hosts shall perform this.[23]

A year later the great scheme was underway, employing scholars from different areas of India, increasing the Serampore printing capacity and enlarging their type foundry, collecting the best library of Indian writings in all languages and training themselves in the habit of translation. A budget of £1,000 a year was estimated. Andrew Fuller felt excited at this bold programme and after a special deputation journey of 1,300 miles (including a visit to Scotland) he succeeded in raising £1,300

---
[21] Dee, SK quoted by Chatterjee, SK Ibid. p171.
[22] Carey, S Pearce p229.
[23] Carey, S Pearce p256.

for the project. At the same time the Rev Brown, the East India Company's Anglican chaplain, urged cooperation with the translation work, which the Calcutta Bible Society began to do, until withdrawing their grant in aid in 1833, as mentioned earlier in this chapter. Attempt great things, indeed!

27
Carey the educationalist

It was financial necessity which had repeatedly led Carey to be a village schoolmaster in England; his interest in schooling Bengali children however, while it answered the lack of education for the children of the common people, was now also pursued as a method of 'pre-evangelism' to support the work of mission. Without literacy how would the Bible be read? Without textbooks on scientific subjects how would Hindu superstitions be exposed as ridiculous? When Carey's sons were later setting off to establish new mission centres on their own, his advice to them was to consider their task as twofold – to establish schools and to spread the gospel message, the former being the means of introducing the latter.

When at the indigo factory in Mudnabatti Carey had set up a school for the local children. Because of the poverty of the families whose children he wished to teach, he proposed to feed and clothe them from his own income as factory manager. Otherwise the children would have had to work as labourers to supplement their family incomes and have no time for schooling. The studies Carey offered were to include Bengali, Sanskrit, Persian, various branches of useful knowledge and the truths of Christianity. Of his school of forty boys[1] Carey reported to Fuller:

> *The school would have been much larger, had we been able to have borne the expense ... the boys have hitherto learned to read and write, especially parts of the*

---
[1] Smith, George p75; also quoting a letter to Fuller, George, Timothy refers to '21 boys' p143.

Scripture and to keep accounts. We may now be able to introduce some other useful branches of knowledge.[2]

However, his work as factory manager meant a constant need to tour his area inspecting the indigo crop; this, together with his efforts at preaching in the surrounding villages and continuing the task of translating the Bible into Bengali, all made it evident that Mudnabatti was not the place nor was he, as a single person, suitable for such a large enterprise.[3] Not until the move to Serampore, where he had the valuable co-operation of Joshua and Hannah Marshman, was it practical for Carey to work out his vision of education as a precursor to evangelism . Joshua had formerly been headmaster of a school in Bristol and had studied in the Baptist College there which was led by Dr John Ryland. William Ward was also a valuable contributor to the fulfilment of Carey's vision, with his previous experience in journalism and printing.

Within five months of setting up the community in Serampore in May 1800, Mr and Mrs Marshman opened two boarding schools, one for Europeans and one for Anglo-Indian young people. This brought in a useful income for the support of the mission. A month later they opened a free vernacular school in which they taught some forty Bengali boys.[4] A few years later a school for girls was opened. By this time, Carey was reporting, about one hundred and forty boys and forty girls were in regular education.[5] Also by this time men and women who were members of the church were being employed as teachers in the schools.

There was excitement in the mission community in 1801 when a request came from the Governor, Lord Wellesley, for a teacher of Bengali at the Government College of Fort William. The purpose of this college was to train young Englishmen, who had come out to India to become Civil Service administrators, to use the local language. The East India Company's Anglican

---

[2] Smith, George p75.
[3] Marshman, John Clark p30.
[4] Jeyaseekaran, TA in Daniel and Hedlund (Eds.) p217.
[5] Smith, George p111.

chaplain had been appointed as Provost of the College and it was his proposal to invite William to be the language teacher. One small problem had to be overcome: regulations required all college staff members to be Anglican and Carey was a Dissenter. Calling him a 'Teacher' and not a 'Professor' and reducing the salary to five hundred rupees per month resolved the matter. (Several years later, when Carey was also asked to teach Sanskrit and Marathi, he was given the title 'Professor' and placed on full salary). He remained teaching in the college for nearly thirty years in all, until 1830. Although this commitment took up three days every week, involving travel by riverboat sixteen miles to the college in Calcutta, there were benefits to the mission. Carey was now earning more money to be devoted to the work of mission than any other member of the Serampore team. (The Marshmans contributed income from their schools, and Ward from his printing). In addition there was the benefit Carey could obtain from detailed study of the languages that he taught from the other skilled college pundits. That knowledge contributed to his translation work. He was also gaining a reputation in Government circles which gave his work as a missionary greater official respect, and providentially that meant that when Serampore was temporarily occupied by the British (owing to the war with Denmark mentioned earlier) the work of the mission continued without difficulty.

One immediate problem for Carey, as he began his college lectures, was the absence not merely of a book of Bengali grammar but also of any other prose book in that language which his students could read – problems which also affected the work of the mission's elementary schools. Alongside his work as a Bible translator Carey therefore began to compile a Bengali grammar and a dictionary of Bengali words. Carey and his son Felix, together with a number of other pundits, produced some sixty prose books: simple stories, fables, essays, a version of Pilgrim's Progress, books on Indian history, a chemistry book and translations of some Sanskrit religious classics.[6] Work was

---

[6] A full list of the authors and their Bengali books published through Serampore press appears in *William Carey and the Linguistic renaissance in India* in Daniel and Hedlund (Eds.) p170-171.

also done in Serampore on vocabularies and grammars in some other Eastern languages – even in Chinese. When Carey began teaching Sanskrit and Marathi the same lack of reference books in those languages also became apparent. To meet these needs he published grammars and dictionaries in Marathi and Sanskrit. There is a very real sense in which the industry of the Serampore men in the years from 1801 to 1834 opened North Indian eyes to the remarkable potential literary excellence of their own various vernacular languages.

> Carey was wholly or partly responsible for the publication of grammars in seven Indian languages and the compilation of dictionaries in Bengali, Sanskrit and Marathi. These would have been signal achievements for a scholar with formal linguistic training; for someone whose formal education had finished at the age of twelve, they must be judged extraordinary.[7]

In 1816, after the East India Company's charter had been amended by Parliament (1813) allowing efforts to bring social improvements to natives in their trading areas as one of the responsibilities of the Company, Joshua Marshman published his *Hints relative to Native schools* in which an appeal was made for funds to finance more mission schools. Many Europeans and Indians responded liberally. The mission's elementary school work began to expand beyond Serampore and Calcutta. By 1818 the mission had organised one hundred and twenty six vernacular schools teaching ten thousand pupils staffed by native teachers under the oversight of Marshman. Carey's syllabus of subjects included writing and spelling, arithmetic, geography, history and scripture. By 1826 the mission had opened twelve schools for girls in which three hundred girls were taught – a fact which began to focus public attention on the need for an improved status for Indian women.[8] But all this did not complete Carey's vision. He was anxious not only to provide facili-

---

[7] Stanley, Brian p51.
[8] Jeyasekaran, T Ambrose in Daniel and Hudlund (Eds.) p219.

ties for elementary education but for higher education as well. Better educated teachers were needed for elementary schools; educated evangelists were needed to spread Christian teaching; non-Christian students (even Hindu and Muslim)[9] needed a centre of higher education where Western knowledge could be taught them alongside Christian students.

In July 1818 a prospectus was published for *A College for the Instruction of Asiatic Christians and other youth in Eastern literature and European science;* the syllabus included studies in Western science,[10] Oriental languages (especially Sanskrit) and Theology. Thus theological studies were to be incorporated with arts and science studies. The medium of studies was to be Bengali though a few advanced students could study in English.[11] The establishment of this Serampore college arose directly from the conviction of the missionaries that Indian Christians would have to shoulder the burden of the evangelisation of India. At the time they wrote:

> *We must form our native brethren to usefulness. Foster every kind of genius, and cherish every gift and grace in them ... It is only by means of native preachers we can hope for the universal spread of the gospel through this immense continent. Europeans are too few, and their subsistence costs too much, for us ever to hope that they can possibly be the instruments of the universal diffusion of the Word among so many millions. The whole administration of the church should assume a native aspect by which means the inhabitants would more readily identify the cause as belonging to their own nation.*[12]

The college project met with criticism because of its breadth

---

[9] George, Timothy p148.
[10] Marshman, John Clark p241. Science then was the science prior to the time of Charles Lyell and Charles Darwin and before Enlightenment atheism had affected philosophical thought
[11] Stanley, Brian p52. Subsequently English was made an optional study for all students
[12] Marshman, John Clark p89.

of appeal, by including Hindu and Muslim students and by combining theological studies with arts and sciences. Some people objected, feeling that the college should be confined to producing only Baptist preachers schooled in Baptist thinking. When some years later new missionaries arrived from England, one of their grievances was that the college project was not a proper project for Baptist missionaries. The Serampore defence was emphatic:

> *The college is made as free as the air, not thinking it right that any should be deprived of its benefits for having had the misfortune to be born and brought up in any particular circles: nor that the gates of knowledge should be barred against those who have a different opinion from themselves ... In a country so destitute and so dependant upon us for both political freedom and moral improvement it is surely our duty to forget the distinctions which divide society in England. It will be time enough a hundred years hence when the country, filled with knowledge and truth had triumphed over every error, to think of sects and parties. Every public institution aiming at India's betterment ought to be constructed on so broad a basis as to invite the aid of all denominations.*[13]

The college began in 1821 with thirty-seven students of whom nineteen were Christian, the rest Hindu.[14] Carey was their Professor of Divinity and also lectured in botany and zoology – lectures that he illustrated from his garden cultivated in the college grounds. The college was housed in a magnificent building which still stands today, paid for from the earnings of the missionaries to the amount of £15,000.[15] A royal charter was presented to the college by the King of Denmark in 1827 empowering it to confer degrees on its graduates and William Carey was appointed President of the college council.

---
[13] Ousseren, AH p110.
[14] Smith, George p279.
[15] Marshman, John Clark p262.

In 1834 when Carey died the college was being used by a total of ninety-four students who were a mixture of European, Eurasian, Indian Christian, or Hindu. After Carey's death the college remained fulfilling his vision until 1883 when it was suspended and became a native Christian Training Institute. But in 1909 it reopened to function in the style of Carey's original plan.

Satisfied that necessary educational materials were now available for students in schools and in the college, Carey and the others realised that there was no literature available for the common people in their mother tongue. Marshman began to produce a periodical magazine called *Dig Darshan* ('The Signpost'), which at Carey's suggestion avoided all political discussion in order not to give any offence to the government. At the same time the Serampore press issued the first newspaper ever printed in non-Christian India – the Bengali *Sumachar Durpun* ('News Mirror'). Governor Hastings regarded the venture with approval, commenting that 'the effect of such a paper must be extensively and importantly useful'.[16] Subsequently Marshman and his son launched a monthly English periodical called *Friend of India*, which, after Joshua Marshman's death, ran for many years being then published by his son.

There were those who accused the Serampore men of making use of education in the college as an underhand way of producing Christians. In the college annual report of 1823 Carey rejected the charge, insisting that there was never:

> ... *any design to make converts by coercion or 'slanting' the syllabus; these methods were not only clean contrary to the Gospel, but quite unnecessary in any case; the Truth manifested in Christianity would be irresistible; all that the college authorities needed to do was to reveal it.*[17]

Once asked if he did not think it wrong to try and make Indians into Christians, Carey is said to have retorted that he

---
[16] Smith, George p204.
[17] Laird, MA in Daniel and Hedlund (Eds.) p207.

had no faith in makings since the pressure of makings makes hypocrites. What he required the right to do was to present the truth, as Christ had commanded, to each person's intelligence and conscience. Does not Carey's great confidence in the power and authority of the gospel message comes down the years to rebuke the spiritual uncertainties and religious hesitations that so often cripple us today?

> *In countries like India ...where civilisation has long ago reached its highest level, and has been declining for the want of the salt of a universal Christianity, it is the missionary who interferes for the highest ends. Mastering the complex classical speech of the learned class ... he takes the popular dialects ... which are the life of the future and brings them under law ... and in time he brings to birth nations worthy of the name by a national language and literature lighted up with the ideas of the Book which he is the first to translate. This was what Carey did for the speech of the Bengalees.*[18]

A significant factor in the ability of the Serampore Three to achieve so much over the thirty or more years in which they were together must be their willingness to agree to work and live together as a team of individuals, but totally dedicated to each other. Their remarkable 'Form of Agreement', which subsequent missionaries found hard to accept, was surely the key that opened the way to what they achieved.

---

[18] Smith, George p201.

28
The form of agreement of 1805

Carey, Marshman, Ward and John Fountain, on first forming the 'family' in Serampore in 1800, entered into an agreement to live together as a community in the Moravian style. As we saw earlier (Chapter twenty-three) this meant, in practical terms, sharing everything together as one family. Since new missionaries were now arriving and joining the group, beginning with John Chamberlain (1803), a new form of agreement was drawn up in 1805 describing the basis on which the community had been originally established and how it was designed to continue. The statement is important because it demonstrates the clear, unambiguous biblical principles that shaped the work of the mission and important also because it became a cause of dispute between its original authors and new missionaries who came to join them later. In 1805, however, the agreement happily bore the signatures of William Carey, Joshua Marshman, William Ward, John Chamberlain, Richard Mardon, John Biss, William Moore, Joshua Rowe and Felix Carey (by then welcomed as a missionary).

Extracts from the Form of Agreement[1]
(NB All footnotes are mine, inserted for the help of today's readers – author)

… We are firmly persuaded that Paul might plant and Apollos might water[2] in vain, in any part of the world, did not God give the increase. We are sure that only those who are ordained to eternal life will believe, and that God alone can add to the

---
[1] Davis, Walter Bruce pp109-127.
[2] 1 Corinthians 3:6

church such as shall be saved. Nevertheless we cannot but observe with admiration that Paul, the great champion for the doctrines of free and sovereign grace, was the most conspicuous for his personal zeal in the work of persuading men to be reconciled to God. In this respect he is a noble example for our imitation ... Upon these [following] points we think it right to fix our serious and abiding intention...

First. In order to be prepared for our great and solemn work, it is absolutely necessary that we set an infinite value upon immortal souls; that we often endeavour to affect our minds with the dreadful loss sustained by an unconverted soul launched into eternal punishment, and to realise frequently the unconceivable [sic] conditions of this vast country, lying in the arms of the wicked one. If we have not this awful sense of the value of souls, it is impossible that we can feel aright in any other part of our work, and in this case it had been better for us to have been in any other situation rather than that of a Missionary ... but while we thus mourn over their miserable condition, we should not be discouraged, as though their recovery were impossible. He who raised the Scottish and brutalised Britons to sit in heavenly places in Christ Jesus,[3] can raise these slaves of superstition, purify their hearts by faith, and make them worshippers of the one God in spirit and in truth. The promises are fully sufficient to remove our doubts, and to make us anticipate that not very distant period when He will famish all the gods of India, and cause these very idolators to cast their idols to the moles and to the bats[4] and renounce for ever the work of their own hands.

Secondly. It is very important that we should gain all the information we can of the snares of delusions in which these heathen are held. By this means we shall be able to converse with them in an intelligent manner. To know their modes of thinking, their habits, their propensities, their antipathies, the way in which they reason about God, sin, holiness, the way of salvation, and the future state, to be aware of the bewitch-

---

[3] Ephesians 2:6
[4] Isaiah 2:20

ing nature of their idolatrous worship, feasts, songs, etc. is of the highest consequence, if we would gain their attention to our discourse and would avoid to be barbarians to them. This knowledge may be easily obtained by conversing with sensible natives, by reading some parts of their works, and by attentively observing their manners and customs.[5]

Thirdly. It is necessary, in our intercourse with the Hindoos, that as far as we are able, we abstain from those things which would increase their prejudices against the Gospel. Those parts of English manners which are most offensive to them should be kept out of sight as much as possible. We should also avoid every degree of cruelty to animals. Nor is it advisable, at once to attack their prejudices, by exhibiting with acrimony, the sins of their gods, neither should we upon any account do violence to their images, nor interrupt their worship. The real conquests of the Gospel are those of love ... In this respect, let us be continually fearful lest one unguarded word, or one unnecessary display of the difference betwixt us, in manners, etc., should set the natives at a greater distance from us. Paul's readiness to become all things to all men,[6] that he might by any means save some, and his disposition to abstain even from necessary comforts that he might not offend the weak, are circumstances worthy of our particular notice. This line of conduct we may be sure was founded on the wisest principles ... He who is too proud to stoop to others in order to draw them to him, though he may know that they are in many respects inferior to himself, is ill-qualified to become a Missionary.

Fourthly. It becomes us to watch all opportunities of doing good. A Missionary would be highly culpable if he contented himself with preaching two or three times a week to those persons whom he might be able to get together in a place of worship. To carry on conversations with the natives almost every hour in the day, to go from village to village, from market to market, from one assembly to another, to talk to servants, la-

---

[5] This point gives the reason for their concern to read Hindu religious writings and to translate such Sanskrit works into Bengali and English – a task not easily appreciated by the Home Committee.
[6] 1 Corinthians 10:19-23

bourers, etc., as often as opportunity offers, and to be instant in season and out of season – this is the life to which we are called in this country. We are apt to relax in these active exertions, especially in a warm climate; but we shall do well always to fix in our minds, that life is short, that all around us are perishing, and that we incur a dreadful woe if we proclaim not the glad tidings of salvation.[7]

Fifthly. In preaching to the heathen, we must keep to the example of St. Paul, and make the greatest subject of our preaching, Christ Crucified.[8] It would be very easy for a Missionary to preach nothing but truths, and that for many years together, without any well-grounded hope of becoming use to one soul. The doctrine of Christ's expiatory death and all-sufficient merits has been, and must ever remain, the great means of conversion. This doctrine, and others immediately connected with it, have constantly nourished and sanctified the church ... It is a well-known fact that the most successful missionaries in the world at the present day make the atonement of Christ their continued theme ... So far as our experience goes in this work, we must freely acknowledge, that every Hindoo among us who has been gained to Christ, has been won by the astonishing and all-constraining love exhibited in our Redeemer's propitiatory death.

Sixthly. It is absolutely necessary that the natives should have an entire confidence in us, and feel quite at home in our company. To gain this confidence we must on all occasions be willing to hear their complaints; we must give them the kindest advice, and we must decide upon everything brought before us in the most open, upright, and impartial manner. We ought to be easy of access, to condescend to them as much as possible, and on all occasions to treat them as our equals. All passionate behaviour will sink our characters exceedingly in their estimation. All force, and everything haughty, reserved, and forbidding, it becomes us ever to shun with the greatest care.

Seventhly. Another important part of our work is to build up, and watch over, the souls that may be gathered. In this work

---

[7] 1 Corinthians 9:16
[8] 1 Corinthians 2:2

we shall do well to simplify our first instructions as much as possible, and to press the great principles of the Gospel upon the minds of the converts till they be thoroughly settled and grounded in the foundation of their hope towards God. We must be willing to spend some time with them daily, if possible, in this work. We must have patience with them, though they may grow very slowly in divine knowledge. We ought also to endeavour as much as possible to form them to habits of industry, and assist them in procuring such employments as may be pursued with the least danger of temptations to evil. Here we shall have occasion to exercise much tenderness and forbearance, knowing that industrious habits are formed with difficulty by all heathen nations.[9] We ought also to remember that these persons have made no common sacrifices in renouncing their connections, their homes, their former situations and means of support, and that it will be very difficult for them to procure employment with heathen masters ... As we consider it our duty to honour the civil magistrate, and in every state and country to render him the readiest obedience, whether we be persecuted or protected, it becomes us to instruct our native brethren in the same principle. A sense of gratitude too presses this obligation upon us in a peculiar manner in return for the liberal protection we have experienced ... To bear the faults of our native brethren so as to reprove them with tenderness, and set them right in the necessity of a holy conversation, is a very necessary duty. We should remember the gross darkness in which they were so lately involved, having never had any just and adequate ideas of the evil of sin, or its consequences ... We ought not, therefore after many falls, to give up and cast away a relapsed convert while he manifests the least inclination to be washed from his filthiness ... In conversing with the wives of native converts, and leading them into the ways of Christ, so that they may be an ornament to the Christ cause and make known the Gospel to the native women, we hope always to have the assistance of

---

[9] This must be understood in the light of the backward social conditions in Carey's day largely due to the stranglehold of caste. Nowadays, as a result of the availability of advanced education and the weakening of caste barriers, India has very many industrious and energetic achievers in all walks of life.

the females who have embarked with us in the mission. We see that in primitive times the Apostles were very much assisted in their great work by several pious females ... It behoves us therefore, to afford to our European sisters all possible assistance in acquiring the language that they may, in every way which Providence may open to them, become instrumental in promoting the salvation of the millions of native women who are in a great measure excluded from all opportunities of hearing the word from the mouths of European missionaries. A European sister may do much for the cause in this respect, by promoting holiness, and stirring up the zeal, of the female converts.

Eighthly. Another part of our work is the forming of our native brethren to usefulness, fostering every kind of genius, and cherishing every gift and grace in them. In this respect we can scarcely be too lavish of our attention to their improvement. It is only by means of native preachers that we can hope for the universal spread of the Gospel throughout this immense continent ... If the practice of confining the ministry of the word to a single individual in a church be once established amongst us, we despair of our Gospel's ever making much progress by our means. Still further to strengthen the cause of Christ in this country, and, as far as in our power, to give it a permanent establishment, even when the efforts of Europeans may fail, we think it our duty, as soon as possible, to advise the native brethren who may be formed in separate churches, to choose their pastors and deacons from amongst their own countrymen, that the word may be steadily preached and the ordinances of Christ administered in each church by the native minister, as much as possible without interference of the Missionary of the district, who will constantly superintend their affairs, give them advice in cases of order and discipline, and to correct any errors into which they may fall, and who joying and beholding their order and their steadfastness of their faith in Christ, may direct his efforts continually to the planting of new churches in other places, and to the spread of the Gospel throughout his district as much as is in his power ... The different native churches will also naturally have to care and provide for their ministers, for their church expenses, the raising of places of worship, etc. and the whole administration will assume a native aspect by which means the inhabitants will more readily identify the cause as belonging to their own nation and their prejudices at falling into the hands of Europeans will entirely vanish.

Under the divine blessing if, in the course of a few years, a number of native churches be thus established, from them the Word of God may sound out even to the extremities of India, and numbers of preachers being raised up and sent forth, may form a body of native missionaries, inured to the climate, acquainted with the customs, language, modes of speech and reasoning of the inhabitants; able to become perfectly familiar with them, to enter their houses, to live upon their food, to sleep with them, or under a tree; and who may travel from one end of the country to the other almost without any expense. These churches will be in no immediate danger of falling into errors of disorders, because the whole of their affairs will be constantly superintended by a European missionary.[10] That we may discharge the important obligations of watching over these infant churches when formed, and of urging them to maintain a steady discipline, to hold forth the clear and cheering light of evangelical truth in this region and shadow of death, and to walk in all respects as those who have been called out of the darkness into marvellous light, we should continually go to the Source of all grace and strength for it.

We have thought it our duty not to change the names of native converts, observing from Scripture that the Apostles did not change those of the first Christians turned from heathenism ... We think the great object which Divine Providence has in view in causing the Gospel to be promulgated in the world, is not the changing of names, the dress, the food, and the innocent usages of mankind, but to produce a moral and divine change in the hearts and conduct of men ... By this they learn to see the evil of a custom, and then to despise and forsake it; whereas in cases wherein force is used, though they may leave off that which is wrong while in our presence, yet not having seen the

---

[10] This paragraph has been shown by subsequent history to be over-optimistic. The movement for the independence of India against the British Raj caused a widespread rejection of European supervision.

evil of it, they are in danger of using hypocrisy, and of doing that out of our presence which they dare not do in it.[11]

Ninthly. It becomes us also to labour with all our might in forwarding translations of the sacred scriptures in the languages of Hindoostan. We consider the publication of the Divine Word throughout India as an object which we ought never to give up till accomplished ... It becomes us to use all assiduity in explaining and distributing the Divine Word on all occasions, and by every means in our power to excite the attention and reverence of the natives towards it, as the fountain of eternal truth and the Message of Salvation to men. It is our duty also to distribute, as extensively as possible, the different religious tracts which are published ... We should endeavour to ascertain where large assemblies of the natives are to be found, that we may attend upon them and gladden whole villages at once with the tidings of salvation. The establishment of native free schools is also an object highly important to the future conquests of the Gospel. Of this very pleasing and interesting part of our missionary labours we should endeavour not to be unmindful ... Some parts of missionary labours very properly tend to present conversion of the heathen, and others to the ushering in the glorious period when 'a nation shall be born in a day'. Of the latter kind are native free schools.

Tenthly. That which, as a means, is to fit us for the discharge of these laborious and unutterably important labours, is the being instant in prayer and the cultivation of personal religion. Prayer, secret, fervent, believing prayer, lies at the root of all personal godliness. A competent knowledge of the languages current where a missionary lives, a mild and winning temper, and a heart given up in closet religion, these are the attainments which, more than all knowledge, or all other gifts, will fit us to become the instruments of God in the great work of Human Redemption.

Finally. Let us never think that our time, our gifts, our strength, our families, or even the clothes we wear, are our own. Let us sanctify ourselves for His work! Let us ever shut out the

---
[11] Compare Philippians 2:12

idea of laying up a dowry for ourselves or our children. If we give up the resolution which was formed on the subject of private trade,[12] when we first united at Serampore, the Mission is from that hour a lost cause. A worldly spirit, quarrels, and every evil work will succeed the moment it is admitted that each brother may do something on his own account. Woe to that man who shall ever make the smallest movement towards such a measure. If in this way we are enabled to glorify God, with our bodies and spirits which are His, our wants will be His care. No private family ever enjoyed a greater portion of happiness than we have done since we resolved to have all things in common and that no one should pursue business for his own exclusive advantage. If we are enabled to persevere in the same principles, we may hope that multitudes of converted souls will have reason to bless God to all eternity for sending His Gospel into this country. To keep these ideas alive in our minds, we resolve that this Agreement shall be read publicly, at every station, at our three annual meetings, viz., on the first Lord's day in January, in May, and October.

---

[12] ie. the resolution that any earnings individual members of the group receive be deposited in a central fund for the financing of the work, and not kept by them as their own.

29
The Mission 'family' grows, but amid opposition

Now to return to our story: as we saw earlier Serampore was not to be the limit of Carey's plans. He began to develop a scheme for reaching out into the whole of Bengal. A mission outpost was to be established every hundred miles or so across Bengal, linked with Serampore in spiritual fellowship and by financial support until each was able to become a self-supporting church in its own right. With the arrival of John Chamberlain from England (1803) the first of these outposts was set up by him (1804) in a town called Katwa, nearly one hundred miles north of Serampore. John was given a capital sum of money to enable him to become self-supporting by engaging in some suitable trade.

> *By August 1805 Carey had framed plans for a further seven stations in addition to those already established in Katwa and Dinajpur[1] and Jessore; the proposed locations ranged from Agra or Delhi in the North-west to Chittagong in the East. Each of these contemplated stations would itself have ten satellite outstations manned by native evangelists.[2]*

But such evangelistic audacity would not be unchallenged for long. Carey's second son William (born while the family were at Moulton in Northamptonshire) and William Moore, an-

---
[1] Dinajpur was where Ignatius Fernandez was based and where the grave of John Fountain was situated (chapter twenty-three).
[2] Stanley, Brian p53.

other of the newly arrived missionaries, began to tour through eastern districts as far as Dacca but were there stopped by the magistrate who found that they were without a licence to preach in East India Company areas.

Similarly, when William Ward went to Jessore to purchase land for the establishment of a missionary outpost he was refused permission to register the purchase, not having a licence to do so from the Company. Richard Mardon went to Malda unnoticed by the authorities, but John Biss and William Moore in Dinajpur were refused permission to settle and had to return to Serampore. The outbreak of official opposition to Serampore evangelism arose from the fact that Lord Cornwallis – a helpful Governor General – had died suddenly at the close of 1805 and was succeeded by acting Governor Sir George Barlow. When working with Lord Cornwallis he had appeared to accept Cornwallis' liberal views. But the weight of the authority of his temporary office caused him to feel that he should adhere more closely to the policy of the English government and the Company by forbidding the proselytisation of the native community. Nor were matters eased when in 1806 Lord Minto, no friend of missions, arrived to be the next Governor General.

The reaction of the Serampore men to these setbacks was to regard them as a possible providential encouragement to look outside India for the hoped-for expansion of the mission, rather than to continue acting in defiance of the Bengal authorities. They wrote home in 1806:

> *The Bengal, in which we have been labouring, is providentially central for all Asia. Orissa, Kurnataka and Mahratta lie to the S. and the S.W.; Hindustan, Bhutan and Thibet [sic] to the N.W. and N.; Assam, Burma, China and the Malay Isles to the N.E. and E. China is only two hundred leagues[3] from Serampore. If we could reach a certain river only thirty leagues from Assam, we could be conveyed into Yunnan[4] ... we have good hope of get-*

---

[3] The term is archaic, one league equal to about three miles
[4] Part of the Chinese empire

> *ting pundits from Bhutan, from Nepal and from Assam. A Burmese Gospel will probably be ready as soon as the earliest recruit from England can arrive.*[5]

It was a cry for more men and for the Society to raise the funds to send them out. Forty new missionaries was their estimate of the number of men required! In the same year James Chater and William Robinson were the next two colleagues to arrive, only to be served immediately with a deportation order. Both European and Indian opponents of missionary work had appealed to the acting Governor General, Sir George Barlow, to enforce the ban against missionaries evangelising in Company areas. The argument was that the recent unrest and rebellion of the Indian sepoys in Vellore was stirred up by Christian workers. (In fact it was due to the change of design of the turban the troops were to wear). Sir George Barlow was persuaded that similar unrest could be caused by the appearance of missionaries outside Serampore. The deportation order was served on Chater and Robinson, and Carey was called before the Governor to account for his actions. Only the fact that he was in Serampore and not in Calcutta saved him. The Governor decreed that Indian Christians might preach outside Serampore, if they so wished, but not the missionaries, nor converts sent out from Serampore. Carey wrote home:

> *We are all of us prisoners at Serampore, and you have sent us two new brethren to keep us company ... the open doors for usefulness, which a few days ago engaged our attention and animated our exertions, are closed by this cruel message.*[6]

Consequently, William Robinson went in 1808 to the hill tribes of Bhutan; James Chater and Richard Mardon went to explore the possibility of establishing a mission in Burma. The Bhutan outreach was abandoned in 1811 for lack of success

---

[5] Carey, S Pearce p269.
[6] Ibid. p272.

and Robinson moved from there to the East Indies, working in Java and then in Sumatra where a mission was established by William Ward's nephew Nathaniel Ward. That work survived until the 1840s. The mission in Java was maintained until 1847 when the work, including the translation of the New Testament into Javanese, was taken over by Dutch missionaries. However success in both these ventures seems to have been limited. Robinson then served in Dacca for some years until he moved to Calcutta to serve as pastor for twelve years in the Lall Bazar chapel (of which more later). Chater moved to Colombo in 1812, founding the Ceylon mission of the Society which eventually was the means of forming an indigenous church in the island.[7] The work in Burma became the responsibility of Felix Carey and then of the American missionary Adoniram Judson and his wife who were, at their request, baptised in the Lall Bazar chapel, having convinced themselves of the rightness of the baptism of believers by immersion while travelling out to India from America.[8]

Opposition to missionary evangelism was to be inflamed still further. Those opposed to the work of the Serampore mission had found a Persian tract that had been printed there, the translation of which showed the tract to make some critical comments about the Prophet Muhammad and Islam. The Bengal authorities judged the tract to be inflammatory and dangerous to public order. Carey was summoned to meet a government official and account for the tract. He replied that:

> *... he and his colleagues entirely disapproved of the use of offensive language in reference to the religion of the Hindoos or Mahomedans, and that this course was entirely foreign to their practice in communications with the natives ... the only means they were disposed*

---

[7] Information drawn from Stanley, Brian pp54-55.
[8] For a while the Judsons worked in Burma supported from Serampore, but eventually the American Baptist Missionary Society was founded in Boston USA whose missionaries later had great success among the Karen people. Smith, George p172.

to use (for the conversion of the natives) was fair argument and persuasion.[9]

Carey agreed to withdraw the offending tract and sent all the remaining stock to the Governor. Investigation revealed that the tract had been written by a Bengali Christian, a convert from Islam, and was printed in Persian without having been revised (admittedly a mistake by Serampore); the Bengali version did not contain the same critical remarks. A tug of war developed between the Governor and the Serampore men over the location of the printing press; the Governor wanted it to be removed to Calcutta so that its use could be closely monitored. Carey and the others wanted it to remain in Serampore under the patronage of the Danish Government. The Danish Governor offered to try and settle the matter amicably by conciliation. Carey and Marshman agreed to leave the matter with him, realising that if they appeared to be defiant in their attitude to Lord Minto, Carey's salary as a professor in the government Fort William college could be lost and the press *forcibly* confiscated. Ward did not agree; he proposed that they ask an audience with Lord Minto to present him with a copy of their English translation of the Sanskrit classic *Ramayana*[10] as a unique example of what their press produced. To this all agreed and a meeting with Lord Minto was arranged. When Lord Minto received the copy of the *Ramayana* he was taken aback, now realising his earlier ignorance of what the missionaries were doing. Marshman went on to explain the origin of the mission, its work in education and in literary productions. The Governor became more friendly and agreed to accept a written statement giving a full account of the mission's work and policies.[11] Ward's diary contains a delightfully revealing account of the interview with Lord Minto:

---

[9] Marshman, John Clark p116.
[10] Regarded by Brahmins as an epic poem of ethical value, dating from 500-300 BC.
[11] The whole incident is explained in great detail in Marshman, John Clark pp120-126.

> Carey and Marshman, having settled their plans and Marshman having borrowed a coat of Mr James Rolt, a Calcutta architect and friend of the mission, they set off ... it was lucky for them that an attendant required them to leave their hats in a passage, or Carey would most likely have stuck his under his left arm-pit, and Marshman would have squeezed his into the size of a black pocket handkerchief – for they were carrying The Ramayana and other Serampore volumes. Making, therefore, very awkward bows they entered into the presence of India's Governor General and offered him the books and the first sheet of Marshman's Chinese New Testament.[12]

Marshman's written statement told the Governor of a hundred Indians so far baptised, both Hindu and Muslim, Brahmin and writer caste, who had come seeking Christian instruction and whose baptisms passed without untoward incident. The statement also explained that the costs of living and working in Calcutta would make it impossible for the mission to continue. Eventually Lord Minto and his government revoked their previous order demanding the removal of the press to Calcutta, being unwilling to provoke a diplomatic incident with Denmark. In 1806 Carey was able to write to Fuller:

> I rejoice to inform you that the storm is over. The Governor of Serampore has received a letter from our government revoking their Order concerning our press, and only requiring to be apprised of what we print...the crests of our challengers have much fallen. Our dispersal of pamphlets in the Company's dominions is now recognised ... I have no doubt that we shall be permitted to print nearly all we desire.[13]

---

[12] Carey, S Pearce p278.
[13] Ibid. p279.

While the printing was now secure, *preaching* outside Serampore was still officially forbidden. And there were still many attempts in England to persuade the English government to ban all missionary work in India, objecting even to the founding of the Bible Society in England because of its support for translations of the Bible being produced in India. One vociferous opponent of missions was an army officer who had become a Hindu while serving in India. He published, anonymously, *A vindication of the Hindus* in which he argued that:

> *Wherever I look around in the vast region of Hindu mythology, I discover piety in the garb of allegory, and I see morality at every turn blended with every tale; and, as far as I can rely on my own judgement, it appears the most complete and ample system of moral allegory the world has even produced.*[14]

All this opposition involved Fuller in frequent visits to London to meet different officials and also in writing a rebuttal of many things that were being said against missionary work. He wrote *An apology for Christian Missions,* which was published in three parts, in which he pleaded for the same toleration for Christians as was given to Hindus and Muslims in their proselytising and effectively rebutted the claims for Hinduism made by the army officer. Other friends of the mission entered the public argument including one who had spent many years in India and who could refute the claims of the anonymous army officer. Eventually the careful conduct of the Serampore men and the strong defence of them by friends in England led to the hostility toward the mission dying down. To the Governor of Serampore's questioning of the British Government as to whether the banning of evangelism in the Company's territory included objection to the circulation of the Holy Scriptures, came the reply:

> *The British Government was not aware of any objection to the circulation of the Holy Scriptures in the vernacular*

---

[14] Marshman, John Clark p132.

tongues, if unaccompanied by any comment on the religion of the country.[15]

The fears of the missionaries began to subside. The passing of the East India Company Act of 1813 which guaranteed the freedom of Christian missionaries to evangelise in India enabled a considerable expansion of the work as envisaged in Carey's initial scheme. By 1813 Mission stations were already opened in Agra, Dinajpur, Jessore and Ceylon. Stations were now planned to be established by 1828 at Dhaka, Monghyr, Patna, Delhi, Howrah, Cuttack, Berhampur, Puri, and Barisal.[16] Once again Carey was 'expecting great things' and 'attempting great things'.

By the end of 1843, fifty years after Carey and John Thomas had arrived in Bengal, the total membership of the BMS churches in the Indian sub-continent was 1,449.[17]

Some have asked why there were not many more converts than this in the fifty years since Carey's arrival in India, in the light of the remarkable success of missionary enterprise known in other parts of the world. Such a question is to forget both the formidable strength of the caste system with which Hindu society was enslaved and the fact that there was, initially, no part of Scripture available in any Indian vernacular. While the early missionaries certainly did not neglect an evangelistic preaching ministry, their main priorities *had* to be those of translating, printing and distributing the Scriptures and establishing a system of education for the natives to learn to read. Only so could their converts be grounded in biblical truth expressed in their mother tongue and also the training of *native* evangelists be made possible.

---

[15] Ibid. p140.
[16] Davis, Walter Bruce p74.
[17] Stanley, Brian p141. John Thomas died in 1801; Carey in 1834. 'BMS churches' refers to those mission stations originally founded by the Serampore mission and linked to the Particular Baptist Society, but later absorbed into the present BMS in 1891.

30
Sunshine and shadows

One curious outcome of Carey's appointment as a teacher and professor in the government's Fort William College in Calcutta was the fact that it allowed him to work outside Serampore, which freedom was normally forbidden to the Serampore men by the Governor. When taking up his college appointment William made it clear that, first and foremost, he was a missionary and could not cease to be so. In 1803 he wrote to Andrew Fuller:

> *We have opened a place of worship in Calcutta, where we have preaching twice on Lord's day in English, on Wednesday evening in Bengali and on Thursday in English.*[1]

The place of the meeting, apparently held with the tacit approval of the Governor, was an undertaker's hall, which was approached through lines of coffins[2] (suitable preparation for thoughts of eternity!). The hall was surrounded by a slum area of Calcutta known as Lall Bazaar, a place of liquor stalls and brothels. Gradually funds were collected from friends and businesses in Calcutta to add to monies that Serampore could provide and by January 1809 what was known as 'Carey's Baptist Chapel' was erected. It was in the baptistery of this chapel that William Ward baptised Adoniram and Ann Judson, at their request.[3] The Serampore men in turn maintained a regular ministry there for a generation, despite the fact that Parliament's

---

[1] George, Timothy p146.
[2] Smith, George p116.
[3] Davis, Walter Bruce p97.

permission for such preaching in Company areas was not given until 1813. William Ward, a warm-hearted soul, expressed his distress that some who attended services in this chapel and who had contributed to its cost, would not be permitted to take communion since they had not been baptised by immersion. Marshman was sympathetic to Ward's distress. After some time Carey himself acquiesced and the practice of restricting communion to believers baptised by immersion was discontinued. Ward wrote home:

> *I rejoice that the first Baptist church in Bengal has shaken off that apparent moroseness of temper which has long made us unlovely in the sight of the Christian world. I am glad that this Church considers real religion alone as the ground of admission to the Lord's table.*[4]

Fuller was not amused. His views had been plainly stated when he accepted the pastorate at Kettering in 1782:

> *I believe the ordinances which Christ ... has instituted for his church throughout the Gospel day are especially two; namely, baptism and the Lord's Supper. I believe the subjects of both to be those who profess repentance towards God and faith towards our Lord Jesus Christ; and on such I consider them incumbent duties. I believe it is essential to Christian baptism that it be by immersion, or burying the person in water, in the name of the Father, the Son and the Holy Ghost. I likewise believe Baptism ... to be pre-requisite to church communion.*[5]

In correspondence with him at the time Fuller argued from Mark 16:16 that what Ward was doing was to separate the two ordinances which Christ had bound together, making one of less importance than the other, which they had no right to do.[6] After a protracted correspondence between Fuller and the Ser-

---
[4] Ibid. p 97.
[5] Naylor, Peter p218.
[6] Ibid p218.

ampore men, Carey agreed with Fuller and the more exclusive practice was resumed.[7]

> *The sentiments of Mr Ward, however, remained unchanged, but with his habitual sweetness of disposition he offered no opposition to the change, and refused to divide the church on this question, simply stipulating that those who were excluded by this rule – the first of whom was an Independent missionary, after he had occupied the pulpit – should be distinctly informed that he was no party to it.*[8]

Before this advance into Calcutta the Danish Governor of Serampore had for some time been proposing that a Danish church should be built in *his* territory. When eventually it was completed (1806) it was handed over to the Serampore men because at that time Serampore had been temporarily taken over by the British (Chapter 23). Carey, Marshman and Ward, followed by their successors, John Mack, John Leechman and 'the learned WH Denham,'[9] also continued to preach there for some forty-five years.

Over against the establishment of these churches in Calcutta and Serampore, which must have brought encouragement to the missionary community and its friends, there was sadness that the end of the twenty-five years of marriage between Dorothy and William was drawing near. The last twelve years of Dorothy's life, especially since the death of their son Peter (1794), were clouded by her growing insanity which sometimes drove her to be violent. On such occasions, robbed of her Christian inhibitions by illness, she would relapse into the typical state of

---

[7] George, Timothy p164. It has to be said that John Ryland Jnr (the Society Chairman) did not agree with Fuller and, as did some other Particular Baptists, he practised 'Open Communion'.

[8] Marshman, John Clark p164.

[9] So described by Smith, George p288; described by Stanley, Brian p157 as 'a theological professor'. He later became the Principal of the Serampore College.

a coarse and ignorant village woman.[10] Those were often sad years for William and his boys. He wrote to his sister:

Poor Mrs Carey is as wretched as insanity can make her, and often makes the family so too, but we are supported by a gracious God.[11]

To his father in England William wrote explaining that Dorothy had to be closely watched at all times and sometimes confined to her room. He was obviously troubled by Dorothy's illness, as any husband would be were his wife so sick. When advised by friends to admit her into the Calcutta mental asylum he refused. He realised that she was in no way to blame for her condition. As one biographer has recorded:

(Carey) was her tender nurse, when many a time the ever-busy scholar would fain have lingered at his desk, or sought the scanty sleep which his jealous devotion to his Master's business allowed him.[12]

The women of the little missionary community, under the leadership of Hannah Marshman, cared for Dorothy as if she were their own and mothered her children. William Ward, who had married John Fountain's widow, became a friendly 'uncle' to the boys. The fact that all four boys were converted and became missionaries themselves must be a significant fact in any assessment of that situation. Dorothy died on 8 December1807 after several days of fever. William Ward recorded in his journal:

This evening Mrs Carey died of the fever under which she has languished for some time. Her death was a very easy one; but there was no appearance of return-

---

[10] Beck, James R *Introduction* pp11-13.

[11] George, Timothy p158.

[12] Quoted from Smith, George in Carey, S Pearce p288.

ing reason, nor anything that could cast a dawn of hope or light on her state.[13]

Today's psychiatric understanding would probably classify Dorothy's insanity as a type of morbid jealousy of which delusions of a partner's infidelity are a symptom. *Depression, with accompanying subjective feelings of inadequacy and failure, may give rise to delusional jealousy or may follow its onset.*[14]

It is not difficult to see how Dorothy could become severely depressed. A long and sometimes stormy sea journey during a time of war with France was an unexpected and frightening experience for a simple English village woman to face. The grinding poverty of several years in a strange and foreign land; the unexpected loss of the close companionship of her sister Kitty by marriage to Charles Short; ignorance of the language spoken all around her; the tragic deaths of three of her seven children; her long years of unrelenting fever and dysentery: these were all cruel events for a mother to endure. The man she had married was a shoemaker and pastor in the familiar surroundings of England and not the learned professor of languages at a college in Calcutta who was now away from home for three days a week. It must be said that in all this Dorothy was by no means the last missionary wife whose loyalty to her husband's calling was at some great personal cost. On Carey's side there seems no evidence of an angry argument with his God; no impetuous asking, Why, O why? He was troubled and saddened – as is evident from his letters – but also submissive, patient and loving to the end. The grace of God proved to be sufficient for him; any Christian believer has to learn, as Carey and even the apostle Paul had to, that the excellence of God's power is made perfect in those heavy trials that could otherwise crush them in all their human weakness.[15]

In May 1808 William caused not a little stir in the Serampore community by his sudden marriage to Miss Charlotte Rhu-

---

[13] George, Timothy p159.
[14] From a paper by Michael Kingham & Harvey Gordon in 'Advances in Psychiatric Treatment' (2004) Vol. 10 pp207-215.
[15] 2 Corinthians 12:9

mohr, a lady of his own age from an historic family in the Danish duchy of Schleswick. Injured as a teenager in a house fire, Charlotte suffered various physical disabilities for the rest of her life and under medical advice had travelled to the warmth of India for the benefit of her health. Originally she intended to reside in Tranquebar, but her ship brought her first to Serampore just after the missionary community had begun there. Colonel Bie introduced her to the community, asking that Carey should teach her English. The spiritual liveliness that she found in the community was an answer to the religious concerns which had arisen in her mind on the outward journey. She resolved to stay in Serampore and join with the community in their times of worship. She was converted, baptised by Carey in the Ganges river[16] and became a close supporter of the mission's work for the rest of her life. Disabled in body, she was possessed of an alert and intelligent mind, was deeply pious in nature and fluent in several European languages, quickly becoming a student of Bengali as well.

> *She was eminently fitted for the companion of a man like Dr Carey, and their happy union enabled him to enjoy that bracing relaxation in the conversation of an accomplished wife to which he had hitherto been a stranger.*[17]

The thirteen wonderful years which followed till her death in 1821 almost exactly balanced the thirteen difficult years of Dorothy's tragic illness. The startled mission community was quickly able to withdraw its concern over the union.

At a walking distance south of Serampore stood an old pagoda which was once the home of a Hindu idol god but was

---

[16] '... very near drowning her in the ceremony'. A quote from Drewery, Mary's 'William Carey' p147.
[17] Marshman, John Clark p145.

now empty and derelict. When Henry Martyn (1781-1812)[18] came to Calcutta in 1806 he chose to live in the deserted pagoda where some rooms had been prepared for him. He used it not merely as a residence but also as a prayer house, writing home that:

The place where once devils were worshipped has now become a Christian oratory.[19]

It was in this 'oratory' that from time to time Calcutta Anglican missionaries and their Dissenter missionary friends from Serampore would meet together for times of united prayer for the progress of the kingdom of God in India, with none of the denominational quarrelling which so often spoiled such unity in the homeland. These must have seemed 'sunshine days' to Carey, Marshman and Ward – but, in fact, storm clouds were gathering…

---

[18] Having been awakened to the need for missionary work by Charles Simeon of Cambridge, Martyn came to Calcutta as an Anglican chaplain. He began translating the New Testament and Psalms into Persian and the former into Arabic. The Book of Common Prayer he translated into Hindustani. He died of a fever while returning to England from Persia.
[19] Smith, George p143.

31
Growing pains and a disaster

Eight new missionaries came out to join the Serampore community between 1810 and 1818. In addition there was the natural growth in the community itself, by the birth of children, the employment of servants, the addition of language pundits, children from the boarding schools run by the Marshmans, and craftsmen employed in the printing and binding workshops. Sometimes as many as sixty adults could be present at a meal.

> *The three elders in their prime ...and their wives ... and the families: Carey's four sons, Marshman's sons, Ward's little children ... more than seventy boarders ... the fiancées of Felix and William Carey Jnr. ... and the many visiting guests ... missionaries of sister societies ... Indian converts and preachers and Indian Christ-seekers.*[1]

Hannah Marshman wrote:

> *In every dinner we expend four very large dishes of boiled rice piled up on a heap; four dishes of curry, three or four joints of meat, sometimes eight or nine large fish, seven or eight dishes of vegetables from our own garden, three tureens of soup with bread ... We have often puddings and pies made by our own cook, very good butter made twice a day ... one plate of toast, six large plates of bread and butter.*[2]

---

[1] Carey, S Pearce pp303-304.
[2] George, Timothy p125.

For Carey, who had known such lonely and hungry days, the sight must have gladdened his heart! But this very expansion in the work brought its own problems. The three men and their wives were content to live Moravian style, each pooling what they earned in the communal fund that financed the work of the mission, while drawing only a pittance for their personal use and then directing the work by a consensus among themselves. The same could not be said however for some of the new men joining the community. They felt it unfair that such self-denial should be expected of them while the original three retained a superior authority to govern the work. As Marshman's son later described the problem, 'They had fallen into the error of creating a system which demanded Moravian self-denial, without conceding Moravian equality'.[3] In response to this problem Carey proposed that henceforth the management of the community should be by a body of those elected from the community. Fuller and the Home Society would not accept this, insisting that the original three men were to retain sole authority for the rest of their lives. Carey then proposed to establish several mission stations in different areas of Bengal away from Serampore but under the direction and support of Serampore, each to be in the care of one of the new missionaries. However, discontent with the restriction against earning a private income remained. In the event the practice of dispersing new missionaries in independent 'outstations' proved difficult for Serampore to support because of the unwillingness of the new missionaries also to agree to the policy of 'self-support' for the work. A scheme to employ Indian preachers was launched, as they were thought to be cheaper to support than European missionaries and would not be affected by the East India Company ban on Europeans engaging in evangelistic outreach. By the close of 1812 six workers were employed supported initially at the personal expense of Carey and his colleagues, until the news of them reached England where it met with Society approval. It was becoming evident that the growth of the community was

---

[3] Marshman, John Clark p147.

bringing with it problems of finance, management and morale which were difficult to overcome.

The translation work of the Serampore Three was also about to suffer a severe blow. By now a translation of the whole Bible was printed and published in Bengali; the New Testament was published in Sanskrit, Oriya, Marathi and Hindi; translated, but not yet printed, were New Testaments in Telegu, Kanarese, Gujarati and Punjabi; work was beginning on translations in Kashmiri, Burmese and even Chinese. Then on the night of Wednesday 11 March 1812 William Ward suddenly found the warehouse and printing office on fire. Despite attempts by him and some native employees to quench the fire by pouring on buckets of water all through the night, large stocks of paper, valuable manuscripts, a library of grammar books and dictionaries and founts of type were lost. The roof of the building collapsed and the whole premises was engulfed in flames. The cause was never discovered. The labour of twelve years was lost in a few hours. In monetary terms the loss was estimated at £10,000; the loss in terms of time and energy over the years and of valuable manuscripts was incalculable.

> *Sikh and Telegu grammars and ten Bible versions were gone ... volumes of the Ramayana translation destroyed for ever ... worst of all was the loss of the Polyglot Dictionary of all the languages derived from Sanskrit which ... would have perpetuated Carey's name in the first rank of philologists.*[4]

Carey's response was typical of the man. He wrote to John Ryland:

> *The Lord has smitten us, he had a right to do so, and we deserve his corrections. I wish to submit to his sovereign will, nay, cordially to acquiesce therein, and to*

---

[4] Smith, George p197.

examine myself rigidly to see what in me has contributed to this evil.[5]

Carey's first sermon after the event was based upon Psalm 46:10[6] dividing his material under two headings – 1. God's right to dispose of us as he pleases, and 2. Man's duty, to acquiesce in his will.[7]

One happy discovery was made – the moulds for casting the type in the various founts were undamaged. A skilled type cutter had been employed for ten years preparing the moulds for the different languages. Their preservation now meant that new types could be cast at once and printing resumed quickly. Five of the presses had also escaped damage. New premises became available, larger than the last; pundits were set to work recommencing translations; and by the end of that year the printing programme was proceeding apace again. Tamil type was the first to be recast;[8] in six months all the oriental types were recast. When news of the fire eventually reached England a huge generosity of giving began not only among Baptist supporting churches but also from Anglican and other Christian groups. Andrew Fuller made herculean efforts in deputation throughout England and Scotland. In India also £800 was raised by interested friends. Within two months the whole amount of the financial loss was raised and Fuller had to exclaim to the committee, 'We must stop the contributions!' He wrote to India:

This fire has given your undertaking a celebrity, which nothing else, it seems, could; a celebrity which makes me tremble. The public is now giving us their praises … if we inhale this incense, will not God withhold his blessing, and then where are we? Ought we not to tremble? Surely all need more grace to go through good report

---

[5] Ibid. p198.
[6] *Be still and know that I am God; I will be exalted among the heathen, I will be exalted in the earth* (AV)
[7] Ousseren, A H p104.
[8] Some Bible portions were translated into Tamil.

> *than through evil ... we are all in danger ... if some new trials were to follow, I should not be surprised.*[9]

Soon Fuller was able to send pages of the reprinted Tamil New Testament to towns and churches which had given so generously. Eventually Carey and his colleagues were able to write that:

> *We found, on making the trial, that the advantages in going over the same ground a second time were so great that they fully counterbalanced the time requisite to be devoted thereto in a second translation.*[10]

Feeling that the Bengal government was becoming friendlier towards the work of the mission, Carey advised Fuller that more missionaries might well be able to join the work. The Governor (Lord Minto) had allowed John Chamberlain to locate in Agra. Young Jabez Carey was due to begin a work in the Moluccas, Felix Carey in Katwa, and then to Burma. But in England a storm was brewing. The charter of the East India Company was up for renewal in 1813 and, anticipating the importance of that, the Company in Bengal resolved to try to deal a fatal blow to the Serampore mission. America's first missionaries who attempted to join the work – the Judsons, the Newells, the Notts, Gordon Hall and Luther Rice, together with John Thompson of the London Missionary Society, were all refused permission to settle in Company areas. Thompson was ordered back to England but died of fever before he could go. The American missionaries were forced to go to Mauritius or, if they could not, to return to England. The Judsons and Luther Rice came to Serampore, as noted earlier. From England, travelling with the Americans, came Mr D Johns (a chemist and surgeon) with his wife, and John Lawson (an artist and engraver). On reaching Serampore they were ordered to be deported. The Johnses left immediately but John Lawson was permitted to stay and work

---

[9] Carey, S Pearce p314.
[10] Smith, George p200.

on the new Chinese type which was being prepared in Serampore. William Robinson, who had gone to Java and Sumatra, would likewise have been deported from thence if he had not been protected by Lieutenant Stamford Raffles there, who was a Christian friend of Serampore. Carey wrote home:

> *I mourn on my country's account, that preaching the Gospel should be regarded in the same light as committing a felony ... while Lord Minto is himself friendly and of liberal enlightenment, the Presidency secretaries are largely infidel and inimical and that they so shape the information and advice they lay before the authorities as almost to necessitate adverse decisions.*[11]

Dr Johns became very bitter, feeling that Serampore should have fought more vigorously for his retention in Bengal. He was a qualified surgeon who could have been of great benefit to India's people. He had raised considerable funds for the Society's work before coming to India. His bitterness was to be a cancer that infected future recruits to the work, as we shall presently see, and knowledge of this made Carey quite ill.

Yet there was comfort to be had. More than five hundred Indians had been baptised in the twelve years since the Serampore work began. The original Calcutta church was now one of eleven churches across Bengal. A hundred enquirers were known to be 'not far from the kingdom.' Translation of the Scriptures was proceeding in eighteen languages and printing in fifteen of them. Eight presses could hardly keep pace with the demand for New Testaments in different languages. Beyond India, the Judsons were settling in Burma. And perhaps greatest joy of all was that in mid 1812 Carey's youngest son Jabez was converted and, as mentioned earlier, was soon to be working with the mission outreach in the Moluccas, recently taken from the Dutch by the Indian Government.[12] Carey was convinced that despite the disaster of the fire and the difficulty of new missionaries

---
[11] Carey, S Pearce p319.
[12] Ibid. Information drawn from pp320-323.

being unable to join them, it was already too late to eradicate the gospel message from Bengal. His confidence was about to be strengthened still further by events in the British Parliament. The Company's charter was up for renewal and a great struggle was about to be fought – and won. William Wilberforce was the champion of the cause of amending the charter to include a duty to allow missionary work in their areas. Argument raged in Parliament for three days. There were insulting and caustic speeches made against the mission, answered repeatedly by Wilberforce calmly and powerfully. In June, by a majority of 53 votes, victory was achieved. On 1 July the debate was resumed and won, with a majority of twenty-two. In the Upper House Lord Wellesley, a former Governor in Calcutta, stood for the defence of missionary activity and won the day. So the struggle was over. Wilberforce's own comment says much:

> *This cause, of the recognition of our Christian obligation to British India, was the greatest I have lived for, not even excepting the emancipation of the slaves.*[13]

For Serampore there seemed to be a newly granted possibility of an officially accepted expansion of Gospel outreach in India. Little did they know that a still more serious quarrel was to threaten to tear the work apart, causing a breach of fellowship both at home and on the mission field.

---

[13] Ibid. p331.

32
The serious quarrel and other sorrows

As soon as the East India Company's charter had been amended, obliging the Company to allow missionary activity among the natives in their trading areas, a flow of new missionaries from the Society came to Bengal. Among the first were Carey's nephew Eustace (1814) and William Yates (1815), a member of Carey's last church in Leicester. Others soon followed: an engineer named Randall who could run the paper mill[1] and who was a convert of John Saffery, a supporter of the Society from Salisbury; James Penney, a trained teacher; and William Hopkins Pearce, an experienced printer from the Clarendon Press.[2] Prospects for the future of the work looked good. The new Governor-General, Earl Moira, had been to inspect the community and its work, being astonished to see translations taking place in twenty-two versions of Scripture. Equally surprised was Calcutta's first Anglican bishop, Dr Middleton, finding on his visit to the community so many pundits working there from many language areas of India.[3]

But in 1814, and again in 1815, sad news from England brought anxiety to Serampore. First, the death of John Sutcliff and the following year that of Andrew Fuller. Carey was losing his personal 'rope holders'. Whoever replaced them would be

---

[1] Smith, George pp182-183. Finding Indian paper unsuitable because of its lack of whiteness Carey was making paper of a better quality from 1820, using a steam engine to drive the process – something unique for India at that time. Paper was also being imported from England.
[2] Carey, S Pearce p332.
[3] Ibid. p332.

unknown to him and he unknown to them. The loss of the close fellowship between Carey and those first two founder members of the Society and the loss of their supreme commitment to its welfare was a heavy blow for him to bear. The Society committee had enlarged itself considerably but none of the new members knew Carey; only Dr John Ryland, now in his few remaining years with the Society, had any intimate knowledge of William. On brief visits to England (concerned with the quarrel yet to figure in the story) Ward and Marshman were the only members of the Serampore Three known to the new committee men.

Something like sixteen hundred people attended Sutcliff's funeral in Olney; he had been pastor to the church there for nearly forty years. His funeral sermon was preached by his close friend Andrew Fuller from the text that Sutcliff had requested – Jude:20-21.[4] Immediately after the funeral Fuller travelled to the north of England on a deputation visit for the Society despite not being in the best of health.[5] The next year he too died and Dr John Ryland was called upon to preach at his funeral. Crowds of mourners were present, people from all parts of the country representing different denominations, Anglicans and Dissenters alike.[6] A mere ten years were to pass before Ryland, too, would die. At the same time as these committed and loved friends in England were passing away, discontent was growing in the Serampore community among the newer missionaries.

Dr Johns' previous critical attitude towards the methods by which Carey, Marshman and Ward chose to live and work, and especially his displeasure at Joshua Marshman's tendency to blunt and plain speaking, seemed fully justified to the new men. They objected to the three senior men not granting them equality in the management of the work. And further unease arose with the arrival of William Pearce (a printer) who came with

---

[4] Haykin, Michael p339 *But ye, beloved, building up yourselves on your most holy faith, praying in the Holy Ghost, keep yourselves in the love of God, looking for the mercy of our Lord Jesus Christ unto eternal life* (AV).

[5] Carey, S Pearce p333. The doctor said Fuller was as completely worn out by intense application as anyone he knew in the last stages of consumption.

[6] Fuller, Thomas Ekins p310.

clear instructions from the new committee to work with Ward in the printing operation (which was, of course, the obvious place for the experienced printer to work). The Serampore Three were startled to realise that this was the first time the home committee had actually dictated where a new missionary was to serve. Such decisions had formerly always been made in Serampore as the normal expression of their self-support and self-governing policy of working.[7] News had reached Serampore of nasty rumours beginning to spread in England (source unknown) that the missionaries were in fact enriching themselves through their business activities and by owning so many properties. Carey responded indignantly:

> *Beloved Fuller, with one scowl of his brow, would have dissipated a thousand such insinuations! I have devoted my all to the cause, and so have my colleagues ... Were I to die today, I should not leave property enough for the purchase of a coffin, and my wife would be entirely unprovided for. We are coarsely clad and certainly not over fed ... I had Rs.6000 once, but now I have none.*[8]

The Society committee was also becoming anxious as to the legal ownership of the various properties which the Serampore community had accumulated. After Fuller's death the new committee members considered that new trust deeds should be created to ensure that the ownership of the properties belonged to the home Society and not merely to the Serampore mission. It was therefore proposed that a majority of the new trustees should be appointed from England, a proposal which further startled Serampore, who responded with a letter drawn up by a Serampore lawyer asserting that all the properties were held in trust on behalf of the Society, by Carey, Marshman and Ward, and such additional trustees as they should appoint. The Serampore community regarded themselves masters of the monies they had accumulated by their labours and directors of the way

---

[7] Stanley, Brian p59.
[8] Carey, S Pearce p336.

those funds were spent in their work, never regarding them as home Society funds. For example, the total amount of financial support that Carey received personally from the Society that sent him out to India was a mere £600, which has to be compared with more than £46,000 that he had spent on the mission's work in India, earned from his time as an indigo producer, by his salary as college professor and by his work as the Bengali translator for the government.[9] Marshman and Ward had also contributed equally generously to the mission's income from the profits from their schools and their printing work respectively. It had always been the intention that the work of the mission should be self-supporting. A clash of ideas was inevitable; an unhappy quarrel was developing between the Society committee and the Serampore community, not helped by the officious style of the letters from the new secretary, John Dyer. Fuller's letters had always been so full of brotherly love and spiritual concern. A distressed Carey wrote to John Ryland:

> *We are your brethren, to live and die with you, but not your servants. I beseech you therefore not to attempt to exercise a power over us to which we shall never submit ...my heart is exceedingly wounded at the Society's proposal of the eight British trustees and at several concomitant symptoms.*[10]

It made matters worse when a group of the new missionaries led by Eustace Carey felt that they must break away from the Serampore community and work separately. Yates, Lawson, Penny and Eustace, with the support of the home committee, began to work in Calcutta as a new missionary group. They withdrew from the Lall Bazaar church and founded another at Entally; they opened schools and intended to establish a press. Yates and Penny had been unhappy with the restricted communion situation at the Lall Bazaar church and Yates had felt it wrong for the new missionaries to be excluded from the man-

---
[9] Smith, George p313.
[10] Stanley, Brian p59 and Carey, S Pearce p338.

agement of the community. On the other hand, it was Carey's suspicion that this group had been sent by the new Society committee in order to make changes in the Serampore pattern of the work.[11] Small wonder that Carey fell ill and was attended by three doctors, one of whom expressed the view that their patient had been 'brought to the brink of the grave'.[12] Nor were the troubles of the community over yet.

William Adam arrived in Bengal as a missionary and joined himself with the separated Calcutta group. He became much attracted to the ideas of a prominent Hindu scholar, Rammohun Roy, who seemed very sympathetic with the Christian teaching against such Hindu practices as suttee, infanticide and idol worship. However, Roy could accept neither the doctrine of the Trinity nor the doctrines of Christ's person and his atonement for sin. Carey wrote to Ryland:

> Brother Adam now denies, or expresses doubts equal to a denial, of the proper deity of Christ. He is now engaged with Rammohun Roy in writing against the Trinity.[13]

Adam organised a Unitarian church in Calcutta and a printing press with which to oppose the publications coming out from Serampore. Joshua Marshman rushed into print to make a strong defence of orthodox belief on behalf of Serampore. Deeply saddened by Adam's departure from biblical truth, William Ward expressed the emotion felt by the community, exclaiming 'the heathen Rammohun Roy has converted a missionary!' It was beginning to look as though all the years of effort in the work and its increasing success were ending in confusion. There was a breach of fellowship between England and Bengal, a breach between missionary groups in Serampore and Calcutta, and now confusion concerning the heart of the gospel message itself. In 1815 the split between the Serampore community and the new missionaries was formalised by the establishment of 'The Calcutta Missionary Union' as distinct from the Serampore

---

[11] Stanley, Brian p60.
[12] Carey, S Pearce p334.
[13] George, Timothy p166.

mission and its outstations. The new missionaries invited Carey to join them but he declined to leave his colleagues Marshman and Ward. An uneasy agreement was reached to accept the existing situation between the two groups. But, significantly, Carey wrote home:

The whole might have been prevented by a little frank conversation with us; and a hundredth part of the self-denial which I found necessary to exercise in the first years of the mission would have prevented the rupture. But there is no doubt there is much on both sides to be forgiven.[14]

Not until 1827 was the breach with the home committee settled, by the committee announcing that henceforth the only missionary work they would support was that which was distinct and independent of the work of the Serampore mission. A new group was formed in England led by Christopher Anderson[15] to continue interest in the work in Serampore. He became the minister of Charlotte Chapel in Edinburgh and was a friend and colleague of Fuller, who had once recommended Christopher to be his successor as secretary – a recommendation that the committee rejected in favour of John Dyer, assistant secretary to the Society from 1817, confirmed as full-time and salaried from 1818. Dyer established an office in London, thus removing the Society from its original Northamptonshire roots.[16] The home committee and the Serampore mission were reunited in 1837 except for the Serampore college which functioned independently until 1855 when it, too, was taken back by the home committee.[17]

---

[14] Ousseren p114.
[15] (1782-1852) On conversion he had hoped to join Carey in Bengal, but ill health prevented that.
[16] John Ryland had previously indicated that 'he trembled for the ark of the mission, when it should be transported to London and fall into the hands of mere counting-house men'. Stanley, Brian p34.
[17] Stanley, Brian p.65

In 1830 Carey, reflecting on the situation, wrote:
Nothing has filled my last years with so much distress as the divisions in the mission brought about by the junior Mission and still maintained with implacable hostility.[18]

Clearly there had been wrong on both sides. But what was really separating the thinking of England and Serampore was an important difference of concept as to the fundamental nature of mission. The Serampore Three regarded the home Society as simply an agency to recruit and send out missionaries to the field. This was also the understanding of the Society itself until after the days of Fuller. After his death however the new committee took the view that the missionary was the servant and employee of the Society that had sent him out. This was not a petty difference, for it meant that the mission was no longer thought of as self-supporting and self-governing. Instead it was to be thought of as wholly financed and controlled from the sending country – a pattern of mission which in the twentieth century has had to be painfully unravelled by redesigning missionary work to become indigenous (a process which has sometimes had hostile consequences) as 'third world' developing countries gained their independence from their home colonial powers.

The agreement of 1827 ... marked the abandonment of Carey's policy concerning the financial support and control of missionary work, a policy, which, had it received the encouragement it deserved, might have resulted in a completely self-supporting Bengali church.[19]

There were three more sorrows to affect Carey and his colleagues in their personal lives during these troubled years. Young Felix Carey had been working in Burma for nearly seven years and had prepared a translation of Matthew's Gospel in Burmese and a manuscript for a dictionary of the Burmese and Pali languages. His preaching and helpfulness among the people had

---
[18] Ibid. p.65
[19] Davis, Walter Bruce p.93

earned him the respect of the king and high officials. The royal wish was that Felix should set up a mission station in the capital of Ava, together with the installation of a printing press. Serampore donated one of their presses and in 1814 Felix conveyed it across to Rangoon accompanied by his second wife, a son from his former marriage, and a new baby. From Rangoon a boat journey was involved on the Irrawaddy river and there tragedy struck the little family. A sudden storm caused the boat to capsize plunging the family and the printing press into the river. Felix supported his wife and baby until he sank with exhaustion. Coming to the surface again he could find neither his wife nor the baby; nor could he reach his son. He struggled to the riverbank only to realise that his new wife, two children, the press and a precious manuscript of Matthew's Gospel had all been lost – a loss which affected him so much that his behaviour became eccentric and unpredictable. The Burmese king, perhaps thinking it to be a form of therapy, sent him back to the familiar Calcutta as an ambassador. Felix resigned from the mission, causing Carey to write to Fuller that 'Felix is shrivelled from a missionary to an ambassador'.[20] In Calcutta's high society life Felix became addicted to drink and accumulated many debts which his father struggled to repay. Returning to Rangoon to report to the king, Felix learned that he was out of favour and fled to the border of Burma and Assam. He drifted about, a lost soul, until in 1818 William Ward came across him when visiting Burma and persuaded him to return to Serampore. The whole story meant an agony of distress for his father. Felix died in 1822 at the early age of thirty-seven. Until the day of his own death in 1834 Carey never lost his sense of grief over the collapse of Felix.[21]

In 1821 William's dearly loved second wife died. With her many talents and her academic abilities she had made the thirteen years of marriage to William the happiest years of his life. Carey was heartbroken. In 1823 he married Grace Hughes, who devotedly cared for him during the remaining years, nurs-

---
[20] Carey, S Pearce p.342
[21] George, Timothy p.168

ing him tenderly through his illnesses. In the same year a third blow fell: William Ward suddenly died, carried off in a few hours by a virulent cholera. After twenty-three years of close fellowship with Ward, this loss was a crushing blow for Carey and Marshman. William Ward's great work *A view of the History, Literature, and Mythology of the Hindoos, including a Minute Description of their Manners and Customs, and Translations from their Principal Works* was published in 1818 and remained the standard work on the subject for fifty years both in India and England.[22] Carey still had his professorships in Fort William College and in Serampore College; he still had manuscripts to revise and matters of social concern about which he must continue to fight with the Government; and there was his remarkable botanical garden. Marshman still had all his responsibilities for schools. He also spent fourteen years translating the Chinese *Works of Confucius,* producing a Chinese grammar and translating the Bible into Chinese.[23] The work must go on. As has been observed:

> *Missionaries whose minds were ... captivated by the sovereignty of God possessed an extraordinary ability to transform discouragements into renewed incentives to faithfulness ... This also helps to explain the remarkable modest self-evaluation displayed by Carey.*[24] *People who thus insisted on their ultimate insignificance in the light of the grandeur of the divine purpose possessed a unique capacity to withstand the immense pressures which were applied to the Indian mission in its early history.*[25]

---

[22] Davis, Walter Bruce p97.
[23] Smith, AC in *The British Particular Baptists* vol.2 Haykin, Michael AG (Ed.) p243.
[24] Such comments in his letters as: 'I have no love. O God, make me a true Christian! God can use weak instruments, but I often question whether it would be for his honour to work by such as me.' And the inscription insisted upon for his tomb was 'A wretched, poor and worthless worm, on Thy kind arms I fall.'
25 A comment by Stanley, Brian p38.

But before we come to the end of our story it is to Carey's botanical interest and his social reforms that we must turn.

33
Carey the botanist

There was a regular daily routine for the community at Serampore. Six o'clock was wake-up time and from then until breakfast at eight o'clock Carey tended his beloved garden and spent time in prayer and meditation; Ward (and later Felix also) would be in the printing office preparing for the coming day's tasks, while the Marshmans prepared material for their schools. Siesta followed an early light lunch and then work until the main meal was served at three o'clock. Evenings were occupied with street preaching and prayer times, as well as meetings with visitors and enquirers.[1] How Carey filled his days with translation work can be seen in his diary entry for Thursday 12 June 1806, written in Calcutta college, which he copied and sent to John Ryland:

> **5.45 – 7.0** Dressed. Read a chapter of the Hebrew Bible. Devotions.
> **7.0 – 10.0** Worship with family and servants in Bengali. Read Persian with munshi. Revised proof in Hindustani. Breakfast. Translated a portion of Ramayana from Sanskrit into English with help of pundit.
> **10 – 1.30** Government College classes.[2] Dinner.
> **2.0 – 6.0** Revised proof of chapter in Jeremiah. Translated most of Matthew 8 into Sanskrit with help of pundit.
> **6.0 – 7.0** Tea. Read Telegu with pundit. Son of Revd Timothy Thomas of London called.
> **7.0 – 9.0** Prepared and preached English sermon; about 40 present.

---

[1] George, Timothy p123.
[2] This was for three days each week, involving a journey by river-boat to Calcutta from Serampore.

9.0 – 11.0 *Translated Ezekiel 11 into Bengali. Have cast aside my first edition translation. Letter to John Ryland. Read a Greek Testament chapter. Commended self to God. I have never more time in a day than this.*[3]

Small wonder that his Sanskrit pundit is reported to have exclaimed one day, 'What kind of a body has Carey Sahib? He never seems hungry or tired and never leaves a thing until it is finished!'

There was one relaxation and recreation which Carey permitted himself – the pleasure of his gardens. He planted a garden wherever his life experiences took him. Yet his great stature as a Baptist missionary has overshadowed his considerable contributions to science.

> ... *no serious research has been undertaken till now on Carey as a naturalist. Recently, however, Chatterjee (1989) and Ghosh (1991) have published their detailed studies on Carey's contribution to the development of Indian science and technology.*[4]

Back in the days of his childhood he would not allow any part of his father's garden to be uncultivated, such was his love of flowers. Every walk in the countryside involved a study of the flowers, the insects and the birds. Talks with his uncle Peter fired his youthful interest in gardening still further. When he became a Christian believer this love of nature was strengthened by a greater motive than just his personal curiosity, for botanical studies became studies in the creative workmanship[5] of his heavenly Father. How could he not be absorbed in the study of nature, being a child of that Father? 'Carey's deep and dogged

---

[3] Several biographers include this schedule in their accounts. This extract from Carey, S Pearce p259.
[4] Michael, George in Daniel, JKT and Hedlund, RE (Eds.) p264.
[5] See Romans 1:20 (NIV) 'what has been made' (Greek *poiema*). Compare Ephesians 2:10 (NIV) 'God's handiwork' (*poiema*). These are the only two uses of the word in the Greek NT. Both the natural creation and the new creation are works of God.

interest in natural sciences ... was rooted in his understanding that this world was his Father's creation.'[6] A few weeks after reaching India Carey was writing home asking:

> ... that they send him certain publications: a polyglot Bible, the Gospels in Malay, Curtis' Botanical Magazine and Sowerby's English Botany.[7]

Soon after arriving in Calcutta Carey heard of a vacancy in the management of the East India Company's botanical garden at Sibpore near Calcutta because of the death of its founder and superintendent Colonel Kyd. Hurrying to make application for the post Carey found, as we saw earlier, that another person, Dr Roxburgh from Madras, had already received the posting. Had Carey succeeded in his application that would have legitimised his presence in Calcutta. The loss of the opportunity did not cause enmity to arise between the two men, however, but instead a strong friendship grew up between them leading to their continually sharing each other's finds and successes in the world of plants, flowers and trees.

Eventually, hearing of a scheme whereby a plot of land in the Sundarbands area could be granted rent free for three years to anyone who would clear it and set up a small holding, Carey applied and was granted a plot on the banks of the river Jabuna, in the Debhatta district some forty miles South East of Calcutta. It was not long until, felling unwanted timber to sell in order to pay for the help of labourers, he was clearing an area of the jungle of all but useful trees such as mango, coconut and tamarind. Soon he began to:

> ... earth-fence a garden, in whose bank he set the quick growing plantains for protection and for fruit and to sow in the garden lentils, mustard, onions and peas. 'I never felt myself more happy' he wrote.[8]

---

[6] Mangalawadi, Vishal in Daniel, JTK and Hedlund, RE (Eds.) p310.
[7] George, Timothy p90.
[8] Carey, S Pearce p153.

With these supplies of fruit and vegetables, plenty of fish from the river, local game and cheap rice, for the first time in India the family began to have a good and varied diet. Within a year however, as we have seen, came the move to Malda and the indigo factory in Mudnabatti, two hundred miles or more north of Calcutta. Once again Carey converted part of the indigo plantation into a garden. Writing home he asked:

> ... for instruments of husbandry, and a yearly assortment of all garden and flowering seeds, and also of fruit, field and forest trees, for the lasting advantage of what I now call my own country.[9] ... He raised flowering fruit and forest trees ...he sent fruits and pressed plants, many of which were rare or single trees of that locality, to Dr Roxburgh for identification and nomenclature. In return he received from Dr Roxburgh many pressed plants for inclusion in his herbarium which he developed in Mudnabatti ... from there he visited Bhutan twice where he discovered twenty-four new plants.[10]

One of those plants was a rare variety which Dr Roxburgh named 'Careya Saulea' in honour of Carey, who later renamed the tree 'Shorea Robuste', not wishing to claim the fame of finding it. Three medicinal herbs which William did identify were 'Careya Harbacea', 'Careya Arborea' and 'Careya Sphoerica'.[11]

In Serampore Carey developed a garden in a five-acre plot which was to become his greatest achievement in gardening. Within six months of being there he was able to write to Dr Roxburgh listing 427 species of plants growing in his garden.[12] The garden was surrounded by trees and had a tree lined avenue across its centre where Carey loved to walk and pray in the early morning hours. Writing to friends in England, in America, and to his sons in Burma and Amboyna (the Dutch East Indies)

---
[9] Ibid. p395.
[10] Das, AR in Daniel, JTK and Hedlund, RE (Eds.) p279.
[11] Palit, Chittabratta Ibid. p286.
[12] Carey, S Pearce p396.

he was constantly pleading for trees, bulbs and seeds, giving detailed instructions as to how they were best to be packaged. In June 1830, just four years before his death and despite his increasing ill-health, he was still writing to an overseas friend:

> *Should, you at anytime, be able to send some seeds, bulbs, or large fleshy roots, packed in, or rather mixed with peat earth, about twice or thrice as much earth as seeds, you would greatly oblige me. I am particularly desirous to get seeds of Geranium, Erodiums, Pelagonium, Solidago, Helianthus, Bush Laburnam and other Syringanacious plants as we are rather poor in plants of that kind.*
> *Believe me, My Dear Sir, W. Carey.*[13]

Carey's studies during all these gardening years enabled him eventually to draw up a syllabus and prepare teaching materials for use in the Serampore College where he lectured on natural history.

> *As a prudent successful botanist Carey's contributions were appreciated not only in India ... but his worth was acknowledged by ... important foreign institutions by electing him as their member. Much has been written about Carey, towards his achievements in various fields, but his contribution to Indian botany has not yet been properly evaluated.*[14]

Carey was often in correspondence, for example, with the Royal Botanic Gardens, Kew, the Liverpool Botanic Gardens and the Regius Professor of Botany at Glasgow University. Typical of his concern that Indian plants should be known in Lon-

---

13 Photocopy of a letter from the archives of the Royal Botanic Gardens, Kew. The more common names of the plants mentioned are, respectively, Geranium, Rock garden plants, Pelagonium, Golden Rod, Sunflower, a kind of Laburnum and Lilacs.
14 Das, AR in Daniel, JKT and Hedlund, RE (Eds.) p283. (R A Dass is a former librarian of the Botanical Survey of India, Sibpore Botanical Garden).

don is Carey's letter of February 1831 in which he wrote (with a certain bluntness that reflects his own perfectionist character):

> *My Dear Sir, By the Princess Charlotte, Captain Mc Kean, I have the pleasure of sending you a bundle of specimens of plants. I have but small hope of there being much in the parcel which is new to you, but I persevere in sending, because there may probably be something among these which I send which you have not seen before. I am convinced that my people are great bunglers in preparing them, still, however they are among the best to be found among the natives of this country but indolence and a stupid inattention to the productions of nature are the prevailing traits of their character ... We have lately received a few [plants] from the West Coast of America and S. America which, in general, succeed well with us ... Accept the Assurance, My Dear Sir, that I am,*
>
> *Yours very sincerely, W. Carey.*[15]

It is evident that Carey's botanical knowledge was such that it earned respect among some of the top botanical scientists in England. This becomes evident in his correspondence with them when he feels able to challenge the accuracy of one of their published findings, as for example the following extract from a letter to *The Botanical Magazine:*

> *Serampore Dec.10th 1829*
>
> *My dear Sirs,*
> *Have you not, my dear Sir, committed an error in the xxx No. of the Botanical Magazine in publishing the foliage of Annona squamosa instead of that of A. reticulata. That represented [on] fol.2911 is undoubtedly the foliage of A. squamosa. The name Annona was undoubtedly formed from nona, the Indian name of the*

---

[15] Photocopy of a letter from the archives of the Royal Botanic Gardens, Kew.

> fruit. The An was prefixed by some Botanist who was ignorant of the oriental language.[16]

Carey's boyhood interest in birds now blossomed in that he was able to build large aviaries near his Serampore house and collect many different kinds of birds. He had trees growing in the aviaries to provide natural surroundings for the captive birds. In 1811 he wrote to Fuller:

> I have for a long time been describing the birds of Asia, and have completed about half of them that are known. I shall, perhaps, publish a series of papers in Asiatic Researches.[17] I have but little time for such pursuits, though a strong natural inclination ... the work proceeds very slowly.[18]

But he was not content with his own personal pleasure in these things; he could see great benefit for India if its agriculture and horticulture could be lifted out of 'the abject and degraded state' in which he saw it. He felt that there should be some Society which could conduct research and experiments in order to improve the state of India's crops and animal husbandry. By 1820, with the encouragement of Lady Hastings (the Governor's wife), the Agri-Horticultural Society was formed with Carey as its initial secretary until Indian members took the responsibility of running the Society's affairs, which was always his aim. An area of land was leased by the Government and given to the Society for its use in experimental research. William defended his involvement in such mundane activities with the comment:

---

[16] Photocopy of a letter from the archives of the Royal Botanic Gardens, Kew.
[17] A publication of the Bengal Asiatic Society which was founded in 1784 to encourage the study of Oriental languages, arts and crafts. This Society helped to finance Carey's translations of Sanskrit literature, such as the Ramayana.
[18] Carey, S Pearce p411.

Few who are extensively acquainted with human life, will esteem these cares either unworthy of religion or incongruous with its highest enjoyments.[19]

Similar Societies were formed in other parts of India, leading to the slow but successful improvement of agriculture generally. By now William Carey's missionary and botanical achievements were being widely recognised and the Brown University in America awarded him the diploma of Doctor of Divinity. He was also elected a corresponding member of the Horticultural Society of London, member of the Geological Society and a Fellow of the Linnaen Society.[20] However the year 1823 was not so much marked out by these honours as by disasters. In the October of the year, returning to Serampore from Calcutta, Carey slipped in the dark and fell on the landing stage severely damaging his thigh. It was the February of the next year before he could begin to limp about. His third wife Grace Hughes, whom he had married shortly before the accident, nursed him tenderly throughout the experience. While he was so incapacitated immense floods from the great Ganges river and the river Hooghli inundated the whole countryside around Carey's estate to the depth of several feet of water, severely damaging Carey's house and virtually destroying his beloved garden. Yet despite being ill with fever consequent upon his accident, Carey set to work at once overseeing the work of coolie labourers and ordering fresh seeds and plants to replace what had been lost. Once the floods had subsided his garden slowly returned to the beautiful state in which it had formerly been kept.[21] Sadly in 1831, just three years before he died, Carey's garden was once again totally destroyed by a tremendous cyclone and tidal wave which caused the Hooghli river to burst its banks and flood the land, bringing down the great trees which once protected the

---

[19] Smith, George p232.
[20] Carl Von Linnaeus (1707-1778), a Swedish naturalist, was the founder of a botanical system of classification of plants, dividing all plants into 24 classes, based on the number or arrangement of their stamens. The English Natural History Society was founded in his honour (1788).
[21] Carey, S Pearce p377.

garden. The garden had gone forever, never being planted out again.[22]

After his death the Bengal Asiatic Society expressed their appreciation of Carey's achievements in their Journal, calling him 'a long time member and an ornament to their institution':

> ... distinguished alike for his high attainments in the Oriental languages ... in opening the stores of Indian literature ... for his extensive acquaintance with the sciences ... and his useful contributions on every hand towards the promotion of the objects of the Society ... placing on record their high sense of his value and merits as a scholar and a man of science.[23]

In similar manner the Agri-Horticultural Society honoured Carey its founder by resolving in 1842 to place a marble bust to his memory in the Society's hall, which was done three years later. The motion to do so described:

> ... the late Revd. Carey as one who unceasingly applied his great talents, abilities, and influence in advancing the happiness of India ... by the spread of an improved system of husbandry and gardening.[24]

But, without belittling in the slightest the heights to which our self-taught shoemaker climbed, we would surely not be wrong to suggest that Carey would have preferred to be known not merely for 'advancing the happiness of India' but more for the blessedness of India in its submission to the Christ who made Carey what he had become. This is not to suggest that Carey was in anyway wrong in what he did: he did it because of his right biblical conviction that the Christian message is for the good of the body as well as the soul, as the example of his Master who went about doing good surely makes so clear. And the gratitude expressed by that marble bust certainly demonstrates

---

[22] Das, AR in Daniel, JKT and Hedlund, RE (Eds.) p282.
[23] Smith, George pp.239-40.
[24] Ibid. p239.

that Carey is to be commended for 'having a good reputation with outsiders'.[25] Carey's influence in the matter of doing good also has to include his influence in the area of social reform which must also be considered.

---
[25] 1 Timothy 3:7

34
Carey the social reformer

In the providence of God, William Carey and his friends (in India and England) began a movement which expressed evangelical views of social concern precisely in the period when India was taking a crucial turn in its development as a nation. The battle of Plassey (1757) produced a new direction to India's history, for it gave to the East India Company – and later to the British Government – a controlling influence in the development of the country. And although the Company steadfastly resisted accepting responsibility for improving the conditions of the natives with whom they traded:

> *Carey was to give impetus and direction to the newly initiated modernization process, amidst the shades of resistance on the part of alien people and the apathy of the British East India Company's government.*[1]

The extent of the social changes initiated by the Christian teaching emanating from the Serampore mission can best be judged by a comparison with India of the pre-British time graphically described by the Indian historian Nemai Sadhan Bose:

> *The decay of knowledge and learning coupled with social degeneration helped the extensive spread of blind superstition and inhuman social customs. Polygamy, early marriage, sati rites, killing female children, throwing the first child into the holy rivers were some of the*

---
[1] Massey, Ashish Kumar in Daniel, JKT and Hedlund, RE (Eds.) p300.

most dreadful and inhuman practices performed in different parts of the country in varying degrees.[2]

Carey's understanding of the truth that human beings are made in the image of God and that therefore all human life is precious inevitably set him on a collision course with the ugly face that Hinduism was presenting in his day. And the hardships of their first six years in Bengal gave to the Carey family a bitter taste of the struggles with poverty, disease and the crippling influence of the caste system that was the plight of so many of India's outcaste people (known today as Dalits).

Some people have been critical of Carey's social reforms, arguing that they were an underhand way of enticing people to accept Christianity. For example in 1965 one Indian writer, Muhammad Mohar Ali, suggested that the motive for social reform was that:

Carey was convinced that the introduction of learning would lead to the dissolution of many popular notions of Hinduism thus paving the way for the dissemination of the truths of Christianity.[3]

While it is true that Carey had realised such a result could follow the acceptance of the Bible truths that he taught, this was not his motive for teaching them. He was driven by the conviction that Christ, his Lord and Master, would condemn the inhuman practices of Hinduism and would have great compassion for the multitudes of outcaste people who accepted those practices for the sake of their supposed salvation from the miseries of this life into a better reincarnation. Such Hindu teaching was oppressive and erroneous. Carey taught that the gospel was a means of liberation from the oppressive ignorance of such Brahmin doctrines into the knowledge and freedom of

---

[2] Ibid. p299. Quoted by Massey, Ashish Kumar.
[3] Quoted by Rajkumar, Evangeline in Daniel, JKT and Hedlund, RE (Eds.) p323.

God's truth.

It was while working as an indigo planter at Malda (1794) that William was one day shocked to find a baby's skeleton in a basket hanging from a tree, its flesh having been devoured by white ants. At a great religious festival or Mela, held where the Hooghli river enters the ocean, he was deeply concerned to see babies being thrown into the water to drown, or to be eaten by crocodiles. The mother, he learned, would have vowed to sacrifice her baby in the river as an offering to the gods: 'the fruit of her body for the sins of her soul'. Carey had seen instances where a sick baby, thought to be affected by an evil spirit, was left exposed to the elements for several days either to die, or unusually, to recover. When he was made a language teacher in the Fort William College (1801) Carey was emboldened to protest to the then Governor Lord Wellesley against the practice of infanticide. Requested to make a survey of such instances, Carey was ready to oblige, and on receiving the result of his survey the Governor ordered the banning of such infanticide. A few years later at the same Mela (1804) Carey was delighted to observe that no babies were sacrificed.[4]

Another of the sights which horrified Carey was that of sati (sometimes spelt suttee), the burning alive of a widow on her husband's funeral pyre. In a letter to John Ryland he wrote a dramatic account of his first coming across this practice.

> *1st April 1799. As I was returning from Calcutta I saw a woman burning herself with the corpse of her husband, for the first time in my life ... we saw a number of people gathered on the riverside. I asked them what they were met for, and they told me 'to burn the body of a dead man'. I inquired if his wife would die with him; they replied 'Yes' and pointed to the woman ... I asked them if this was the woman's choice ... they answered that it was perfectly voluntary ... they told me it was a great act of holiness, and added in a very surly manner, that if I did not like to see it I might go further off ... she, in the*

---

[4] Mangalawadi, Ruth in Daniel, JKT and Hedlund, RE (Eds.) p338.

most calm manner, mounted the pile and danced on it ... she lay down by the corpse, and put one arm under its neck and the other over it, when a quantity of dried cocoa leaves and other substances were heaped over them ... two bamboos were put over them and held fast down, and fire put to the pile, which immediately blazed very fiercely ... we could not bear to see more, but left them exclaiming loudly against the murder, and full of horror at what we had seen.[5]

William was heartbroken at what he had seen and at his failure to prevent it despite having 'exclaimed with all my might at what they were doing'. He would not rest from then on until he had succeeded in having the practice banished. In some parts of India it was already forbidden but not in the East India Company areas.[6] Carey began to make a survey, again at the request of Governor Wellesley, to discover how frequently 'sati' occurred and was shocked to find it happening more commonly than generally thought. There had been a total of 438 cases in the area around Calcutta in one year.[7] With the help of one of his pundits he also discovered in 1816 that there was no obligation in any of the Hindu holy books for sati to be performed, merely an acknowledgement that the practice did exist. Many debates about the matter took place in the British Parliament and in India (William Ward was visiting England on deputation at the time). Nevertheless not until December 1829 that the Governor Lord Bentinck ordered the abolishment of the rite.[8] As official government translator, Carey received the news on Sunday evening 6 December. Cancelling his preaching engagement, he sat down at once and while another person preached on his behalf that evening Carey completed the translation of Regulation XXVII of the Bengal Code 1829. There must be no delay!

---

[5] Extract from Rajkumar, Evangeline in Daniel, JKT and Hedlund, RE (Eds.) pp326-7.
[6] Beck, James R p170.
[7] Mangalawadi, Ruth in Daniel, JKT and Hedlund, RE (Eds.) p340.
[8] Rajkumar, Evangeline in Daniel, JKT and Hedlund, RE (Eds.) p328.

> *The practice of suttee, or the burning or burying alive [9] of widows of Hindus, is hereby illegal, and punishable by the criminal courts.*

There could possibly be arguments for sati arising from the miserable conditions under which a widow was forced to live – head shaven, wearing white, jewellery forbidden, under 'house arrest', socially shunned, no dowry available for a second marriage. Under such conditions self-immolation might seem preferable. One Indian writer, Narasimhan Singh, describes the thinking of the time as:

> *All actions of a woman should be the same as that of her husband. If her husband is happy, she should be happy; if he is sad, she should be sad; and if he is dead, she should also die.*[10]

But it was surely impossible that Carey could condone such thinking, believing as he did that all human life was precious because it was God-given. The emancipation of Indian women from these social restraints was a great reform for which Carey fought tirelessly.

The lack of education for Indian girls was also a cause of offence to Carey's Christian thinking, denying as it did equal rights for women as for men. Child marriages, for example, inevitably meant no opportunity for schooling even if there had been schools for girls to go to. The girl could become a child widow or possibly even a mother before ever being a mature person.

> *The last census of the 19th century in Bengal revealed that there were 10,000 widows under the age of four and over 50,000 between the ages of five and nine around Calcutta.*[11]

---

[9] There was one caste which buried rather than burned their dead and so the widow was buried alive with the corpse of her husband. Smith. George p54.
[10] Quoted by Mangalawadi, Ruth ibid. p339.
[11] Ibid. p341.

The concern of Carey and the Marshmans to establish schools for girls was in fact a determined attack upon this female 'slavery'. Polygamy was another practice which reduced women to chattels since it was an honour to give female children to a Brahmin as his wives. Encouraging female education was Carey's way to fight these abuses. From 1820-1830 Serampore took the lead in bringing modern education to the village women of Bengal, which in turn led to schools for girls commencing in Benares, Dacca, and Allahabad as the work of the mission spread.[12]

At Katwa in 1812 William Carey watched the burning of a leper in a pit and discovered that this was not an uncommon practice.

> *Taught that a violent end purifies the body and ensures transmigration into a healthy new existence, while natural death by disease results in four successive births and a fifth as a leper again, the leper, like the even more wretched widow, has always courted suicide.*[13]

We know that before he died Carey took an active part in attempting to found a leper hospital in Calcutta, though some of his biographers maintain that there is no firm evidence that the attempt came to fruition.

It is clear from all this that the same Carey who, while he worked as a journeyman shoemaker denied himself and his family the pleasure of using sugar because it was the product of slavery in the West Indies, was concerned to the end of his days with all social injustices and was resolved that the power of the gospel must provide the remedy. Even when confronted by the long established and powerful culture of the Hinduism of his day he was not deterred from opposing it as ungodly, unjust and inhuman. We give the last word on this matter to J B Middlebrook, writing in 1961:

---

[12] Ibid. p342.
[13] Smith, George p214.

> *Carey had a vision of the gospel as the new humanity created in Christ, the new Adam, and visualised it as a human community transcending religious, cultural, class, caste and sexist barriers ... he saw the church's mission as that of providing the ferment of the gospel for the humanist transformation of India's traditional society and culture so that through Christ's renewing power the chain of caste and other exploitative structures might be broken. Therefore he asked, 'Would not the spread of the Gospel be the most effectual means of their civilisation?'*[14]

Significantly, the original statute of the Serampore College expressed something of this Christian liberality by declaring 'No caste, colour or country shall bar any man from admission to Serampore College.'

And now our tale is nearly told; only the few closing years of a remarkable life remain.

---

[14] Quoted by M M Thomas in Daniel, JKT and Hedlund, RE (Eds.) p348.

35
Epilogue

The years from 1821 to the end of Carey's life were hard, busy years. There was the construction of the splendid building to house the Serampore College (nearly forty students had already been registered to begin studies there); there was the death of Carey's second wife, the much loved Charlotte; then the marriage to Grace Hughes who 'was the best nurse a man of sixty-two could have had for his remaining years'.[1] William Ward had been on deputation to England and had now plunged back again into the work of the busy print shop until in March 1823 he was suddenly struck down by a severe bout of cholera which sadly ended his life; while later that same year Carey himself was incapacitated by his serious accident, and a severe flood damaged his house and destroyed his garden as we have already noted (Chapter thirty-three).

There was also the worry of financial embarrassment for the community since the considerable translation and printing work was proving more costly than had been estimated. There were ten outstations requiring financial support, plus the financing of the college building and the essential repairs needed for Carey's damaged house and ruined garden. On his deputation time in England Ward had learned that, apart from the support of Christopher Anderson and his friends as already mentioned (Chapter thirty-two) the Society was in no mood to offer financial support for the Serampore College and on his return to Bengal Ward made it clear that he was left in no doubt that Carey, Marshman and he must finance the college project themselves, which they did at an expense of £15,000. Eventually a grant from the Bible Society of England for the translation work enabled Carey

---
[1] Marshman, John Clark p266.

and Marshman to clear the community's overdraft at the bank. The Bengal government, by appointing Carey as their official translator in the Bengali language, provided further financial resources, and the home committee also made a special grant of £1000 available for the repair of Carey's flood-damaged house, indicating that this could become an annual grant. However, on his return to England because of ill health, Eustace Carey (the leader of the breakaway group from the Serampore community) influenced the home committee once more to adopt an unfriendly attitude towards the Serampore Three. It was at this point that Carey seriously considered abandoning Serampore and living privately nearer to Calcutta. His colleagues Joshua Marshman and John Mack with difficulty persuaded him to relinquish such an idea.

Marshman later proceeded to England on a deputation visit and in 1826 succeeded in negotiating a happier financial arrangement with the home committee. One tenth of all monies received by them would be made available to Serampore for the support of the outstations and it was agreed that the Serampore College could raise its own separate support fund with the committee's agreement. Marshman expressed his pleasure in a letter to Carey, though in the event that pleasure proved to be premature.

> *All is settled between the Society and us on the most solid and equitable basis. I am convinced that, with reference to the troubles with which Serampore has been exercised these last years, 'the days of her mourning are ended'.*[2]

From this point Marshman travelled to Denmark and negotiated for a royal charter for the College (granted in 1827) permitting the College to issue its own degrees to successful students. On his return to England from Denmark Marshman was bitterly disappointed to find that in his absence a fresh series of criticisms of the Serampore College had arisen there and were

---

[2] Marshman, John Clark p287.

circulating through denominational magazines. There were scandalous charges against him personally, possibly designed to prevent him from receiving funds for the College. As Eustace Carey and the separated missionaries had suggested, the nature of the College syllabus was the problem. The Society committee came to the view that such a College offering secular as well as Christian instruction to all, regardless of their faith, was not a fit object for missionary support. The committee did not share Carey's objective that future Christian leaders should be educated widely in order to withstand the errors of Hinduism and atheism alike. Marshman felt that no reply of his would be considered calmly while such a storm of criticism lasted. Deeply troubled and on the verge of exhaustion, he left England suddenly and returned to India (1829) where his friends remarked that he looked 'fifteen years older'.[3]

As that year closed two further blows struck the troubled Serampore community. Funds for the mission's work and for the College were lost as the result of the sudden failure of five Calcutta banks, and Carey's salary as the official translator to the Bengal Government was reduced – a measure forced by the lack of Government money due to the heavy cost of a Burmese war which was currently being fought.[4] The missionaries met to plead with God and a newly arrived missionary recruit recorded:

> *The two old men were dissolved in tears while they engaged in prayer and Dr Marshman, in particular, could not give expression to his feelings. It was, indeed, affecting to see these good men – the fathers of the mission – entreating with tears that God would not forsake them, now gray hairs were come upon them, but that He would silence the tongue of calumny, and furnish them with the means of carrying on His own work.*[5]

Appeals to friends in England and America resulted in gen-

---

[3] Ibid. p301.
[4] Smith, George pp296-7.
[5] Marshman, John Clark p305.

erous donations being given and eventually Serampore was rescued from insolvency. However, the growing attraction for education using the English medium meant that in succeeding years the College, using only the teaching mediums of Bengali and Sanskrit languages which were suitable for the training of men expected to work in the vernacular among lowly village congregations, became unpopular among students. The arrival in Calcutta of Alexander Duff in 1830 and his subsequent opening of a school and a college with English as a teaching medium hastened the decline of the Serampore College. The royal charter issued by the king of Denmark became virtually defunct. The home committee had to struggle with what to do with the College: lack of student support for vernacular theological training meant that Carey's vision was getting lost. After Carey's death the committee resolved to abandon the present College and establish instead a vernacular Christian Training Institution. Not until 1910/11 was the College reconstituted and furnished with finance to open Arts and Theological departments linked with Calcutta University, and the conferring of degrees began again in 1915.[6]

By the year of Carey's death Serampore was financing eighteen missionary outstations around Calcutta and extending out to Delhi, managed by fifty workers, of whom a quarter were Indo-European and a half were pure Indian. A nineteenth station was opened in Agra led by Marshman's son-in-law. Together with this expansion of outreach was the tremendous output of translations of the Bible.[7] Both of these endeavours were remarkable achievements from Carey's thirty-four years of labour and that of his colleagues Marshman and Ward.[8] Yet the three men sought no praise for themselves. Writing a few months before he died to Christopher Anderson, the secretary of the continuing Serampore work, Carey expressed some typical sentiments that we can recognise as his constant theme:

---

[6] Material drawn from Stanley, Brian pp156-162.
[7] Now whole Bibles in six languages; New Testaments & partial Old Testaments in five languages; New Testaments in 19 languages; five translations of one or more Gospels in further languages. Carey, S Pearce p424.
[8] Ibid. p433.

> *As everything connected with the divine promises depends on the almighty power of God, pray that I and all the ministers of the Word may take hold of His strength and go about our work as fully expecting the accomplishment of them all, which, however difficult and improbable it may appear, is certain, as all the promises of God are in him, Yea and Amen.*[9]

The ageing warrior was weakening physically. The last three years of his life were marked by several attacks of enervating fever and at least once it was feared that he had suffered a minor stroke. In mid-1833 he wrote to his two sisters in England:

> *About a week ago a great change took place in me that I concluded it was the immediate stroke of death and all my children were informed of it and have been here to see me. I have since revived in an almost miraculous manner, or I could not have written this. But I cannot expect it to continue. The will of the Lord be done. Adieu, until I meet you in a better world.*[10]

Later that same year Carey again spoke of a sense of extreme fatigue and exhaustion. He could hardly walk and often had to be carried in a wheelchair or left to rest on a couch outside his room. He had many visitors in these last months, including the Governor's wife, the Bishop of Calcutta and the now renowned Alexander Duff. Encouraging news came to Carey of generous support for the work from friends in England. Such was his contentment of spirit that he could say 'I have hardly a wish ungratified'.[11] Dr Marshman was a regular visitor, often coming two or three times a day. Finally, with his three sons William, Jabez and Jonathan at his side, early on the morning of 9 June 1834, Carey's weariness was suddenly gone: he was with his Lord. The next day the streets of Serampore were crowded with onlookers as his coffin was carried to the

---

[9] Smith, George p308.
[10] Ibid. p307.
[11] Carey, S Pearce p437.

cemetery. Instructing in his will that he should be buried by the side of his second wife Charlotte, Carey requested that his name and two lines of one of Isaac Watt's hymns, and nothing more, be added to her memorial stone:

> WILLIAM CAREY, BORN 17th AUGUST, 1761;
> DIED 9th JUNE 1834
> *A wretched, poor and helpless worm*
> *On Thy kind arms I fall.*[12]

The last of the Serampore Three, Dr Marshman, was now approaching his seventieth birthday and became troubled with depression and bodily weakness. In December 1837 he too died:

> ... *like his colleagues, in graceful poverty, after having, in conjunction with Mrs Marshman, devoted a sum a little short of £40,000 to the mission.*[13]

The death of his widow followed in 1847.

And so the remarkable Serampore Three had 'fought the fight and finished the race'. Remarkable, because of their ability always to work consistently together in a spiritual harmony that was outstanding; remarkable, too, for the harmonious use of the distinctive gifts each one possessed. Carey was the mission strategist, translator and preacher; Ward, the diligent and ceaseless worker in the print and binding shop, friend of Carey's boys, preacher and sensitively respectful of all that was good in the Indian culture; Marshman, the enthusiastic preacher and apologist for the Faith and educational organiser of the young; Hannah Marshman, the tireless 'mother' of the community. God's wise providence had assembled a powerful force to begin the great task of shining a light into India's darkness such as would challenge the worldwide church to awake to its duty of making Christ known everywhere. A fascinating glimpse of

---
[12] Smith, George p311.
[13] Marshman, John Clark p327.

how each of the Three evaluated their own gifts correctly and never sought to possess another's is in a letter written by Carey to Andrew Fuller, August 1804:

> *A want of character and firmness has always predominated in me. I have not resolution enough to reprove sin, to introduce serious and evangelistic conversation in carnal company, especially among the great to whom I sometimes have access. I sometimes labour with myself long, and at last cannot prevail sufficiently to break silence; or, if I introduce a subject, want resolution to keep it up, if the company do not show a readiness thereto.*[14]

The gift that Carey thought he did not have belonged to Dr Marshman who seemed constantly to be watching for opportunities to speak of Christ to unbelievers. Carey's expertise was in languages and the translation of God's Word. Dr Marshman did translate the Scriptures into Chinese but only after many years of effort and possibly with less than the best results. And Ward with his friendly, sympathetic and sensitive nature, gave the growing boys in the mission community what busy community life could not give. But as a team, each with complementary gifts, they had remarkable success together.

At this point the original Serampore Three were succeeded by three 'Johns' who were all regarded in the community with pleasure and confidence. John Mack, from Edinburgh University, Bristol Baptist College and Guy's Hospital; John Leechman from Glasgow University; and John Clark Marshman, (Joshua Marshman's son) who was much loved and respected in Serampore. All were 'animated with one spirit and their energies concentrated on one object'.[15] William Robinson, formerly missionary in Java and Sumatra, who in the time of the great quarrel had stoutly defended the original Three, now came to Serampore to join forces with the new three, taking up the pastorate of

---

[14] Beck, James R p133. Carey asked that this letter should not be made public till after his death.
[15] Carey S Pearce p431.

the Lall Bazar chapel. And here we leave the story of Carey and the early years of the Particular Baptist Society. Certain changes had already occurred, and more now were taking place among Baptists in England. After the death of Fuller and the establishment of the mission headquarters in London under John Dyer (Chapter thirty-two) the founding Society had become:

> ... cut free from the apron-strings of the Northamptonshire Association which had nursed it, and was now established at the heart of evangelical philanthropy and respectable society.[16]

In the years that followed different theological movements were taking place among Baptist churches in England. From the General (Arminian) Baptist churches sprang the New Connection Baptist churches led by Dan Taylor energised by the effect upon them of the Great Evangelical Awakening of the late 18th century and early 19th century. From these New Connection churches, inspired by the work of the Serampore Three, emerged the New Connection General Baptist Missionary Society (1816) whose first missionaries, William Bampton and James Peggs, began a successful work south of Bengal in the Indian state of Orissa (1821). The Serampore translation of the Bible into that language already being available made Orissa a suitable place for Carey and Ward to recommend that work be done there when Bampton and Peggs sought their advice.[17] In England some of the original General Baptist churches drifted into Unitarianism and fell into other forms of doctrinal error. The fact that the New Connection Baptist churches and the Particular Baptist Society both had overseas work in India led to the proposal that the two should amalgamate, for the strengthening of the Baptist missionary work generally. In 1891, there was a coming together of the General Baptists with Particular Baptists and the New Connection General Baptist Missionary Society with the Particular Baptist Society. An extract from the

---

[16] Stanley, Brian p35.
[17] Ibid. p56.

new Baptist Missionary Society's Constitution of 1891 reads:

> 1. The name by which this society is designated is 'The Baptist Missionary Society', including 'the Particular Baptist Missionary Society for the propagating of the Gospel among the Heathen' formed in 1792, 'The General Baptist Missionary Society' formed in 1816, 'The Baptist Zenana Mission' formed in 1867, and 'The Bible Translation Society' formed in 1840.[18]

This new Baptist Missionary Society celebrated Centenary celebrations in 1892 (calculated from the time of the foundation of the Particular Baptist Society in 1792) with great excitement.

> John Clifford, the brightest star in the General Baptists firmament, was invited to preach the missionary sermon at Nottingham on 31st May 1892, in commemoration of Carey's sermon of 100 years earlier. Clifford preached on Carey's text of Isaiah 54: 2-3, and delivered a rousing message on Carey's new vision of the universality of God's fatherly love for the family of mankind. It was a sermon which appeared to make Carey into an honorary member of the General Baptists, but few among Clifford's hearers would have perceived any incongruity.[19]

Those who might have perceived that incongruity were probably not present at the meeting. Prior to this Centenary meeting some Strict Baptist churches in London resolved in 1860/61 to form 'The Strict Baptist Mission' (now 'Grace Baptist Mission') on behalf of those Strict Baptist churches in England which, because of differences in doctrinal understanding and lack of regular news from India, felt unable any longer to support the mission work of other Baptist churches. In 1861 a committee was appointed and SBM work began. (See Appendix H).

---

[18] Ibid. p225.
[19] Ibid. p226.

We ought not to leave the story of William Carey without emphasising, firstly, the conviction that his remarkable life's work was done in the context of the outstanding fellowship of those dedicated friends who with him first formed the Society, and the similarly rich fellowship of his colleagues in Serampore. The spiritual warmth of Kettering and of Serampore was a vital component of the success of Carey's achievements. Secondly, to this we must add the significant fact that God's providentially arranged circumstances were so often just ahead of the next steps that Carey was to take, ensuring their success. That was his continual expectation as he set out to attempt his next task. And thirdly, we must not overlook the solemn fact that once the Christian message was planted in India God's providences began to test the genuiness of the work by providing various tough trials – a thing which, as Carey would have understood, God had the right to do. *Any Christian ministry loses too much if it loses the awareness of the importance of those three precious experiences.*

Appendices

A. The Leicester Covenant

B. Carey's Catholicity

C. The Communion Question

D. William Carey's Will

E. Extract from 'Sumachar Durpun'

F. A.N. Groves and His Unwilling Wife

G. The Society and Home Mission

H. Grace Baptist Mission

Appendix A

The Leicester Covenant, 1791[1]

We, the Church of Jesus Christ meeting in Harvey Lane, Leicester, being convinced of the importance of impartial Discipline, and pure Doctrine in order to our Peace, and Prosperity in the Ways of God: do in the Presence of God, and of one another, solemnly Covenant and agree, in Manner and Form as follows:

I. That we receive the Bible as the Word of God, and the only Rule of Faith, and Practice, in which we find the following Doctrines taught, namely, that in the Deity are three equal Persons, the Father, the Son, and the Holy Spirit, Who sustain distinct offices in the economy of Human Salvation; We believe that all Things were fully known to God from the foundation of the world, that he from Eternity chose his People in Christ to Salvation through sanctification of the Spirit and belief of the Truth; that all rational Creatures are under indispensable Obligation to obey the Law of God, which is Holy, just and good, but that all Men have broken it and are liable to eternal Punishment; that in the fullness of Time God sent his Son to redeem his People whose Blood was a sufficient Atonement for sin, and by the imputation of whose righteousness we are accounted righteous before God, and accepted with him; and that being Justified by Faith we have Peace with God through our Lord Jesus Christ. We further believe that Men are totally depraved, and that the carnal Mind is enmity against God, and that we are convicted, and converted only by the sovereign operations of the Holy Spirit upon our Hearts, being made willing in the Day of his Power, and that the life of Grace is maintained by the same Divine Spirit, who is the Finisher as well as the Author of our faith, that those who are received thus shall persevere in the way of Holiness, and at last obtain everlasting Happiness through the mercy of God.

---

[1] From a photocopy of the original church minute book held in the County Records Office

II. That we will pay the strictest regard to our conduct in the World, acting with the strictest Honesty and integrity in all our Worldly Dealings, we will likewise abstain from all unlawful Amusements and diversions by which Time would be wasted, Money spent, our Minds carnalized, our Brethren's minds hurt, or religion dishonoured. We will abstain from worldly Labour on the Lord's Day, and carefully sanctify it, we will pay the strictest regard to our Promises, and by an holy conduct endeavour to honour the cause of God.

III. Also that we will endeavour to train up our Families in the Fear of the Lord, and to instruct and govern our Households as little charges entrusted to us.

IV. That we consistently attend the Worship of God on Sundays, at Church Meetings, and other Meetings appointed by the Church; if we ever are absent we will be ready to give a Reason why, if required; if we are absent from public worship three Sabbaths, or should attend but only in three Weeks for six Weeks together, or if we are once absent from the Lord's Supper or twice from Church Meetings without Just cause, it should be a sufficient reason why the Church should visit and enquire the reason, and deal accordingly, as shall be required. At our Church meetings only one of our Brethren shall speak at a time, and if in any matter a difference should take place, we will endeavour to weigh the matter deliberately and fully, and then put it to the Vote that it may be determined by the Majority to which the Minority shall peacefully accede; all our Sisters shall have the same right to vote as the Brethren, and be as capable of giving evidence in any matter; yet they shall not be permitted to dictate. We will not watch for each other's Faults, but will visit each other, mourning with the Mourners and joining in the joy of them that rejoice; we will warn, rebuke, exhort, and encourage with long suffering, and desire to keep the Unity of the Spirit in the Bond of Peace. If called to act against those who break the Law of our Lord's House we will do it in the spirit of the Gospel, admonishing, Suspending, or Excluding, as the matter of the case requires.

V. We will regard and highly esteem our Minister for his Work's sake, constantly attending on his Ministry and freely consulting him on the concern of our Souls, contributing according to our ability to his comfortable support, and avoiding all that may weaken his hands, or discourage his Mind; in a Word we will all seek the good of the Body with which we are connected and if the good of the Body calls us to sacrifice our own case or interest, we will cheerfully do it; esteeming the honour of Christ as far preferable to our own.

VI. We will seek out those in our Congregation who appear under concern of soul, and having good evidence of a work of Grace on their Hearts, will set before them the Privileges they have a right to, and the Duties they ought to be found in, and endeavour to remove the Stumbling Blocks out of their Way that they may enjoy the Communion of Saints.

VII. To receive such, and only such into our Communion who make a credible profession of Repentance towards God, and Faith in our Lord Jesus Christ, and who have been baptised according to the primitive Mode of administering that Ordinance, that is, by immersing them in Water, in the Name of the Father, the Son, and the Holy Spirit.

VIII. That in all personal Misunderstandings the person offended shall go to the Offender, and in a Spirit of Love seek to be reconciled, before the matter be reported to any other. That all debates of the church shall be kept as secret as possible. That no person under censure shall have a Voice in the Church. That this Covenant be READ at the admission of Members, and that all things be done decently, and in order.

These things and whatsoever else we find contained in the Word of God, we (in a dependence on divine support) solemnly Promise in the Presence of almighty God to observe, and do, but knowing our insufficiency to do any things without divine help, we look up to the strong, for strength, and daily influence – Hold thou us up O Lord, and we shall be safe, Amen.

At a Church Meeting on Lords Day Oct.3, 1790 and after the Church Book had not been read for more than nine years and much damage had been done by erasing the Names of the Members the above covenant was added and signed by the above Members all of whom had been joined for some years before – and as several refused to join with us it was agreed that two months should be allowed for them to determine whether they will join or not – after which they must be received in the ordinary way of receiving Members.

On Tuesday May 22,1791 Our Brother Wm Carey was solemnly Ordained to the Pastoral Office over this Church. Mr Hopper of Nottingham proposed the Questions to the People & Minister Mr Sutcliff of Olney preached to the Minister and Mr Fuller of Kettering to the People and Mr Ryland of Northampton pray'd THE Ordination Prayer.

Signed: Saml Hull Ben^j Connor Thos Carnal James Essex Wm Carey Joseph Morley Thomas Powell Wm Hind Peter Bedalls Margery Neal Sarah Clark Elizabeth Payne Elizabeth Scott(dead) Mary Prowitt Mary Pick(died 1794) Ann Yates Ann Emmiot Mary Purser Elizabeth Carnall Ann Carnall Ann Dickson Elizabeth Jackson Ann Hayes Mercy Wonner Margaret Noon(x) Elizabeth Knott(x)

Appendix B

Carey's Catholicity

Perhaps one of the unexpected facets of Carey's attitude toward other Protestant Christians of different theological thinking from his own was his willingness to encourage and enjoy sincere friendship with them. The Leicester Covenant which Carey drew up when the church there was re-established makes his own theological views and his church practice very clear (chapter ten & Appendix A). It might have been expected that his Calvinistic theology, his church practice of baptism of believers by immersion and of restricting access to church communion for such baptised persons only would have meant considerable isolationism in his attitude. He could be severely critical of Roman Catholicism and of the Pope. But he was eager for a prayerful relationship with other spiritually minded Christians whether Anglican or Dissenter, Arminian or Calvinistic. Wherever he found true believers who were eager to tell the world of salvation through Jesus Christ his heart warmed towards them. From his earliest days as a Christian minister Carey had what might best be described as a 'kingdom mentality' rather than a denominational one. Among the ministers present at his ordination service, as he was appointed pastor of the Moulton church, was the previous Arminian pastor of that church when it had been a General Baptist church. His was one of the hands laid on Carey's head as the ordination prayer was offered (chapter six). Much later, writing to his father from India (1802), Carey comments that his attitude to other Christians was:

> ... to cherish a catholic spirit toward them, and engage in a ready cooperation with them in everything which did not require a sacrifice of religious principle ... Missionary concern led Carey to forge channels of cooperation with other Christians who were committed to the same goal. At the same time it also made him wary of others ... whose betrayal of the Gospel seemed to undermine

the very purpose of mission.[1]

His vision was of the whole Church of God reaching the whole of the world with the gospel message. In 1806 the Cape of South Africa fell into British hands. A number of different denominations had by then founded their own missions (following the lead in India of the Particular Baptists). Carey proposed to Fuller that a general association of them all should meet in South Africa every ten years to coordinate their individual efforts with the aim of the gospel message reaching the whole world.

An interesting little insight into the practical out-working of the openness to other believers is given us from the reaction of the Serampore three to the arrival of Adoniram Judson and his wife in Serampore. Knowing that these friends were from the Congregational Church of New England, America, Carey and his colleagues ... *made it a point to guard against obtruding on missionary brethren of different sentiments any conversation relative to baptism.*[2]

In the event no such conversation was necessary since through their own study of the Bible while travelling to India the Judsons arrived already convinced of the rightness of the baptism of believers by immersion (chapter 29). Another glimpse of Carey's readiness to enjoy fellowship with an evangelical brother of another persuasion appears with the arrival of Henry Martyn in Calcutta (chapter thirty). A paedobaptist Anglican, he was appointed as military chaplain by the government. Martyn at once sought out Carey, having previously heard of him through the ministry of Charles Simeon in Cambridge. Soon a disused former Hindu shrine on the banks of the Hooghli river, which Martyn used as his residence, became a prayer house in which he, the Serampore Three and some other Christians in the area, would regularly meet for times of earnest prayer for the progress of the kingdom of God in India. Carey wrote home of Martyn as ... *very honest, evangelical and bold. As the shadow of bigotry*

---

[1] George, Timothy p162.
[2] Smith, George p127.

never falls upon us here, we take sweet counsel and go together to God's House as friends.[3]

In his turn Martyn was enthusiastic about Carey's proposal for a world missionary conference in South Africa every ten years for all the different church groups working in mission. As Carey expressed it to Fuller, *We should [then] understand one another better in two hours than by two years of letters.*

It seems that Carey was of a similar spirit as that which the Evangelical Awakening brought to many church groups in England, where an evangelical ecumenism was abroad in some quarters. The Haldane brothers are an example of this: Robert (1764-1842)[4] and James (1768-1851), founders in 1797 of the Society for the Propagation of the Gospel at Home, held the view that:

> *The pulpit was open to all preachers, without regard to their denominational label, whose message was Christ and him crucified. They had a profound regard for denominationalism and held to a broader sense of Christian unity. Andrew Fuller, Charles Simeon, John Newton, David Bogue and the maverick preacher Rowland Hill were all within the bounds of their fellowship.*[5]

In a similar way, Joseph Hughes, one of the founders of the Religious Tract Society (1799) could happily write:

> *I long to see the day in which Episcopalians, Presbyterians, Methodists, Independents and Baptists will exchange pulpits and meet at the same sacramental board.*[6]

---

[3] Carey, S Pearce p268.
[4] Robert had hoped to go to India to assist William Carey but was prevented because his political views, arising from Baptist views of the freedom of the individual, were considered by some as too revolutionary. Haykin, Michael (Ed.) *The British Particular Baptists* vol.2 p225.
[5] Ibid. p225.
[6] Brown, Raymond p138.

It has to be kept in mind that Carey's catholicity was based upon finding, in those with whom he would have eager fellowship, a similar passion and earnestness as his own for the biblical message of salvation for hell-deserving sinners through faith in Jesus Christ alone. Such a catholicity can thrive in a spiritual atmosphere as that engendered by the Evangelical Awakening. His was not a catholicity based upon the lowest common theological denominator in a time of poverty of spiritual power.

In 1861 C H Spurgeon was asked to give a speech in appreciation of the life and ministry of William Carey. In it he said the following:

> *I admire Carey for being a Baptist: he had none of the false charity which might prompt some to conceal their belief for fear of offending others; but at the same time he was a man who loved all who loved the Lord Jesus Christ.*[7]

---

[7] 'C.H. Spurgeon's tribute to William Carey' *Baptist Times* (16 April 1992) Supplement p. 1, quoted by Haykin, Michael AG in *British Particular Baptists* vol. 3 pp.xvii &xviii.

Appendix C

The Communion Question

The Particular Baptist churches were not all of one mind with regard to who was entitled to share in church communion. Some churches were of a closed table persuasion which restricted communicants to only those believers who had been baptised by immersion. Others practised an open or free table, allowing all who professed faith in Christ, including those not baptised, to share in the celebration.[1] Andrew Fuller, secretary of the Society, was of the former mind: when he became pastor at Kettering his statement was unambiguous, saying: 'I believe baptism ... to be a requisite to church communion'.[2] Carey also took that view, as did many of the Particular Baptist churches. Dr John Ryland, however, the chairman of the Society committee, practised an open table in his church. The policy of the Serampore Three for their first years was to practise a restricted access to the Lord's Table as Fuller and many home churches did. But to refuse communion to non-Baptist sea captains and other Christian friends visiting Calcutta, as well as local Anglican friends (who had contributed to the costs of the mission) was a cause of embarrassment particularly to William Ward and in some measure to Joshua Marshman. Eventually Carey agreed to go along with them and the Lord's Table was declared to be open to unbaptised believers, Anglicans and Baptists alike. Ward wrote:

> *We could not doubt that Watts, Edwards, Brainerd, Doddridge and Whitefield, although not Baptists, had been welcome to his table by the Lord. On what grounds could we exclude such? ... Let us conscientiously profess our own convictions ... while we love him exceed-*

---

[1] A detailed survey of the controversy in the 1700s and 1800s is available in Naylor, Peter *Picking up a pin for the Lord,* Grace Publications ISBN 0-9505476-3-8

[2] Naylor, Peter p218.

ingly, in whom we see much of Christ, although some of his opinions are contrary to our own.[3]

In his journal Ward recorded his view that:

With regard to a church state, a stricter union may be required; but to partake of the Lord's Supper worthily, it requires only that a man's heart be right towards God.[4]

Andrew Fuller wrote in response to Ward's comments:

... the neglect of what Christ has commanded (i.e. baptism) to all his followers, and this, it may be knowingly, is to put asunder what Christ has joined together – Mark 16:16.[5]

However, after a few years of keeping an open table, Serampore returned to the practice of a restricted communion again, not so much because of Fuller's words but, as Pearce Carey informs us (though without any detail of the reason), because *abnormal and distressing circumstances, alas! drove them, a few years later, reluctantly to bend back from this happier course.*[6]

It is perhaps not out of place to note briefly that the origin of the practice of restricting participation in church communion derives not simply from an examination of Scripture but also from the practice in earliest church times as historically recorded. It is clearly indicated in *The Didache* or *The teaching of the twelve Apostles* where we find, stated in its chapter nine:

---

[3] Carey, S Pearce p263.
[4] Marshman, John Clark p83. He seems to distinguish between church *membership* and the taking of communion.
[5] Naylor, Peter p218.
[6] Carey, S Pearce p263. By referring to 'this *happier* course' the 'open table' situation is meant. Presumably Pearce Carey is expressing his own personal opinion.

But let no one eat or drink of your Eucharist except those baptized into the name of the Lord.[7]

There is confirmation that this was the practice of the early church from the writings of Justin Martyr (circa 100-163 AD) who was an apologist for Christian teaching and behaviour. He describes the structure of a church service as in two parts. The first part, he writes, was a time for singing, reading from Scripture and the delivery of the sermon, after which unbaptised persons would leave. The second part, only for those who had been baptised, consisted of prayers and the Eucharist.[8] In Carey's time a prominent London pastor, Abraham Booth (1734-1806), who became a supporter of the missionary Society, published in 1778 *A defence for the Baptists* in which he defended Baptists from the charge that they laid too great a stress on the necessity of baptism before communion and were guilty of bigotry in refusing communion to Paedobaptists.[9] It is a comprehensive and powerful work, the compelling thrust of which is inescapable once its arguments – biblical, historical and logical – are seriously evaluated. At least, for the purpose of this biography, we can better understand Carey's practice in this matter when the biblical and historical evidence for it is examined.

---

[7] There is some discussion as to the date of *The Didache* but at least it is suggested as somewhere between 100 and 200 AD.
[8] Needham, NR vol.1 p69.
[9] It could be argued that not Baptists but Paedobaptists themselves prevent their taking communion with Baptists, because of their different understanding of what the nature of baptism is.

Appendix D

William Carey's Will[1]

'I William, Carey, Doctor of Divinity, residing at Serampore, in the province of Bengal,
being in good health and of sound mind, do make this my last will and testament in manner and form following:

First, I utterly disclaim all or any right or title to the premises at Serampore, called the Mission Premises, and every part and parcel thereof; and do hereby declare that I never had, or supposed myself to have, any such right or title.[2]

Secondly, I disclaim all right and title to the property belonging to my present wife, Grace Carey, amounting to 25,000 rupees, more or less, which was settled upon her by a particular deed, executed previously to my marriage with her.

Thirdly, I give and bequeath to the College of Serampore, the whole of my museum, consisting of minerals, shells, corals, insects, and other natural curiosities and a Hortus Seccus. Also the folio edition of 'Hortus Woburnensis', which was presented to me by Lord Hastings, Taylor's Hebrew Concordance, my collection of Bibles in foreign languages, and all my books in the Italian and German languages.

Fourthly, I desire that my wife, Grace Carey, will collect from my library whatever books in the English language she wishes for, and keep them for her own use.

Fifthly, From the failure of funds to carry my further intentions into effect, I direct that my library, with the exception above made, be sold by public auction, unless it, or any part of it can be advantageously disposed of by private sale; and that from the proceeds 1500 rupees be paid as a legacy to my son Jabez Carey, a like sum having heretofore been paid to my sons Felix and William.

---

[1] From AH Oussoren p121.
[2] This is his answer to the Home committee's accusation that the Three were enriching themselves as owners of all the mission properties in Serampore.

Sixthly, It was my intention to have bequeathed a similar sum to my son Jonathan Carey; but God has so prospered him that he is in no immediate want of it. I direct that if anything remains, it be given to my wife, Grace Carey, to whom I also bequeath all my household furniture, wearing apparel, and whatever other effects I may possess, for her purpose and behoof.[3]

Seventhly, I direct that, before every other thing, all my lawful debts may be paid; that my funeral be as plain as possible; that I may be buried by the side of my second wife, Charlotte Emilia Carey; and that the following inscription, and nothing more, may be cut on the stone which commemorates her, either above or below, as there may be room - viz:

'William Carey, born August 17th, 1761; died ...
A wretched, poor and helpless worm,
On Thy kind arms I fall.'

Eighthly, I hereby constitute and appoint my dear friends the Rev. WILLIAM ROBINSON of Calcutta, and the Rev. JOHN MACK of Serampore, executors, to this my last will and testament, and request them to perform all therein desired and ordered by me, to the utmost of their power.

Ninthly, I hereby declare this to be my last will and testament and revoke all other wills and testaments of a date prior to this.

(Signed) William Carey.
(Signed) W.H. Jones, S.M. M'intosh

---

[3] An archaic term meaning 'benefit'

Appendix E

Extract from 'Sumachar Durpun'[1]

Wednesday 11 June 1834

WE have to communicate intelligence to-day, which will be received with general lamentation, not only throughout India, but throughout the world. Dr Carey has finished his pilgrimage on earth, having gently expired early last Monday morning. For several years past, his health has been infirm; and his strength has gradually sunk, until the weary wheels of nature stood still from mere debility, and not from disease. The peculiarly trying hot weather and rainy season of 1833, reduced him to such extreme weakness, that in September last he experienced a stroke of apoplexy, and, for some time after, his death was expected daily. It pleased God, however, to revive him for a little. During the past cold season, he could again take an evening and morning ride in his palanquin carriage, and spend much of the day reclining in an easy chair with a book in his hand or conversing cheerfully with any friend that called. As however the hot weather advanced, he sunk daily into still greater debility than before: he could take no nourishment: he lay helpless and speechless on his bed, until his skin was worn off his body, and death was a merciful relief. His dearest friends could not but rejoice that his sufferings were ended, although they mourn his loss to themselves and to mankind.

    The career which Dr. Carey has run, is worthy of most honourable notice. He was a man who stood prominently forward from the mass of the several generations of men with whom he lived; and both for his private and his public character he deserves to be had in lasting remembrance ...

    1801 Dr. Carey was chosen as Bengalee Teacher in the newly instituted College of Fort William. He was enabled to translate the Scriptures into all the principal languages of northern Hindoosthan. For the Students in the College, he had to

---

[1] Extracts from the newspaper *News Mirror* published in Serampore. Chapter 27 refers.

compile grammars of the languages he taught them; and after many years he completed his voluminous Bengalee Dictionary. By means of these and other works, he became known throughout the world as an oriental scholar of the first eminence. He was not less celebrated as a man of science. Botany and Natural History he began to study long before he left England; and India opened to him a wide field of observation, which he examined with untiring assiduity from his first arrival, until his strength utterly failed him. In these pursuits, he was the coadjutor and personal friend of Roxburgh, Buchanan, Hardwick, and Wallich, and the correspondent of several of the first men in Europe, with whom he was continually exchanging botanical treasures.

As a philanthropist, Dr. Carey is entitled to a high rank. He sought and gained the prevention of infanticide at Gunga Sangur. He was amongst the first, if not the first, that engaged in seeking the abolition of suttees, and chiefly through his exertions the Marquis of Wellesley left to his successors in the government of India, a minute declaring his conviction that he [?it] thus might and ought to be abolished. Had he continued in the Government, he would have abolished them. Dr. Carey also took an active part in attempting the establishment of a leper hospital in Calcutta. He was the founder of the Agricultural Society. And indeed scarcely any undertaking for the benefit of the country has been engaged in, of which he was not either a prime mover, or a zealous promoter.

It was however as a Christian, a Missionary, and a Translator of the Sacred Scriptures, that Dr. Carey shone pre-eminently. Their obligations to him in these respects the people of India have yet in a great degree to learn. They will however learn them; and future generations will arise to bless his name. All Bengalees at least may thank him for this: before his days, the Bengalee language was unknown, and had never been reduced to grammatical rule. Pundits would not write it, and there was scarcely a book in it worth reading. It is now rich, refined, and expressive; and scholarship in it is generally sought both by natives and foreigners;and to Dr. Carey and the pundits whom he employed, and whose labours he directed, the change is principally owing.

Appendix F

A.N.Groves and his Unwilling Wife

Anthony Norris Groves (1795-1853), the pioneer Brethren missionary, was brother-in-law to the well-known George Muller of Bristol who was renowned for his orphanage work that he conducted by a remarkable life of prayer. When Groves was a schoolboy he would sometimes attend the preaching of a Mr Owen at Fulham and on one such occasion, while still unconverted, he was impressed by the thought that he should one day go to India. Having become a successful business man but still in a state of rebellion against God, he again heard a sermon by Mr Owen and found himself thinking that 'it would be a worthy object to die for, to go to India, to win but one idolater from hopeless death to life and peace'. He consulted two godly ministers in Plymouth and 'in good faith gave myself to the Lord and missionary work abroad'.

But earlier he had married a young lady whom for some time he had greatly loved. He wrote afterwards:

> *We were soon married, before I was twenty two, and in the joy of possessing one who had so truly loved me, after five years of trial,[1] I for a moment quite forgot all my promises to the Lord and his work abroad ... I do not think I was wrong in marrying my dearest Mary, for I had truly felt we were married in the sight of God years before: but I did a right thing in a wrong spirit. I ought to have asked my Lord and told him my difficulties and he would, I know, have eased my way and still have let me have all I sought.[2]*

Groves could, after a few years, record that it became increasingly clear that Mary was determined to prevent him from

---

[1] He had to wait five years before the marriage could take place with the approval of Mary's father.
[2] Lang, GH pp231-2.

becoming a missionary. He was greatly prospering in his work[3] yet had to record that 'often I did, with every earthly thing that a man could desire, feel most miserable. I had a wife who loved me ... and a most lucrative profession, yet I had not the Lord's presence as in days past'. For some six years Groves felt increasing difficulties daily, though never losing the thought that nothing is too hard for God. He describes how a change came about in the life of his wife:

> *Mary was accustomed to go and hear a Mr Marriot and one day he expounded the concluding verses of 1 Corinthians 1 – 'God hath chosen the weak things' etc. 'If this be the plan of God's government' she thought to herself, 'then there is hope that he may, for his name's sake, glorify himself in me, the vilest the most worthless of his creatures'.*[4]

Yet she said nothing to her husband, fearing to revive his missionary hopes. Some time later she and Anthony together heard Mr Marriot again, speaking on the same chapter. This time Mary could resist no longer but told Anthony her feelings had changed. From that time on she was no longer against him, but for him. Groves resigned from his business, recognising the incongruity (as he saw it) of a believer supporting the work of places that sold alcohol by selling them his insurance policies, and so Mary and he began a missionary career together.

At first they were directed to work in Baghdad, where his wife shortly died of a fever. But Anthony felt that his ministry was to be independent from any organisation, allowing him to go when and where he felt the Spirit of God would guide him. He made three visits to India – the country of his first impressions – in 1822, 1826 and 1849. He travelled widely in India, evangelising and also working briefly with various Christian groups that he found. In the Tamil Nadu of South India it was his ministry which was the means of J.C. Arulappen being con-

---
[3] He had a business selling fire insurance for public houses.
[4] Ibid. p237.

verted and carrying out a life of fruitful evangelism. But it was the ten years that he had to wait for his wife to accompany him unreservedly which contrasts him with William Carey. Are there lessons to be learned from the lives of these two great pioneers?

Dorothy Carey, a few years older than her husband – whose horizons were limited to a difficult village life, a woman of limited academic skills, a loving mother of her children but fearful of the exposure of the family to situations with which she was not familiar, spiritually 'an infant' compared with her husband – was distressed, no doubt, by the persistent pressure of William's enthusiasm for missionary work though finally compelled to go with him by the blunt words of persuasion uttered by Dr Thomas and helped by the promise of her sister Kitty's companionship. So near to the delivery of another child, she eventually, *within twenty four hours*, packed her things and joined William in the stage coach to the south coast and the dreaded unknown!

Mary Groves – a young, talented woman, used to the risks and gains of her husband's business life, enjoying the fruits of his lucrative successes and mother of his children – was able to resist her older husband's interest in mission work for years, free from any persuasion on his part on the matter. Yet eventually, through God's touch upon her spirit, she was able to accept her husband's rejection of business success, his resignation from secular work and to live with him in dependence upon God for their financial support, wholeheartedly joining in the work of mission.

Both women faced situations the like of which had not been faced before by their kind, one moved by blunt argument and fear of loss; the other, after years of rebellion, moved by spiritual conviction to a willing agreement with an abstemious way of life. One said, 'I will go' but never really went wholeheartedly; the other said 'I will not go' but was moved by the Spirit and went with all her heart and soul. But who is so wise and free from fault as to be fit to judge either woman?

Appendix G

The Society and Home Mission

One of the effects of the formation of the Particular Baptist Missionary Society and of the growing concern for overseas mission among many of the Particular Baptist churches in the United Kingdom, was the awakening realisation that not all the world's heathen lived overseas. For example, from the committee of the Society:

> *It has been objected to us, that while we are seeking the good of the heathen abroad, we are not sufficiently attentive to a kind of characters at home, who, though they sustain the Christian name, yet are heathens in reality, nearly as much as the inhabitants of India or Africa. We cannot admit that this objection applies with any justice against a foreign mission; and we could say in truth, that since this undertaking has been on foot, there has been more of a spirit for carrying the gospel into the dark corners of our own land, than there was before.*[1]

Some itinerant evangelism was being conducted in parts of England before the Missionary Society was formed. The Baptist Western Association and the Northamptonshire Baptist Association issued circular letters to their churches in 1775 and 1779 respectively reminding the churches that there were funds available for 'itinerant preaching in those places where it might be judged necessary and desirable'.[2]

Evidently the reminder was necessary!

> *To take the Western Association as a good example of this point in practice, it appears that William Steadman*[3]

---

[1] Talbot, Brian in *The British Particular Baptists* Haykin, Michael AG (Ed.) vol.3 p.61.
[2] Ibid. p62.
[3] 1764-1837

and John Saffery[4] were possibly the only two ministers who, in the 1790s, engaged in regular itinerant work.[5]

Both men eventually left that area to minister elsewhere and the enthusiasm for itinerant evangelism in the Western Association was in danger of sinking very low. One reason for the uncertainty about the biblical rightness of such evangelism and the consequent lack of enthusiasm for it was the High Calvinistic thinking which influenced some of the Particular Baptist churches at that time. In the light of God's sovereignty in the election of his people, could it be right to present the open invitations of the gospel to *all* hearers of the preaching? In 1792 Steadman learned of the formation of the Particular Baptist Missionary Society and subsequently wrote in his journal of his reaction to that news:

> *It revived me, and did my heart good to think that God had put it into the heart of any to attempt that good work; and I cannot but look upon this as one of the many favourable indications of the approach of the universal spread of the Gospel and of the latter day glory.*[6]

Steadman's confidence in an evangelistic Calvinism was clearly encouraged by the formation of the Particular Baptist Missionary Society. Other notable Particular Baptist leaders responded with enthusiasm to the challenge of mission in the United Kingdom, prominent among them being John Fawcett of Hebden Bridge and Samuel Pearce of Birmingham.

One example of the interest of the Society in home mission, as well as mission overseas, was the decision taken in 1795 to finance the work of two Baptist ministers to spend some weeks in the summer on an evangelistic tour of Cornwall, while their home pulpits were to be served by students on their summer vacation from the Bristol Baptist College. William Steadman and

---
[4] 1763-1825
[5] Ibid. p62.
[6] Talbot, Brian in *The British Particular Baptists* Haykin, Michael, AG (Ed.) vol 3 p65.

John Saffery were the chosen men, because of their previous experience at itinerant preaching. Dr John Ryland (Chairman of the Missionary Society) wrote to Saffery in 1796:

> *Our brethren highly approve of the plan, and we all want you and brother Steadman to set out as soon as possible, and the Society will thankfully pay all charges. We hope you will be able to spend two whole months itinerating in Cornwall.*[7]

In June 1796 the two men set out on what became an eight week tour in which they preached 139 times in 59 places, using Baptist chapels, Independent and Methodist chapels, town halls, private dwellings and the open air, including a meeting in the famous Gwennap Pit – a huge natural amphitheatre which could accommodate a large audience (famously used by John Wesley in his previous open air preaching tours). According to a report in the *Periodical accounts of the Baptist Missionary Society* in 1800 it was estimated that more than 20,000 people must have listened to the two men.[8] The whole experience revealed what a large task still awaited Particular Baptists if they were ever to spread the Christian message to all parts of the United Kingdom. The passionate energy of William Carey and his friends for the gospel to reach the heathen overseas had, in those early years of the Society, also brought to birth a growing concern for the heathen of England. It has been suggested that by 1830:

> *Over seventy organisations, active in itinerant evangelism, were formed ... by Calvinistic dissenters.*[9]

---

[7] Ibid. p67.
[8] Talbot, Brian in *The British Particular Baptists 1638-1910* Haykin, Michael AG (Ed.) vol 3 p69.
[9] James, Sharon in *British Particular Baptists 1638-1910* Haykin, Michael, AG (Ed.) vol 2 p163.

Appendix H

Grace Baptist Mission

... it is not consistent or desirable that the Auxiliaries existing in the aid of these societies in connection with this church should continue longer in operation.[1]

So the Baptist church at Keppel Street, London resolved to sever its connection with the Baptist Foreign Missionary Society and some other Baptist Societies in 1860. Their report of this appears in *The Gospel Herald* under the heading of 'Religious Intelligence'. In January 1833 this magazine had been founded in Ipswich and now circulated among Baptist churches in various parts of the country.[2] Its stance was Baptist and Calvinistic but rejected the theologies of Andrew Fuller and of William Gadsby.[3] The fear was that the teaching of the former would lead to Arminianism, and that that of the latter, who taught that the gospel not the Old Testament moral law was the believer's rule of conduct, would lead to Antinomianism. The action of the Keppel Street church was symptomatic of the unrest that was growing among other Strict Baptist churches, and which *The Gospel Herald* was expressing. It was their view that the Baptist movement at large was departing from the theology and practice of the founders of the Particular Baptist Society and its missionary outreach, and also that Baptist Colleges were tending so to emphasise the need for academic achievement as to neglect the need for the students to be spiritually qualified for the work of ministry.[4]

A later issue of *The Gospel Herald* includes the following announcement:

---

[1] Extract from a photocopy of *The Gospel Herald* 1860 p146, from the archives of the Strict Baptist Historical Society
[2] Oliver, RW p263.
[3] (1773-1844)
[4] Ibid. p265.

> The church meeting at Keppel Street chapel, London, having dissolved its connection with the Baptist Foreign Missionary Society, on the grounds already stated, has formed an independent Society in connection with this place of worship, to be called 'The Keppel Street Strict Baptist Missionary Society'.[5]

It is clear that the church resolved to take this step from the conviction that the Baptist Foreign Missionary Society increasingly ignored the views they held of divine truth and biblical practice:

> ... and also that the more simple and Scriptural plan is for churches themselves, as such, to conduct their own missionary operations in their own way and by their own chosen agents, instead of confiding this important work to a separate Society, over whose proceedings and organisation they had, practically, so little control.[6]

Thus, difference in doctrinal understanding was not the only problem. Both Fuller and Carey had been aware that if their Society were to outlive them changes would have to be made. But in the event the brotherly and informal spirit that they had cultivated over the years, which had enabled the Serampore work to thrive, was lost in successive generations, replaced by a more formal, 'professional' approach. The mission was turning from a church base to a supra-church Mission base. Intimate touch between the churches at home and the work on the foreign fields was lost: clearly Keppel Street friends were unhappy with that, feeling that the tendency of large missionary Societies was to lodge power in the hands of a few individuals at the top.[7] A letter unexpectedly reached the Keppel Street friends from a Mr

---

[5] Extract from a photocopy of *The Gospel Herald* 1860 p169, from the archives of the Strict Baptist Historical Society
[6] Ibid. 1861 p212.
[7] Taken from an unpublished paper by (BA Hons) student Thurairatnam B Surendran of the Evangelical Theological College of Wales, *An examination of the Grace Baptist Mission work among the Tamils in South India* p4 .

Fenwick in Ceylon who was a missionary formerly employed by the Free Church of Scotland but who had become convinced of the rightness of believers baptism and strict communion. The ensuing correspondence led to Mr Fenwick being supported by the Keppel Street Strict Baptist Mission. The first annual meeting of this mission was held in June 1862 in which a report was presented giving an account of the church's support of Mr Fenwick, details of the work he was to undertake and the news of other churches joining in the support of this work.[8] Thus the work of the Strict Baptist Mission began and has since grown over the years, but known today under the name of Grace Baptist Mission, maintaining the doctrinal position and church practice of the courageous Northhamptonshire pioneers of 1792.[9]

The many years of work of the Strict Baptist Mission among the Tamils in South India can be divided into four distinct periods of emphasis:

>   1861 – 1894 Indian workers employed by the mission to carry on the work
>   1895 – 1937 English missionaries sent out to join the work
>   1938 – 1950 The training of Indian pastors, teachers and Bible women to
> equip the Tamil churches for self government
>   1951 – 1970 The gradual devolvement of responsibility into Indian hands for church affairs, for mission properties and for school managements.

Grace Baptist Mission exists to help Grace Baptist churches support and care for their missionaries worldwide. Its council is composed only of representatives from those churches and is elected in the annual business meeting that is attended by

---

[8] Extract from a photocopy of *The Gospel Herald* 1862 p164, from the archives of the Strict Baptist Historical Society

[9] The 'anti-Fullerism' motivation of Keppel Street friends is perhaps indicated by the clause in their doctrinal basis that 'saving faith is not a legal duty' which appears in their statement of 1885; that clause no longer appears in the published summary of Grace Baptist Mission's doctrinal position.

delegates from those churches. This structure helps to preserve the direct 'family relationship' between the churches and the missionaries that the Keppel Street church sought to institute in 1861. The basis of GBM includes the following article:

> *We believe in church based mission – that it is the responsibility of the local church to be obedient to Christ's commission to go into all the world and preach the gospel to all mankind, seeking to disciple and baptise believers, establishing them into local churches.*[10]

Currently (2007) there are missionaries from Grace Baptist churches working in fifteen different countries, including the UK. Based in Abingdon, Oxfordshire, a programme of literature production reaches into many countries worldwide and a recording studio supplies programmes in English and French to Christian and secular transmitters in many countries. Further information may be obtained from the Abingdon office at 12 Abbey Close, Oxon, OX14 3JD; telephone 01235 520147; email infodesk@gbm.org.uk There is a web site at www.gbm.org.uk

---

[10] From GBM Annual Report and Handbook 2007